Reminiscences

of

Admiral Roy L. Johnson, USN (Ret.)

U.S. Naval Institute
Annapolis, Maryland

Preface

This volume contains a transcript of taped interviews with Admiral Roy L. Johnson, USN (Ret.). They were held at his home in Virginia Beach, Virginia in December, 1980. The Admiral has corrected the initial transcript; the text has been re-typed and an index added for convenience.

Admiral Johnson has had a most notable career in naval aviation. He saw heavy action in World War II, in Korea and ultimately in Vietnam when he served as Commander of the 7th fleet. His last active duty was as Commander-in-Chief of the Pacific Fleet during 1965-67. Other significant assignments in his career came as Director of the Long Range Objectives Group, office of CNO, and as Deputy Director of Joint Strategic Target Planning at Offutt Air Force Base, Omaha, Nebraska.

John T. Mason, Jr.
Director of Oral History

April 6, 1982.

ADMIRAL ROY L. JOHNSON, UNITED STATES NAVY, RETIRED

Roy Lee Johnson was born in Big Bend, Louisiana, on March 18, 1906, son of John E. and Hettie Mae (Long) Johnson. He entered the U. S. Naval Academy, Annapolis, Maryland, On June 15, 1925, on appointment from Louisiana, and as a Midshipman played varsity baseball and was a member of the "Lucky Bag" Staff. He was graduated and commissioned Ensign on June 6, 1929, and subsequently advanced in rank to that of Rear Admiral, to date from January 1, 1956; Vice Admiral, from December 15, 1961, and to Admiral, to date from March 31, 1965.

Upon graduation from the Naval Academy in June 1929, he was assigned to the USS TENNESSEE, and served as a junior officer in that battleship until May 1930. He was then transferred to the USS WEST VIRGINIA for communication duty on the Staff of Commander Battleship Divisions, Battle Fleet. On January 28, 1931, he began flight training at the Naval Air Station, Pensacola, Florida, having had preliminary training at the Naval Air Station, San Diego, California, in 1930, and on January 25, 1932, was designated Naval Aviator.

From March to June 1932 he had duty at the Naval Air Station, Hampton Roads, Virginia, and upon detachment was ordered to the USS SALT LAKE CITY for three years' duty with Scouting Squadron TEN-S, aviation unit of that cruiser. He returned to the Naval Air Station, Pensacola, on June 20, 1935, and for two years served as a Flight Instructor. In May 1937, he joined Scouting Squadron SIX, for three years' duty, while that squadron was based alternately on the USS ENTERPRISE and USS YORKTOWN.

On June 29, 1940, he was ordered to Patrol Squadron TWELVE, and completing that assignment, he reported on March 28, 1941, to the Bureau of Aeronautics, Navy Department, Washington, D.C., where he was on duty when the United States entered World War II. He remained in the Bureau until May 1943, when he was transferred to the Fleet Air Command, Quonset Point, Rhode Island, and assigned duty as Commander Carrier Air Group TWO. He continued in command when his Air Group joined the USS HORNET early in 1944, and from May of that year until May 1945 he served as Air Officer of that carrier, and for four months thereafter served as Executive Officer of the same ship.

For meritorious service while in command of Carrier Air Group TWO, and as Air Officer of the USS HORNET, he was awarded the Air Medal, the Bronze Star Medal, with Combat "V", the Legion of Merit, also with Combat "V", and a Gold Star in lieu of the Second Legion of Merit. The citations follow, in part:

Adm. R. L. Johnson, USN, Ret.   Page 2

Air Medal: "For meritorious achievement in aerial flight as Commander of a Carrier Based Air Group, attached to the USS HORNET, in action against enemy Japanese forces at Palau, Woleai, Wakde and Truk, from March to May 1944. Coordinating and leading fighter sweeps against enemy airfields and airborne craft, and bombing missions against enemy shipping and shore installations, (he) directed the operations of his squadron in the air over the target, took photographs of the targets in the face of intense antiaircraft fire and made valuable and timely reports of his flights to the Task Group Commander..."

Bronze Star Medal: "For meritorious service as Air Group Commander and later as Air Officer on board the USS HORNET...from March 5 to July 20, 1944. Serving with distinction in an assignmen of vital importance, (he) rendered invaluable service in connection with the organization, training and operation of his air group and contributed materially to the successful record of accomplishment attained by the HORNET and the aircraft on board..."

Legion of Merit: "For exceptionally meritorious conduct... as Air Officer of the USS HORNET, assigned to second Carrier Task Force, Pacific Fleet, during operations...from June 5 to September 24, 1944..(he) contributed materially to the high degree of operating efficiency attained by the Air Group..."

Gold star in lieu of Second Legion of Merit: "...as Air Officer of the USS HORNET during operations against enemy Japanese forces in the Philippine Islands, Iwo Jima and Okinawa Campaigns from October 2, 1944 to April 22, 1945...(He) operated the air department at the peak of efficiency during this period of extensive air activities and consistently maintained a high degree of availability and performance of aircraft...(contributing) materially to the infliction of damage upon the enemy by the air groups serving on his ship..."

He is also entitled to the Ribbon for, and a facsimile of the Presidential Unit Citation awarded the USS HORNET for "extraordinary heroism in action against enemy Japanese forces in the air, ashore and afloat in the Pacific War Area from March 29, 1944 to June 10, 1945..."

Returning to the Navy Department, he reported on October 3, 1945 for duty at Headquarters, Commander in Chief, United States Fleet. He was transferred to the Office of the Chief of Naval Operations when the two offices were combined under the latter name on October 10, 1945, and later had duty in the Office of the Joint Chiefs of Staff. In July 1947 he was ordered to Norfolk, Virginia, where he served as Aviation Operations Office on the Staff of Commander SECOND Task Fleet.

In January 1950 he reported as Training Officer on the Staff of the Chief of Naval Air Reserve Training, at Glenview, Illinois. In that capacity he had additional duty at Pensacola, Florida, and various other places until detached in October 1951. On November 15, that year, he became Commanding Officer of the USS BADOENG STRAIT, which under his command participated in operations in the Korean Area. After his detachment in July 1952 he had instruction at the National War College, Washington, D.C., for a year.

During the next two years he served as Head of the Air Weapons Systems Analysis Staff, Office of the Deputy Chief of Naval Operations (Air). In May 1955 he reported as Prospective Commanding Officer of the USS FORRESTAL (CVA-59), and assumed command of that giant flat-top (the first of the super aircraft carriers of 60,000 tons to be completed), at her commissioning at Norfolk, Virginia, on October 1, 1955. He commanded the FORRESTAL until June 1956, then had duty as Director of the Long Range Objectives Group, Office of the Chief of Naval Operations.

From December 1958 until January 1960 he commanded Carrier Division FOUR, after which he was Assistant Chief of Naval Operations (Plans and Policy), Navy Department. In January 1962 he became Deputy Director of Joint Strategic Target Planning, with headquarters at Offutt Air Force Base, Omaha, Nebraska, and continued to serve as such until July 1963, when he assumed duty as Deputy Commander in Chief, U.S. Pacific Fleet and Chief of staff and Aide to the Commander in Chief, U.S. Pacific Fleet. In April 1964, he reported as Commander SEVENTH Fleet and for "exceptionally meritorious service...(in that capacity)...from June 15, 1964 to March 1, 1965..." he was awarded the Distinguished Service Medal. The citation further states:

"During this period of ever-increasing tension in Southeast Asia, Vice Admiral Johnson provided dynamic leadership to the world's largest and most powerful task fleet, responsible for security of one-fifth of the earth's surface. Under his superb direction, forces of the SEVENTH Fleet maintained constant vigilance and continued readiness for instant response at a sustained tempo of operations heretofore unknown to a peacetime world. The decision of the United States Government to retaliate to the unprovoked attack on U.S. Naval ships in the Gulf of Tonkin on August 5, 1964 was translated into a swift and appropriate action by the ever-ready forces under Vice Admiral Johnson's command. The combat air strikes were carried out in an exemplary manner, clearly indicative of a high state of professional skill. Subsequent combat air operations have similarly been conducted in an unsurpassed fashion..."

On March 30, 1965 he became Commander in Chief, U.S. Pacific Fleet and for "exceptionally meritorious service...(in that capacity) from March 1965 to November 1967..." he was awarded a Gold Star in lieu of the Second Distinguished Service Medal. The citation continues:

"During this period, Admiral Johnson has demonstrated dynamic leadership, outstanding executive ability, and exceptional foresight in the directing the complex and manifold operations of the Pacific ocean area. Through his far-sighted and imaginative planning, he has successfully coped with the myriad of problems generated by the continuing intensification of combat operations and the concomitant buildup of forces and facilities in Southeast Asia. Under his brilliant direction, the Pacific Fleet has been molded into an integrated, highly trained, professional force, operating ships and equipment which are the most advanced the world has ever seen. In the past thirty-two months, the Pacific Fleet has landed and subsequently furnished logistical support to over 78,000 Fleet Marine Force personnel in South Vietnam; naval gunfire operations have been expanded from support of our forces in South Vietnam to include targets along a portion of the North Vietnamese coastline, amphibious assault operations have been conducted along the entire South Vietnamese coastline in order to search for and destroy enemy personnel and equipment; naval forces have been introduced into the swamps, rivers and canals of the Mekong River Delta in order to interdict enemy logist traffic and to support Army operations in that area; and air strike operations against heavily defended targets in North Vietnam have been greatly expanded. Many of the operations conducted by the Pacific Fleet were without precedent in modern naval history, requiring the development and employment of new tactics, techniques and equipment. Nuclear powered ships, the Naval Tactical Data System, and navigation and communications by sattelite have been introduced into combat for the first time in history, and new techniques of ocean surveillance, intelligence collection and electronic warfare were developed and placed in operation. Coordin electronic and tactical measures have been successfully developed to counter the surface-to-air missile threat and a positive radar surveillance and identification system has been establsihed for all air operations over the Gulf of Tonkin and North Vietnam. These achievements are the direct result of Admiral Johnson's ability to master the complexities of integrating and employing new techniques, tactics and equipment to meet the challenges posed by a fast-changing combat environment. In addition to his deep involvements in and massive contribution to the advances mentioned above, Admiral Johnson has been most effective in revising command relationships, when required, in order to provide improved control and faster reaction of the Pacific Fleet. The command relationships within the antisubmarine warfare forces of the Pacific Fleet have undergone a major revision which resulted in a vastly increase effectiveness in the control and utilization of these diverse forces. Admiral Johnson has also achieved effective coordination and cooperation with the other component commanders of the Pacific Command required to attain the maximum effectiveness and efficiency of combined operations against the common enemy. He has continuous demonstrated the great tact diplomacy necessary to protect our vital national and naval interests in the Pacific Ocean area. Through persuasive negotiation and personal leadership, he has served with distinction in nurturing effective channels for liaison and in furthering the United States goodwill and prestige with foreign nations..."

He was transferred to the Retired List of the U.S. Navy, effective December 1, 1967.

In addition to the Distinguished Service Medal with Gold Star, the Legion of Merit with Gold Star and Combat "V", the Bronze Star Medal with Combat "V", the Air Medal; and the Presidential Unit Citation Ribbon, Admiral Johnson has the American Defense Service Medal, Fleet Clasp; American Campaign Medal; Asiatic-Pacific Campaign Medal; World War II Victory Medal; China Service Medal; Navy Occupation Service Medal; National Defense Service Medal with bronze star; Korean Service Medal; United Nations Service Medal; Vietnam Service Medal with three stars and the Philippine Liberation Ribbon with two stars. He also has the Korean Presidential Unit Citation Badge and the Republic of Vietnam Campaign Medal.

Admiral Johnson and his wife, the former Miss Margaret Louise Gross of Washington, D.C., have two children, Mrs. Jo-Anne Lee (Johnson) Coe and Roy Lee Johnson, Jr. His home address is Eunice, Louisiana.

NAVY - Office of Information
Internal Relations Division (OI-430)
4 March 1968

DECLARATION OF TRUST

The undersigned does hereby appoint and designate as his (her) Trustee herein, the Secretary-Treasurer and Publisher of the United States Naval Institute to perform and discharge the following duties, powers, and privileges in connection with the possession and use of a certain taped interview between the undersigned and the Oral History Department of the United States Naval Institute.

1. Classification of Transcript.

   ( )a. If classified <u>OPEN</u>, the transcript(s) may be read or the recording(s) audited by the qualified personnel upon presentation of proper credentials, as determined by the Secretary-Treasurer of the U.S. Naval Institute.

   (X)b. If classified <u>PERMISSION REQUIRED TO CITE OR QUOTE</u>, the user will be required to obtain permission in writing from the interviewee prior to quoting or citing from either the transcript(s) or the recording(s).

   ( )c. If classified <u>PERMISSION REQUIRED</u>, permission must be obtained in writing from the interviewee before the transcribed interview(s) can be examined or the tape recording(s) audited.

   ( )d. If classified <u>CLOSED</u>, the transcribed interview(s) and the tape recording(s) will be sealed until a time specified by the interviewee. This may be until the death of the interviewee or for any specified number of years.

2. It is expressly understood that in giving this authorization, I am in no way precluded from placing such restrictions as I may desire upon use of the interview at any time during my lifetime, nor does this authorization in any way affect my rights to the copyright of my literary expressions that may be contained in the interview.

Witness my hand and seal this 25 day of Jan. 1982.

Roy L. Johnson

I hereby accept and consent to the foregoing Declaration of Trust and the powers therein conferred upon me as Trustee:

R. E. Bowler Jr.

Interview No. 1 with Admiral Roy L. Johnson, U.S. Navy (Retired)

Place: His home in Virginia Beach, Virginia

Date: Thursday morning, 4 December 1980

Subject: Biography

By: John T. Mason, Jr.

Q: Well, at long last we're going to get under way, Sir, and I'm delighted. Would you begin in the proper way, this being a spoken biography, by giving me the date of your birth and the place of your birth, and then tell me something about your family background.

Adm. J.: I was born in the state of Louisiana on 18 March 1906 in a place that I'm not sure is even on the map these days, Big Ben, Louisiana. At that time, my father and mother were involved in farming. Based on what I learned later, this farm, this place, was located not too far from the Mississippi River. They didn't stay there very long because in those days the Mississippi River on pretty regular occasions would flood and this flooded out this whole area, so they had to move and that ended their farming.

Q: What kind of farming was it in that area?

Adm. J.: Typical Mississippi Delta in those days, sugar cane, cotton, and corn. Of course, you go down there today and it's difficult to find cotton growing in any of those places. Sugar cane, yes, of course a lot of corn, but mostly sugar cane.

So, after this disaster, I suppose you'd call it -

Q: Indeed it was a disaster!

Adm. J.: He moved farther south. How this connection came about I don't know, but he got into the lumber business, saw-milling, and as long as I can remember after that, as a kid growing up, he was always in the lumber business, moving from one place to another because you'd have these big lumber mills and they'd buy up large tracts of timber. In time, they would cut it out -

Q: Largely pine, I suppose, wasn't it?

Adm. J.: Depending on the location. In Eunice, Louisiana, and that's where I finished high school before going to the Naval Academy, they had pine and they had hardwood. In another place, another big lumber mill that he was connected with before that, this was about eighty miles north of New Orleans, this was the cypress swamps, nothing but cypress. They would log out these tremendous cypress trees, some of them as much as thirty feet in diamater. Of course, you don't see any more of that. It's all cut out, and not too many years ago they finally realized they'd better start reforesting, like Weyerhauser and some of these other big outfits. Of course, with cypress it will take you a hundred years and that's the thing that's been happening to our natural resources.

Anyway, we moved about -

Q: How many members were there?

Adm. J.: The family was increasing all the time, and, by the time I went to the Naval Academy, I was the oldest of twelve.

Q: Twelve children?

Adm. J.: Yes, six boys and six girls. Finishing high school of course, I didn't want to stay in Eunice, Louisiana, which is a wonderful little place. I go back to it every now and again. It's right in the middle of what they call the Cajun country.

Q: Oh, yes.

Adm. J.: Lafayette, Opelousas. But I didn't want to stay there. I wanted to go some place and try to get some kind of an education.

Q: What impelled you to move out from there?

Adm. J.: Well, I just didn't feel that if I stayed there, having seen what other people did, you know, and followed in the footsteps of two or three generations in operating a clothing store or a fuel and feed store or something like that. I didn't want to get in the lumber business, I can tell you that, because after having worked two or three summers at a dollar and a half or two dollars a day at hard labor, I couldn't see any future in that.

So, finishing high school, I did have a scholarship to Southwestern Louisiana Institute in Lafayette, and this professor in the high school, a very wonderful man, wonderful to me, Professor Jeanmard, a French name, you know, his father lived in Lafayette and his father's brother lived there also, who was a Catholic priest, Father Jeanmard. So, during the summer, he said:

"Let's go down and get you checked in, look the place over, and see what we can do lining up a job for you."

So, we went to his father's place, and Father Jeanmard was there also, and for lunch this one day there was Congressman Lazaro, a U.S. congressman, from Opalousas. He was visiting there, and he asked me what I was going to do. I told him that I was going to go to SLI and take engineering. So he said:

"Well, I don't suppose you have any desire to go to West Point?"

I said, "Sure, I'd like to try."

He said, "Well, I've got a vacancy for West Point, and you'll make five people who are interested in this appointment. Take the competitive exam and whoever comes out No. 1, of course, will get the appointment."

So I went back, and I didn't really think about it too seriously at the time, but I boned up a little bit on the math and a few things like that, then took the exam. One day a secretary called from Opalousas and said:

"The congressman said to inform you that you came out No. 1, but he made a mistake. This vacancy is not for West Point, it's for Annapolis."

I said, "where is that?"

Of course, I then had to take the entrance exams for the academy, passed those, and that's how I got into the Naval Academy.

Q: How did your family react? What did your mother think about this military thing?

Adm. R.: Well, the first reaction was that you stayed close to home and didn't go away, but my mother was pretty broadminded about it. My father was more that way than my mother. She was happy to see me go some place and do what I wanted to do.

I went up there, and Congressman Lazaro and Mrs. Lazaro would come down every two months or so on Sunday to see me. They'd take me out to lunch and they were very good to me.

Q: That was most unusual, a personal interest.

Adm. J.: Yes, I was the first midshipman that he appointed to ever finish the Naval Academy. Every other one busted out. So I guess that's one reason why he was interested in me. He followed my carrer as long as the old gentleman lived. He was really quite a wonderful person.

So, I guess, among other things, I lost my Southern accent, as my mother used to say, and I belonged to the navy. Of course, in the navy you don't have an opportunity to get home as often as you would in some other occupations, and they were always disappointed I did not come home as often as they would like. But, as I just said, in the navy that's a different situation, a different environment.

Q: Did any of the other brothers or sisters get away, too?

Adm. J.: Not really. My third brother wanted to go to Annapolis but he didn' make it. He very much wanted to go, but he got in the insurance business and did very well in Jackson, Mississippi. My family had eventually left Louisiana and moved to Mississippi.

Q: Oh, I see.

Adm. J.: First, to Morton, Mississippi, and that's where they lived until they died, they're buried there. Some of my brothers and sisters lived there. A brother of mine, next to me, moved to Yazoo City, and did very well. He became involved in real estate and was mayor of Yazoo City for, gee, I don't know how many years. I don't think they could get rid of him! He was a Democrat then, even though in later years, his leanings went from Democrat to Republican. Those people down there, at one time, there "was stamp the rooster". No matter who it was, if they were a Democrat, that's who you voted for.

Q: It's changed since.

Adm. J.: So my brother Floyd began to change that way, even at the time Carter came in, but he had to make all the arrangements for Jimmy Carter, when he came down to Yazoo City, and spoke to a gathering in this big townhall. I remember seeing it on TV. There he was sitting up there. He looked as though he enjoyed it very much. He did all right. Of course, he's retired now and lives in Hattiesburg, Mississippi, and travels around quite a bit.

Q: Tell me about your early years in the academy.

Adm. J.: They were pretty tough because -

Q: What about - ?

Adm. J.: Academically, because in the first place, a lot of people going to the Naval Academy then were in a much higher age group than they are today, which meant that many of them had been to college.

Q: At least one or two years?

Adm. J.: At least one or two years. I can well remember the fellow who stood No. 1 in the class of '30, the class behind me, '29, he's gone to LSU for four years. Well, I came right out of high school and, of course, your first year in the Naval Academy you're introduced to solid geometry in one month, and trig, and things like that. Well, the high schools down there didn't teach them. You got a smattering of plane geometry and that's all. None of this other stuff. So that was a pretty roughroad for the first year, particularly in mathematics. After the first year, you begin to learn how to study, and with help from a wonderful roommate that I found when I arrived in Annapolis, Sam Lincoln from Alton, Iowa - he had gone to the University of Iowa for two years. He had all this solid geometry and stuff. He never had to even open a book.

Q: So he helped you!

Adm. J.: Oh, yes. He was a very wonderful person. I hear from him to this day. A kind of an interesting thing happened because — I'm getting too far ahead now - World War II, I went up to Quonset to form and commission, Air Group 2, and we were going to go aboard a carrier, going to fly west and then go aboard a carrier. Well, I arrived up there and in, oh, I guess we were there two or three days. One Saturday evening, I went into the Officers' Club and saw this naval officer in a white uniform up at the bar. I didn't think anything of that, but he stayed at the bar and tossed one right after the other. Pretty soon, the guy was really in bad shape, staggering all over the place. One of the squadron commanders was with me and I said:

"Who in the world is that?"

He said: "He's just arrived. He's your administrative officer."

I said, "He was."

So I called down to BuPers, to a classmate of mine who had an assignment there, and said"

"Look, get me another administrative officer. I need him in a hurry because we're getting organized."

He said, "I have just the person. He just applied for active duty, we've brought him on, and I'm sending him up there next week, and he's your old roommate."

He had to get out of the Naval Academy when he graduated because of his eyes.

Q: I see. Yes, they were very strict.

Adm. J.: His eyes went bad the second year he was in the Naval Academy. It was amazing to me that he was able to pass the eye exams. Of course, you can get waivers now, but in those days you couldn't. You were 20/20 or you didn't stay in. But he memorized that eye chart and if he knew where the fellow put the pointer, he could rattle it off forwards, backwards, diagonally, any way. He had the whole thing memorized, and that's the way he finished the Naval Academy.

He became my administrative officer and was really a wonderful person.

Q: What a great association, too, to see him again.

Johnson #1 -10-

Adm. J.: Yes. He was with me all the time that I had Air Group 2 in the Hornet.

Q: You say the first year was a tough year. What about adjusting to the kind of routine they had at the academy in those days, the regimentation and hazing?

Adm. J.: Oh, well, some of it was irritating, but it really didn't bother me too much.

In those days, except for some being more severe, the harsh physical forms of hazing, a lot of this was accepted as a thing that a plebe had to go through as part of his indoctrination.

Q: Toughening him up?

Adm. J.: Discipline. Of course, there were extremes and there was no place for that, absolutely no place. It should have been regulated and, in time, it was. Some people seemed to get some great big kick out of swatting somebody twenty times with a broom.

Q: Memorizing a lot of silly things and all that?

Adm. J.: I didn't think that was too bad. In other words, at the table where I sat in the messhall they made a big point of your learning about naval history. Of course, I new nothing about Lord Nelson and those people. They'd ask you question after question about that. You had to prep yourself and, of course, if you didn't have most of the answers you were in trouble. Then, the old business

Johnson #1 -11-

of having to walk with a military posture and so forth. I don't think there's anything too wrong with that. Marching to and from class, it's a military institution, so I didn't see anything wrong with that. Today, of course, that's all gone. Except for the uniform, you would hardly know it was the naval academy.

Q: I agree with you. I knew it in those days, too, as a visitor there.

Adm. J.: Either you have a military institution or you don't, and I think we've let the pendulum swing too far in that direction, liberal and so forth. Jimmy Holloway brought it back quite a way but it seems to me now that it's swinging the other way a little bit much again.

I admire Bill Lawrence very much, he and Diane. I'm very fond of them, but they've got some liberal ideas about the way the Naval Academy should be run.

Q: Of course, the excuse that is offered is that you have to bend somewhat to be more in keeping with the outside world. Youngsters come in from the outside world and they're acclimated in a certain direction.

Adm. J.: Well, I would say there's probably a lot in that that is true and probably makes sense because there is the changing mood of the country, unfortunately. Unfortunately, that is a thing that's happening in the country that's not very good, along with the weakening of our moral fiber and so forth.

I think you have to accommodate to a degree to this sort of thing. On the other hand, I don't think you have to go as far as a lot of people think you do, because they are still able to recruit and entice enough high-quality men and women to come in to the military schools. They're still able to do that.

Q: Well, its quite an education that's provided!

Adm. J.: Oh, yes.

Q: That in itself is a great inducement.

Adm. J.: That's another area that I think we've gone to extremes in, and this is due to the influence of Rickover. I think they went to extremes, namely, the liberal arts and so forth. He didn't say so in so many words, but he thought that seamanship, navigation and leadership are things you could possibly acquire after you left the Naval Academy; in other words, the professional subjects. Holloway and Bill Lawrence put more and more emphasis on professional subjects, the adjustment and balance in the cirriculum. They still have the others. They have these elective subjects like in languages and so forth, and that's probably all right. But I think he went too far in that direction and really didn't seem to realize the importance of these various things along with leadership.

Q: That is the essential element.

Johnson #1 -13-

Adm. J.: Yes.

Q: Tommy Hart told me many years ago that he had two things in mind, training a young man for leadership and to be a gentleman. Those were the two elements he had in mind.

Adm. J.: We used to say "gentlemen by act of Congress."

Q: Well, tell me more about your academic years there. What did you excel in?

Adm. J.: Nothing, really. I wasn't any star man or anything like that.

Of course, those were lean years in the Naval Academy because '29 and those were depression years, and the regiment - it was a regiment of midshipmen then - was half of what it is now. Our class, as I recall, was 420 or something like that, and out of that number we graduated, I think, about 280. Out of that, I stood 61, so you can see I wasn't any great scholar in the academic sense.

Q: What academic subjects appealed to you most?

Adm. J.: The professional, really.

Q: Engineering and -?

Adm. J.: Engineering, navigation, electrical engineering, language didn't give me any problem.

Q: What did you do, French?

Adm. J.: French, yes, and I guess that was a mistake because I came from the Cajun country and was able to speak the patois down there, Cajun.

Q: Which isn't exactly French, is it?

Adm. J.: To come up there and get involved in grammatical French and so forth gave me problems. I'd have been better off if I'd taken Spanish. Those were the only two you could take in those days.

History, I liked history. English I had a bad time with at times. My lowest marks, I guess, were actually in English. Of course, it was a great day when you finished there.

Q: What about athletics?

Adm. J.: I always liked athletics, from the days in high school —of course, I wasn't big enough to do anything in football, only class football and basketball. I was on the varsity baseball team. I was a pitcher on the baseball team and played baseball all four years there. I liked that.

I think athletics are very important, part of being in an institution. Other people, particular classmates of mine, would almost glue themselves to books and, I must say, some of them came out with very high marks. But, thinking back to the first eight or ten people in my class, right now I can't think of one of them who ever got very far in the navy. One ended up in St. Elizabeth's, one committed suicide, for example.

Q: Oh, my!

Adm. J.: And the others just ended up not going very far.

Q: Athletics contribute to a sense of team participation.

Adm. J.: Team participation, knowing people, getting to know people, in addition to rounding out your makeup. In other words, the mental and physical part, and it's a healthy thing.

Q: It also turns right over into your profession, doesn't it, on board ship? It's a team that's operating, isn't it?

Adm. J.: Yes, working with people.

Q: Tell me about the summers. Did you have a cruise?

Adm. J.: In those days -

Q: Plebe summer first.

Adm. J.: Plebe summer? Let's see, we went aboard three battleships, the old battleships _Florida_, _Utah_, and one other one. I was in the _Florida_. It wasn't much of a cruise because, once again, everything was in the direction of austerity.

Q: The depression?

Adm. J.: Because of the economic situation.

Q: Yes.

Adm. J.: So all we did was cruise the East Atlantic Coast and then go to Guantanamo.

Q: You were going to see that many times afterwards, weren't you?

Adm. J.: Oh, yes. We went down there and then, after Guantanamo, after Gitmo, we came up and we visited Marblehead, on the Cape, Pronvincetown, Camden, Maine, and Newport. We had a great time in Newport because I remember the Vanderbilts and the great big mansion where they gave two great big lawn parties and invited all the midshipmen. So we went there.

In Gitmo - of course, that marked the end of the last coalburning cruise by midshipmen. That was the last one.

Q: You had to work!

Adm. J.: Oh, coaling ship, gee it's the worst thing I ever experienced, I think.

Q: Worse than working in a lumber yard, was it?

Adm. J.: Yes.

Q: Dirtier, certainly.

Adm. J.: Yes, because you'd get up at daylight and start loading the stuff, with the tropical heat and all this coal dust. You'd go on September leave, and you still hadn't gotten rid of all the coal dust. You were really pooped out after all this.

Johnson #1   17-

and then the ordeal of having to clean ship and get all this dust out of compartments. It was just an awful ordeal.

Q: And the knowledge that it was going to happen again!

Adm. J.: Yes, and, of course, during this cruise, you spent part of the time in the gunnery department, on a turret, actually firing the big guns. We actually did that, and then we had to spend two weeks down in the fire rooms, shoveling coal. Of course, a lot of them in the ship were old. You'd see some of these old brawny watertenders and firemen and so forth. They were brought up with this kind of thing, but a midshipman wasn't.

Q: It must have discouraged some from going on into a naval career?

Adm. J.: Well, some of the ones who weren't too enthusiastic about it, that's true, they fell by the wayside. You always have that number.

But, going back to adjusting to the way of life in the country today, surprisingly enough, Bill Lawrence just put out these statistics that show that the attrition last year at the Academy was the lowest it's been in many years, below 30 per cent. So I think the people there are really becoming more motivated. The girls, the women, I can't speak for them. I guess they're motivated, even though an increasing number of them seems to dislike the idea of going to sea. The initial reaction is, oh, this is terrific, we'll be the same as the other people, and I guess a lot of them do. But there's no use fighting the idea of women in the Naval Academy. It's a fact.

Q: It's a fact, yes.

Adm J.: But the idea of women aboard combatant ships simply makes no sense at all.

Q: No, it only makes for problems.

Adm. J.: Particularly if you say that today, the first day of any sort of war or combat, they come off. You can imagine the difficulty that would create, and our Congress will probably change that, or try to. There are just too many problems involved The Vulcan, a repair ship, left Norfolk - this was last year - and they had sixty-four women on board, going to the Med, a Med deployment. Well, on the front page of the Norfolk paper, "Six Women Removed from Vulcan Because of Pregnancy Before Going on Cruise." And, of course, going over there for deployment, as Arleigh Burke said, maybe the problem was that they made the deployment nine months long, it should have been shorter. Sounds like Arleigh, but that's typical of some of the problems they're having and will continue to have.

Q: Well, now, your second summer?

Adm. J.: The second year wasn't much better. That was the Oklahoma and Nevada, and we made the cruise this time to the Panama Canal and the West Coast. In those days, every summer

Johnson #1 -19-

you made a cruise in the battleships.

Q: And you got introduced to aviation, too?

Adm. J.: We didn't have an aviation summer then.

Q: You didn't?

Adm. J.: No. Aviation was really in its infancy. They only had one carrier, the old converted Langley. Of course, midshipmen were aware of it.

Q: But not encouraged to think about it?

Adm. J.: Not all all. We weren't exposed to anything in the way of aviation.

We had a good cruise to the West Coast and back. First-class cruise, I've forgotten what ships we were in.

Q: Did you get to Europe?

Adm. J.: No, it was too austere in those days. They wouldn't send us over there. And, of course, now they keep some of them back there and put them on carriers and destroyers, which is a good thing. They keep one class back there, I think, the "segundos," the second class, I think it is. And they used to have aviation summers.

Q: There's much to be said, however, for the whole group of midshipmen going off on a battleship together?

Adm. J.: I thought it was great then, terrific. You were integrated as part of the crew. You actually - well, you holystoned decks, you worked in the fire room, you stood junior officer of the deck watches on the bridge, and you actually got in a turret. I was a pointer in a 5-inch gun turret and I fired the guns at a target, things like that. That was a great experience for a young kid.

Q: Sure.

Adm. J.: Great. I guess they do quite a bit of that today.

Q: It isn't any longer possible, not having battleships available.

Adm. J.: No, no and with your deployments of carriers - that's the thing that's made it very difficult, if not impossible. In those days, you had the Atlantic Fleet and the Pacific Fleet, and they stayed on the coast. They went up and down. Maybe they would go down to the Panama Canal, cross over to the Caribbean to join up with the Atlantic Fleet. It was a rare thing that any part of the Atlantic Fleet went over to Europe. Maybe one or two ships on a special mission or something, but not as a general thing.

In other words, you would have to take the midshipmen, as they do now, to the ship, instead of bringing them into Annapolis Roads, going out in boats, and embarking.

They finally began to introduce avaition to midshipmen, the Aviation Department, and that's when they brought the

Johnson #1 -21-

old seaplanes there and everybody got a ride in an airplane. That's when aviation began to expand, even though in those days the kind of airplanes we were flying weren't exactly -

Q: They were crates!

Adm. J.: Yes, they were.

I left the Naval Academy - and you would draw to see what ship you were going aboard, and everybody went to a battleship, everybody in my class.

Q: That was the first assignment.

Adm. J.: Yes, and there being only 200 of us it wasn't any great problem. I went to the Tennessee, which was a good ship one of the better battleships out there.

Q: Who was skipper of the Tennessee?

Adm. J.: At that time, the first skipper was a fellow they called Handsome Charlie Courtney, Captain Courtney, and he was really quite a handsome figure. He was married to a very, very wealthy socialite from New York.

I stayed on there less than a year because I was put in the gunnery department, down in the plotting room, where they worked out all the fire-control solutions for the turrets firing and so forth, and I applied for aviation flight training. Well in those days, before you could go to Pensacola you had to go to either San Diego or Norfolk and you got ten hours of dual instruction and then you either soloed or you didn't.

Johnson #1 -22-

If you were not cleared for solo, you couldn't go to Pensacola.

Q: That was a culling-out process?

Adm. J.: Yes. That many people applied for flight training in those days.

Q: What induced you to apply for aviation?

Adm. J.: It was just a challenge. Glamor, that was it, the days of glamor of aviation, to fly.

Q: Submarines didn't appeal to you?

Adm. J.: No, not to me. Well, to some people it did, yes. It was volunteer, you see, and we had more volunteers than we needed to fill the quotas. In every department, the gunnery officer - of course, in those days the old battleship people in the Gun Club, the Gun Club guys, you know -

Q: They were supreme at that time.

Adm. J.: They were the top-notch guys. He said:

"Well, Johnson, you're of no potential use to me. You're interested in aviation. They've asked for nominees for the communications department of Commander, Battleships, on the West Virginia, and for that reason your name has been submitted." And that's where they sent me. I was a communicator on the West Virginia.

Johnson #1 -23-

Q: He didn't want anything more to do with you because you were -

Adm. J.: No, because I'd put in for aviation.

I went over there and stayed for about seven months, a communicator handling messages, moving traffic, and so forth, on Admiral Leigh's staff, and Admiral E. C. Kalbfus, a wonderful man, was the chief of staff, a great tactician, a Norwegian.

I finally got orders to go to San Diego for flight training, and I left the West Virginia. Good-bye battleships.

Q: Did any of your classmates go with you?

Adm. J.: Oh, yes. You went more or less as a class, except for a few stragglers, latercomers who had all of a sudden decided they wanted to get into aviation, too.

So we went down, and, as I remember, there were twenty-one or twenty-two of us in what they called the flight-elimination course, and I think twelve of us soloed. Then you waited for orders to go to Pensacola.

Q: This was out of North Island?

Adm. J.: Yes.

Q: Who was out there then, Charlie Mason?

Adm. J.: No, Buddy Weiber was there. Charlie Mason was at North Island. He was on the other side with one of his squadrons over there. Yes, he was there.

I had an instructor whose name was Peterson, another great pilot there was a fellow named Syd Harvey. These were really people who counted, we thought they were next to the man up above.

Q: They had made it.

Adm. J.: They wore these puttees, you know, the boots, which were later abandoned because if you ever went in the water with those it was not good.

Let's see. John Cassidy was out there. He was later well known in World War II. Anyway, the day came and this was my last day of dual instruction, either I solo or I don't, and I'll never forget this fellow got out and said:

"All right, go on, see if you can land this thing, and I hope you don't kill yourself."

So, off we go down the runway. You had to make three landings within two white lines on this field, otherwise you didn't pass. I went up, came down, landed, after the first one I had confidence. I yelled as loud as I could. Came down and so enthusiastic I almost grounded this thing. You didn't have any brakes, you know. He came over and said:

"OK, take me home. You're all right." That's all he said. We went back to North Island, landed, and I very soon got orders to go to Pensacola.

In the class down there, were fifty-some of us, most of them out of my class. A few began to dribble in from the class of '30. Out of fifty-one, fifty-two, or something

Johnson #1 -25-

like that, a little more than half finished, two were killed.

Q: Give me some idea of the training course at that point.

Adm. J.: You went down to Squadron 1 and the old N-2Y seaplanes, two-place seaplanes. Of course, it was almost complete fundamentals of flying, taking off and landing. Then you'd progress into more precision flying like flying around pylons, to be able to take account of wind and so forth, then going up to 2,500 feet, cutting the engine, the switch, and coming down and landing in a certain place to simulate an emergency. And finally, a little bit of formation flying. No acrobatics over there, in the seaplanes. In other words, it was primary flying.

Q: You'd hardly do acrobatics in seaplanes!

Adm. J.: Oh, you could, they were pretty light planes.

There were different phases in this training, like once again you had to solo the seaplanes, and then check out in the next phase, more precision flying. Each time you had to take a check, and unless you passed the check or they were good enough to give you extra time, you were washed out. You were through.

Q: Just one failure and you were through?

Adm. J.: Well, for one down, as they called it, you had to fly two up-checks. That meant you had to take three checks with three different instructors, and then, after you had one down, to fly two ups after that, the odds were kind of against you there.

Anyway, when you left Squadron 1, you'd go to Corey Field. Now you were in primarily land flights, the same airplane, except on wheels. Here you begin to get into formation flying, and then you had to go into acrobatics, you know, the loops and rolls, etc.

In other words, it was a different stage you had to take a check in, and if you progressed satisfactorily, you'd proceed to the next stage. If they gave you a down, and some of them were pretty tough because they were turning out more aviators than the navy needed, so they could be selective. In those days, the attrition was 35 per cent or something like that. Today it is only ten or fifteen.

Q: Did you have any ground classes?

Adm. J.: Oh, yes, from the very beginning you had to -

Q: Half a day, wasn't it?

Adm. J.: Yes. We had to go to ground school for aeronautical engineering, aerial navigation, all about engines, and the whole gamut of things like that, most related to aviation because you already had the other background for the navy, as opposed to what they did with an aviation cadet. When he goes down there, of course, he knows nothing about the navy and he's got to be schooled in all these other different things fundamental to the navy, and it's a very good school that they have for that. They were out of the Naval Academy so they just concentrated on the specialized things in aviation.

Q: Did you have anything to do with gliders?

Adm. J.: Only one time. You see, I left Pensacola and went to Salt Lake City in cruiser aviation, which was not very good. I wanted to go to carriers, but they didn't have very many. After three years on the Salt Lake City, I came back as an instructor at Pensacola.

This was about the time that the Germans went into Crete, remember, all the gliders and all the other things associated with it. This created all this tremendous enthusiasm for gliders. There was a fellow in the navy named Ralph Barnaby. He was dowm there. There was nothing to do - we've got to try gliders (because, just think of the economy involved in it. The fundamentals of flying are taught in the same way. It's the same in a glider, whether you have an engine in front of you or not. So I was part of this experiment to see how this would work with students.

Sure, you could teach them pretty much the fundamentals of flying, aerodynamics and so forth, in a glider, but there was still no way of shortcutting what you had to do and learn how to do in handling an airplane that had an engine in it. You still had to go through that phase, so you weren't shortcutting anything.

Well, that was a bitter blow to the man.

Q: Ralph never got over that, either.

Adm. J.: No, but it just didn't work out. So that was the end of trying to introduce or to integrate gliders into primary flight trtaining down at Pensacola.

Q: That was only for a period of a year or so, wasn't it?

Adm. J.: Oh, less than that, only about three months, that's how long it took to convince you that it just wasn't a thing to do.

Q: Did you have any close calls during your training period?

Adm. J.: You mean as a student?

Q: As a student, yes.

Adm. J.: Oh, I clipped off a couple of pine-tree tops, thing like that, and ground looped a couple of times. I had one engine failure. Fortunately, I was close to the field and came down and landed. That was the only close call, if you want to call it that, I had as a student.

Of course, as instructor, that's different because some of them were very much on the marginal side, they just didn't have the coordination. Probably the most trouble I had with students happened to be with captains sent down there by Ernie King.

Q: The senior types?

Adm. J.: Senior types, yes.

Q: You mean their reflexes were not as great?

Johnson #1 -29-

Adm. J.: They can't possibly be the same as a young man's. We had Halsey, McCain, Shermam Brown, and Lee Hoyes, Gunther. Oh, there were eight or ten of them. They'd never had anything at all to do with aviation.

Q: King had already been through the mill?

Adm. J.: Oh, yes. He had qualified in submarines and aviation.

We were beginning to come out with more carriers, the Lexington, the Saratoga, and the Ranger, and there were very few people who were born in aviation who had reached the rank of captain then. So this is how he filled that void, even though he could have taken some of these other people and made captains out of them, and they'd have been a lot better qualified.

Q: He was head of Aeronautics at that point?

Adm. J.: Yes, and made them skippers of these carriers. So they sent these people down there and the idea was that they'd take the same courses as all the other students. Well, that was a mistake.

I was in Squadron 3 and we were flying the PS-2U, a Chance Vought scout airplane, carrier type. They'd put them through the primary part of it and then they came over to us, and I had McCain as a student, I had Admiral Noyes as a student, I had Sherman as a student, and Gunther. He couldn't even taxi the airplane. You were sitting in the rear seat and he was up forward, and he's taxi like this, weaving. Couldn't even taxi the airplane.

But I must say these people wanted to fly.

Q: Were you more lenient with them as a result of their age?

Adm. J.: We had to be. You've got a certain number of pilots in any one phase as a regular student, and then, if you couldn't pass the check, that's all you got, unless they were lenient enough to give you extra time. But these people, we were stuck with the. They would go out ten hours, fifteen hours, or twenty hours until they passed.

So John Sidney McCain came out and I took him out to what we called shoot the circle. You'd go up, climb up to 1,500 feet, you'd cut the engine back and you'd glide down, and you were supposed to land inside this 200-foot circle. I worked on him and worked with him and I finally got him to the point where in this one field he could hit the circle about two out of three times. I could see what he was doing because he cut his power and he's glide down and once he got over this little farmhouse he would be at a certain altitude and then over this road down here at a certain altitude, and he was all right.

So he went out one afternoon and he came back and the check pilot said:

"Gee, he couldn't even land in the field, leave alone hit the circle." So I went over and asked him and he said:

"The altimeter must have been out, Son."

What had happened was the wind had changed 180 degrees and he lost all his check points!

Johnson #1 -31-

Q: He really was at sea!

Adm. J.: Yes. Then they put him in fighters. You see, the last squadron you went to in flight instruction were single-seat fighters. You got in that thing and off you went. That was the last squadron you went to.

They started out putting these people in these fighters. Well, they decided very quickly they'd better shortcircuit that idea and just give them a few flights.

Q: You mean they'd lose all of them?

Adm. J.: Well, there was a good chance of it.

They tell a story about Admiral Halsey and he went up -Evans, I guess, was his instructor, who had Squadron, fighters, and he would give cockpit checkout and tell you what to do and so forth, and Halsey asked him:

"how do you take this thing off?"

And he says, "Well, Captain, I tell you what, you get in there, you get all set, and you head it down the runway, and you give it full throttle, push the stick forward and I defy you to keep that thing on the ground."

Well, off he went and the next thing people saw was the plane up on its nose.

They finally graduated all these people out of Pensacola.

Q: They must have been a disruptive element for the regular students down there, weren't they?

Johnson #1 -32-

Adm. J.: Yes, a little bit, because they saw what was happening. Here, with the regular students at that time we had more than enough students to take care of the quota but we prety well needed all we had and they were pretty stringent in their requirements of them. They had to cut the mustard, and to see the treatment being given to these people, that didn't sit too well with some of them.

Q: There must have been another way of dealing with this situation?

Adm. J.: Well, that was King's way of dealing with it. As I said before, there were people who had been in aviation long enough, Herbster, and Charlie Mason was getting close to it, they could have promoted them to captain and sent them out to command the carriers.

Q: What about Ballentine? He was still younger.

Adm. J.: Ballentine was almost at that point, yes.

Q: He was from 1921.

Adm. J.: Yes, and Radford. They had people out of the class of '18. But you see, and they're still thinking even today that you do not have to be an aviator to command a carrier battle group - they call them battle groups now - or the carrier itself. There's still that feeling, which is completely erroneous. That's a very fallacious thing. It has been tried in the case of the carrier battle groups and it just doesn't work out because so many things can happen so fast involving airplanes, particularly in the day of jets, that unless you have some understanidng of jets you can really get a lot of people in trouble. It's bad enough in peacetime but even more so if you were in a combat situation.

Q: Yes, but I was wondering if it wouldn't be possible for these older men, given a course of sprouts to learn all about planes and so forth without necessarily learning to fly.

Adm. J.: Yes, at first, but as I said, they changed their minds about it later on. That was going a little bit too far. This was due to Ernie King and, boy, you know how demanding he was. In a lot of ways, he was a great naval officer and probably the person that the navy needed at a time when no one else could probably have done the job as well as he did. I think President Roosevelt knew that at the time he brought him in as CinCAtlantic. He was a pretty irascible gentleman, I'll tell you that.

Q: That was quite a tour you had down there as an instructor. How long was it?

Adm. J.: Two years, but that's what I liked to do because you got plenty of flying under all kinds of conditions, night flying, etc. It was nothing at all to get in 100 hours a month with students.

Q: Did you operate from Corpus Christi?

Adm. J.: No. Corpus Christi didn't exist then. All we had was the Penscola complex. It was about that time we began to expand rapidly with the approach of World War II. During World War II that we got into Meridian, Mississippi, and Corpus; also the other operating base places like Jacksonville. Of course, Jacksonville was never training, just a big carrier base. But soon we had so many carriers that you couldn't base them all here at Norfolk and at San Diego, and the next thing we opened up was Alameda and Quonset Point in addition to Mayport (Jacksonville). Quonset Point, now, has been pretty well abandoned, which is too bad because we may need it one of these days again.

So I finished flight training and went to the Salt Lake City, which was a bitter disappointment.

Q: Why?

Adm. J.: Because I wanted to go to a carrier. That was the glamour part of naval aviation -

Q: How many planes were there on the Salt Lake City?

Adm. J.: Four planes and, let's see, there were two fresh-caught aviators out of Penscaola plus two, they called them APs, enliste pilots. About once a year they'd send a whole class of nothing but enlisted men down there, and they made good pilots.

Johnson #1 -35-

Q: Later, I think.

Adm. J.: Yes. So we had a total of eight pilots and four airplanes, two catapults, four seaplanes. Most of the time you would ride in the rear seat operating an old key radio set.
We were part of the Scouting Force then. The Salt Lake City was one of the two first treaty cruisers, 8,000 tons.

Q: Was she in the Pacific?

Adm. J.: Yes. I finished flight training and waited in Norfolk about four months for her to come around and she never made it. I was running out of money and couldn't take any more leave, so I went to the West Coast and joined her out there. Most of the fleet was in the Pacific then, the same as it was for a long time. Only during the Neutrality Patrol, when Roosevelt ordered quite a few ships into the Atlantic providing convoy and so forth, did we have any ships in the Atlantic.
Anyway, I went aboard the Salt Lake City, and we were just a complete nuisance aboard the ship in the eyes of most of the people.

Q: Did you stand watch and do things like that?

Adm. J.: We stood watch in port, but we weren't qualified to stand watch under way.

Q: Some of the skippers insisted upon it, didn't they?

Adm. J.: Well, later on they did and it was a requirement that you had to spend so much time on the bridge, but not in those days.

Q: You were a different kind of breed on board ship?

Adm. J.: You were pretty much a stepchild, I can tell you that. You were just something they had to put up with and really needed only in longe-range battle practice. They had 8-inch guns on there that could shoot a distance of 28,000 yards, but, in order to spot any gunfire at that range - you couldn't see anything from the ship since it was below the horizon so they'd put us up and we'd do the spotting and we'd send the spot back by radio key.

Q: Well, you performing a useful function?

Adm. J.: Oh, sure. That was our act, and they'd let you fly as long as you were doing something like that.

The gunnery officer on there was Jerauld Wright. He was really the aviators' boss. He was pretty good with us. He looked after us, because all the aviation on there was part of the gunnery department. So we came under him. But he was the only one on there who thought we served any useful purpose. The rest of the people - we'd get all the bad watches, and they loved to give you the mid watches because there was a fleet order put out that anyone flying the next morning could not stand any watch after midnight.

Johnson #1 -37-

Q: Privileged in that sense?

Adm. J.: Yes. This, of course, meant that they couldn't put you on the mid watch. They didn't like that. So any time you weren't flying, they just waited, and, boy, you could be sure you were going to be on the mid watch every time. That was quite an experience. But it began to improve as time went on with different skippers. The last skipper I had on there was a namesake of mine, Captaom Ike Johnson. He liked the aviators, and he had us up on the bridge standing JO watches and pretty soon some of us qualified for top watch. He was very good. Any place he had to go, he's always ask me to fly him. He loved to fly. The Salt Lake City came around, the whole fleet came around, and that's the time they had the big fleet parade up in New York City.

Q: Oh, yes.

Adm. J.: Before that, we were anchored in Hampton Roads and the old man, Captain Ike, said:

"Well, I've got to go to Washington, to a big costume ball." He was a bachelor. "I want you to fly me up."

This was Saturday afternoon.

Q: Was he going to take you to the ball, too?

Adm. J.: No. My wife's family lived up there. I was going to see them.

I told him I'd get an airplane ready, which I did. So he gets in the rear seat, I'm in the front seat and they hoist us over the side by crane instead of catapult. And, of course Hampton Roads is noted for tremendous currents, 4 and 5 knots. I didn't like that too well, so I said:

"Now, look, be sure that when you hoist me over and you put me down in the water, this airplane is not towed out because that current is going to catch me and I'm not going to have enough slack in this hook to disengage it."

Well, they did exactly that. The more cable they let out. The more the airplane went out away from the ship, and pretty soon that airplane was up like this. I looked back and there the captain was. You could see his knuckles were white, and I finally said:

"Captain, get out, bail out," and so he got back in the water. I did, too, because I thought we'd be upended, and, of course, the concern was to get the captain back aboard. They threw all these lines out and everything. They weren't concerned with me. I went floating off the stern and finally grabbed a line on a whaleboat on the next ship astern, the Northampton. Well, they threw these lines to the captain, and finally hauled him up. But right under a scupper, going full blast over the side.

Well, I finally got back and told the people in charge that experience should be a lesson.

Q: You'd served warning!

Adm. J.: I got back and, heck, he was already changed. He said:

"Run down and change clothes. Get up here as soon as you can. We're going to take of."

Q: Do it again!

Adm. J.: I said, "OK, this time we'll go on the cat."

Went to the catapult and off we went. No problem.

Q: Why didn't you use the catapult the first time?

Adm. J.: The people in charge of the deck just didn't want to do it. They didn't want to go to the trouble of getting the thing ready.

Q: Oh, I see.

Adm. J.: So we took off, landed in the Anacostia River. The navy had the air station on the river. It was dark, I landed, taxied it up, and the old man got out and went to his costume ball, and Monday morning came back. He still had lipstick all over him. Apparently, he'd had himself a great time, and back to the ship we went.

Q: Now, let's lap back because you told me that you were married by that time. Tell me something about that. This being a biography, that part of your life has to come in, too.

Adm. J.: Last year, we celebrated our fiftieth wedding anniversary. I graduted June 6th and we were married June 6th 1929.

Q: Oh, you were?

Adm. J.: This girl that lives in this house here - well, I met her up in Washington -

Q: It was permitted in those days then?

Adm. J.: Yes, the two-year thing had been changed two or three years before that. Of course, even after they changed it, there were two in my class who were married the second year they were at the Naval Academy. It was a secret and they never did find out..

Q: If they had found out they would have left.

Adm. J.: There's a case of a graduate of the Naval Academy in the Marine Corps - I don't know why they made such a court case out of it - but several years later, they discovered that he had been married while he was in the Naval Academy. I can't remember exactly what the penalty was, but I think they took away from him all of the extra money he'd got at sea by virtue of being married. He lost it.

Anyway, I met Peg up in Washington. Midshipmen on Christmas leave used to go over to Washington, and -

Q: The ones who didn't go back home?

Adm. J.: Yes, that's right. It was too far for me to go back home. I didn't have that kind of money.

Johnson #1 -41-

Then, of course, after the academic year started all these girls would flock down for the hops and the football games and things. So we got married when I graduated.

Q: She was down in Pensacola then?

Adm. J.: Oh, yes. We had two lovely children.

Q: Had they arrived by that time?

Adm. J.: Let's see. one of them, my daughter, was born while I was in the Salt Lake City. Then I went as an instructor. I was an instructor for two years and I came back right here to Norfolk and went into a squadron on the old Enterprise, and that was when our son was born.

Q: And he's Roy Jr.?

Adm. J.: Yes. He is living on the West Coast, in San Jose, and he's an engineer working for a subsidiary company of the Dillingham Corporation.

Q: Are they related to the Hawaiian family of Dillinghams?

Adm. J.: That's where they're based, that's where the parent headquarters are. Mr. Lowell Dillingham founded the company. It's a big corporation. At the moment, he's in charge of the building of - I think right now it's the biggest hospital under construction in the United States, 700 or 800 rooms, in San Jose.

Johnson #1 -42-

They have two children and we're crazy about them. One of them is five and the other one is four.

My daughter Jo Anne is in Washington. She's office manager for Senator Dole.

Q: Oh, really?

Adm. J.: Yes.

Q: She's got an active boss!

Adm. J.: Oh, yes. At the moment she's over with Elizabeth, Mrs. Dole, who's quite a woman. They're running the transition, of course. That's what they're doing now.

Q: It's been rumored that Mrs. Dole is going to get some kind of a job in the new administration.

Adm. J.: She's a very capable woman. She was head of the Federal Trade Commission before she married Senator Dole.

Jo Anne has a daughter. Both of them are divorced. The daughter, Kathy, is twenty-six, so we've got quite a spread in grandchildren. One of twenty-six and the others four and five. She's quite a live wire. I can't keep up with her. She's too much for me because she's about the No. 1 lobbyist up on the Hill for the National Rifle Association.

Q: She must have worked hand in hand with Lloyd Mustin, then, at one point?

Adm. J.: Oh, yes, she sure did. I think some army general has relieved Lloyd.

Q: Yes, I think so, too.

Adm. J.: She's very active in politics, and I think she'd prefer to be in some senator's office or something like that. She's working with the transition team, too, in addition to the other. The NRA has loaned her to this transition outfit. You know, that's a great big outfit up there, a lot of people in it. I don't think they need that many, but I guess somebody thinks they do.

At one time, she was vice president of the Young Republicans of Virginia. That's how active she's been in all these different campaigns. The two of them, of course, were very active for Obernsheim, who was really a very fine man.

Q: He was the one who was killed, and Warner came in?

Adm. J.: Yes, and John Warner, I would say, up to this point has turned out to be a very good senator.

Q: Well, back to your career now! Having been down in Pensacola as an instructor, in May of 1937 you joined Scouting Squadron 6, and that took you to the Enterprise.

Adm. J. That's right, which was built at Newport News along with the old Yorktown and commissioned right here. I stayed on her quite a while.

Adm. J.: The Essex was the first of the old Essex class. Prior to that, you had the Yorktown, the Enterprise, and the Hornet those three. Of course, the Yorktown and the Hornet were both sunk. The first Hornet in Santa Cruz and the Yorktown at Midway. She was abandoned by Captain Buckmaster and his people. He was a student down there as another one of Ernie King's people.

At first we operated on the East Coast with the Atlantic Fleet, and Commander Carriers, Atlantic Fleet, as "Bull" Halsey. He was an admiral by then. That consisted of the Yorktown and Enterprise On the West Coast, you had the Lex, Saratoga, and the Ranger, and every so often all of those carriers would come through the canal and we'd all join up in the Caribbean for a big war game.

Q: Defending the canal?

Adm. J.: Well, that was part of it. Then you'd chose up sides and go at each other. It began to dawn on people then that the carriers really had an offensive capability rather than just being the eyes of the fleet. For a long time they were the scouts of the fleet, and, of course, they served that purpose very well.

Q: Yes, that was a crucial watershed time, wasn't it?

Adm. J.: Oh, it certainly was.

Q: The battleship was beginning to be less -

Adm. J.: No, not yet. They still had the battle line.

Q: But the carriers were beginning to be recognized.

Adm. J.: That's right, because of the tremendous fight put up by people like Ernie King, Jocko Clark, Reeves - Billygoat Reeves -

Q: Jack Towers?

Adm. J.: Jack Towers, yes. All those people fought for Naval Aviation, and they were just beginning to come into their own. Once again, you had people like Jack Towers, why didn't they make him captain of one of the carriers.

Q: For a very good reason, I guess.

Adm. J.: I guess so.

Q: There was personal animosity between Towers and King.

Adm. J.: I think that is true.
Things were beginning to get a little bit tense over in Europe. The Germans went into Poland, didn't they?

Q: First, yes.

Adm. J.: OK. FDR sent all the carriers to the West Coast, sent us out there. The family drove across country and met me in Coronado.

That's when we began a pretty big building program of carriers, about the time that FDR said we were going to produce so many thousand airplanes in a year, 100,000 or something like that. We weren't out there very long, less than a month, when FDR ordered the whole outfit out to Pearl. You remember, over the objection of Admiral Richardson?

Q: Richardson, yes.

Adm. J.: He said to keep them on the West Coast. So they sent all these carriers out there plus the battleships. I was out there quite a while and, about a year and a half before Pearl Harbor, I was ordered out of Scouting Squadron 6 to VP-12. About that time there was another new glamour element in aviation, the P-boats, the PBYs. In other words, you didn't have a rounded-out career in aviation until you'd been in PBYs. Why I don't know, but anyway the skipper of my squadron, Theta Combs, said:

"You ought to go to PBYs, and I'll see to it that you get orders."

So, sure enough, I got orders to VP-12 in San Diego, which never thrilled me too much. Of course, we were doing a lot of flying because that's when Ernie King had all this emphasis on night flying and all-weather flying. People were taking off when you couldn't see the end of Point Loma because of fog, and they had two bad collisions. A lot of people killed, but he still said, "Keep doing it."

I stayed one year in VP-12 and, out of that, back to BuAer. That was the first of my several tours in Washington.

Q: Say a little more about the flying boats and the role they did play at that time.

Adm. J.: At that time, even though they participated in war games, I think they completely exaggerated the potential of the flying boat and minimized the tremendous vulnerability of them. We used to go out and practice by the hour in high altitude horizontal bombing. Well, gee, you were a sitting duck at that kind of stuff. For long-range patrols out of Pearl, if they'd been doing them, they would have seen the Japs. That's all right. That's sort of, you might say, a defensive role, but offensive role, to go out and attack something, no, you'd never make it. You'd never survive. The same thing happened to all of them. They were stationed in the Philippines when the war started. Only one ever got out of there and got to Australia.

They thought that they could protect themselves because you had two waist gunners, a bow gunner and you had a tail gunner, but it was too slow and it was easy to shoot them down.

Q: They were long-distance flyers?

Adm. J.: Long-distance flyers for a scouting, reconnaissance role, and antisubmarine long-range patrols, they were good for that. They carried depth bombs, yes, they were good in the Atlantic for that, but for any role other than that they just couldn't survive. Besides, in some areas of the world where you might have to operate, you couldn't find any suitable water. They tried it up in Kodiak, they tried it in Iceland. You'd never get off because of the freezing water on the wings and the spray. That's why, even though the navy had pioneered in seaplanes and built all these bases, Alameda, San Juan, for seaplanes on the old Hepburn Board's recommendation, they were gradually phased out and, even though at one time there were still some enthusiasts who came up with the Martin jet seaplanes –

Q: The jet, yes, but that was not an immediate success, was it? What was it called?

Adm. J.: It was the Seamaster, and before that we did have the four-engine jobs. That gave them more range and so forth, the PB4-Y. The last real seaplane, I guess, was the Martin PBM. But about that time, based on the lessons of World War II from the British, they began to put in more turrets. You couldn't put a gun in any airplane unless there was a turret. They began to put in self-sealing fuel tanks, which made sense. They began to put in all this armor, and this was adding hundreds and hundreds of pounds of weight and, finally, the poor PBM simply could not take off. The engines overheated and there you were. So they had to change the engines or doctor the engines up.

Q: That's when they experimented with the jet?

Adm. J.: The Jato. It was used during the war, but only in a limited sense because it just didn't fill the need. That's when the navy got into the land-plane business, which was very difficult, and Admiral Towers with George Anderson negotiated a very, very difficult agreement with the army air corps then - it wasn't air force yet - with General Kuter and some of the other people. They did not want the navy to have anything to do with big land planes. And even though they had a B-24 Liberator plant at San Diego and could produce any number of them they wanted at that time, they still wouldn't let us have them. So I think Admiral Towers and George Anderson deserve great credit for really negotiating that agreement whereby they would let us have Liberators and let us operate them.

From then on, of course, down in South China, I mean in Southeast Asia at places like Espiritu Santo that's what the navy operated, land planes, not the PBYs. The only PBY Catalinas down there were the Black Cats, which used to operate at night in a chain up from Guadalcanal, a hazardous thing even at night. So that was the phasing-out of seaplanes, as such, into land planes.

Q: And it remained for Bob Pirie to give it the coup de grace at the end!

Adm. J.: Yes, right. Cost-effectively, it just didn't make any sense.

Q: Are there any foreign navies that use them?

Adm. J.: Not militarily, no, not even the Japanese. The Japanese, you know, at one time were building what looked to be a very, very efficient seaplane. They were going to use it for ASW. It had a new hydrodynamic design on the hull, whereby it could operate in much rougher waters. I saw movies of the test and it looked very good, but then I think they decided not to pursue it. The only place I know where any seaplanes at all operate - and I'm not sure they're still in operation - they used to operate between LA and Catalina Island, between Hong Kong and Macao, places like that. But now the hydrofoil is taking over there, or the air-cushion vehicles have taken over. So I think the seaplane today has gone. It's hard to find one around, as a matter of fact.

I can tell you the only place they're used that I can think of right now is down in the Carribbean(St. Croix, St. John's), and I've forgotten the name of the airline, but the fellow had accumulated thousands and thousands of hours flying for Pan Am, in pioneering for Pan Am, and he was married to the movie actress, Arlene Dahl. He had this airline, which is still operating between the islands down there. He was

Johnson #1 -51-

flying the Grumman amphibian, I think it was the Goose -

Q: The Grumman Goose, that's right.

Adm. J.: - and - I can't think of the fellow's name but he was well known - he was killed in a crash a little over a year ago, a well-known pioneer in aviation. Charlie Blair is the closest I can come to his name.

Q: Talk some more about that period when you were out with the fleet, out in Hawaii.

Adm. J.: It was known as the Hawaiian Detachment, and Admiral Adolphus Andrews was head of it. At that time, of course, the Japanese were acting up. They'd been acting up. They'd been in China for a long time and -

Q: Oh, yes.

Adm. J.: Flexing their muscle and everything. That, of course, is when FDR really began to impose the embargo on oil and it was a question of how long the Japanese could stand that. Not having any source of fuel oil themselves and their reserves were getting low.

Q: It was stangling them, in a sense.

Adm. J.: That's right. So they began to make noises out there and that's why FDR sent the fleet out to Honolulu, hoping that that would show that we meant to do something if they acted up. You might say that that was the genesis of their planning whereby they were going to attack. Of course, all the books and all the war games that you ever read, none of them ever envisaged the idea that the Japanese would attack Pearl Harbor, even though it had proven to be entirely feasible by carrier forces in all the war games that we conducted against the Panama Canal Zone and also Pearl Harbor.

Q: Yes, and using French Frigate Shoals in your exercises.

Adm. J.: Yes, but only for seaplanes.

Tension was mounting all the time and the left hand didn't know what the right hand was doing out there because there was no joint planning, there was no joint operations center, and, really, no realization that there was a possibility that the Japanese might do something like that. Unified Command was totally absent.

Q: Except Richardson seemed to have some idea, didn't he?

Adm. J.: Yes, he did. I guess he was probably the only one who did because he just did not want to expose the Pacific Fleet that far away, and, for what little good you were doing insofar as intimidation and pressure and so forth or whatever you were trying to do with the Japanese -

Q: An image, we'd say now!

Adm. J.: We could probably accomplish just as much on the West Coast and the extra distance provided an additional cushion of time.

Q: What sort of observation flights were taken at that point?

Adm. J.: Well, the PBYs were flying out of Kaneohe. They were flying, but only covering a certain sector and I'm not sure they were even done on a daily basis. It was kind of a random thing and, as it happened, they just weren't out there the morning the Japanese came in, from the direction they came. There was just nobody out there in the NW sector.

I wasn't out there at that time. I'd left there then. I don't know whether the patrols even went out far enough. They must have gone far enough because the Japanese, the range of their carrier aircraft was 100 miles at most, and there'd be no problem for PBYs to fly that sort of a patrol. But they just didn't think there was that possibility, even though all the ships were on varying degrees of alert.

Q: Well, you came back to the Bureau of Aeronautics?

Adm. J.: Yes.

Q: Was this something you wanted to do?

Adm. J.: No, I wanted to stay out in the fleet because I could see that something was going to happen. It was only a question of time.

I came back to BuAer and, at that time, I was spending practically all my time in the Plans Division, trying to take care of all the different things that Harry Hopkins and others were pushing us to produce to give to the British. All this equipment, Grumman airplanes, fighters and all the different spare parts they needed and, of course, they did need the stuff. There's no question about that.

About that time, when I was listening to the Redskins' football game, they announced Pearl Harbor. Everybody ran down to the old building on the avenue there -

Q: Constitution Avenue, yes.

Adm. J.: Constitution, yes, and, gee, I've never seen people who looked so helpless. There was nothing you could do in the face of this disaster we'd just suffered.

Q: Everybody was in a state of shock.

Adm. J.: They said, "Break out the war plan." Well, they broke out the war plan. It was a very general thing, and finally George Anderson and Towers said:

"Well, let's get busy and size up the situation here, what we've got, and make sure what we have left of the carriers."

Fortunately, Halsey didn't come in. That was kind of an accident.

Q: But at that point you didn't know.

Adm. J.: And they turned this whole thing around and diverted these airplanes to us, not the British or somebody else.

Of course, the main thing was right away to call these companies and get them to accelerate their production line, which Grumman did within a matter of days. That's how good Grumman was. But it took time to recover from this. In the meantime, the Japanese could move pretty much as they wanted to and as they did in the Philippines and then down in Southeast Asia. We had practically nothing down there. We had the Houston, and the old Langley was down there, some other old ships, and they combined with the Dutch. Of course, the Japanese did away with them in quick order.

So, at that time, with the war going on, my idea was to get back out in the fleet.

Q: Naturally, but you were doing a real job there.

Adm. J.: Well, it was a necessary job, yes, it was.

Q: So you had to stay.

Adm. J.: Yes.

Q: George Anderson did, too, didn't he?

Adm. J.: Yes, George Anderson did, Abe Vosseller, and the head of the Plans Division that I was in was Duke Ramsey. Let's see. Jack Towers was head of BuAer at the time.

Of course, we had to really beef up and expand the training setup, and Admiral Radford and some others did a tremendous job in that respect. They started the V-5 program in all the different universities around the country, recruited people for it. Tom Hamilton was very much involved in that.

Q: Very much indeed, yes.

Adm. J.: Then they opened up all these E bases, all these little fields throughout the country and put cadets in them. All the technical training in Memphis and other places, training mechanics and so forth, in addition to the real expanded carrier-building program. That's when the Kaisers came in and the converted CVLs.

Q: The jeep carriers.

Adm. J.: The jeep carriers, yes.

Q: What was your particular role in BuAer at that point?

Adm. J.: I was in the Plans Division, in equipment. George Anderson was on the other side, he was in program allocations. He was the guy trying to get the airplanes produced and allocate them to the proper place. On my side of it, we had to make sure we had the latest in the way of radio equipment, armor, to put in .50-caliber guns instead of .30-caliber. One thing we went through that was agonizing, but we finally got it, was the matter of radar. The British had radar, but adapting radar to airplanes was a different thing.

Q: All of it being in a state of infancy, anyway.

Adm. J.: Oh, yes. And to put in new kinds of navigational equipment, identification equipment, and so forth. We'd begun to work on some of this but with not any great degree of

Johnson #1 -57-

urgency, because some of these things the British had started and we were trying to pick it up. But they were so involved in trying to do it themselves and with us trying to help them and put it in airplanes we were giving them, that we were doing very little, if anything, for the ones that we had.

So it took quite a while before the navy, and aviation itself, began to build up.

Q: You got involved directly with manufacturers, then?

Adm. J.: Oh, yes, all the time. Well, every week, because you were doing this on a crash basis, to make it fit, you know, and then to go ahead and produce it as soon as you can, hoping you didn't make too many errors in doing so.

Q: The regular governmental procedure of contracts and bidding and all that was done away with?

Adm. J.: That was out. Cost plus. They made a lot of money on that, I'm sure, but you couldn't afford to waste time on bidding and so forth.

Q: You had to travel around a lot, too?

Adm. J.: Oh, yes. I'd go up to Grumman and Curtiss and get other producers in the act. You had four different outfits producing the F6-F airplane, General Motors and companies like that. They really got cranked up in a big hurry and, of course, once again you had competition because you had the army air corps. They were going into a tremendous expansion, too.

Note: page 58 was omitted as a number in re-typing...text continuous from page 57 to 59

Q: You ran into Gene Wilson, I suppose. Was he a help?

Adm. J.: Yes, but only in a casual way. I do know he had an awful lot of foresight about things. He had been very instrumental, of course, along with one or two other people in the navy, in saying that the way to go in power plants was air-cooled. Before that, on the other side, the army air corps had nothing to do with anything except liquid cooled, and it took them a long time to come around to the other. Their reasoning was that you could not get enough horsepower. Well, that was proved different because you finally had Pratt and Whitney producing - well, we had double-banked air-cooled engines and four-bladed propellers way up in the horsepower.

Gene Wilson was very instrumental in this sort of thing. There were a lot of the real pioneers, Mr. Roy Gumman was one, Curtiss, and the people down at Consolidated, Douglas, and those people. Ed Heineman. Ed had written a book, and well he could write one, about the things he did in evolving the design of airplanes for the navy. People were always saying, "You simply will never be able to operate this airplane off a carrier, no way," just like some of the foremost naval aviators we had expressed severe doubt that you'd ever operate a jet off a carrier.

Q: You say the British helped a great deal?

Adm. J.: Yes, because -

Q: They'd been there before.

Adm. J.: With high-performance airplanes, particularly after we went into the jets, you simply could not have operated jet airplanes efficiently without the steam catapult or the angled deck. Well, they first operated jets without the angled deck.

Q: Yes, they did and so did we.

Adm. J.: But you had a tough time with the nose gear, getting the right kind of barrier, and that just wasn't a very good operation. They'd already gone about as far as you could possibly go with the combination of air-hydraulic catapults. Due to the tremendous pressure generated, they'd already had two very bad explosions, one on the Boxer, with those catapults. So, here, the British came along with the steam catapult and the angled deck that solved a lot of your problems. And they helped us in many other ways, of course.

Q: Another element was introduced into the picture at that point, after Pearl Harbor, and that was the needs of the Russians. How did they infringe on your -?

Adm. J.: As I remember, I don't think the navy was involved in that very much. This was practically all army air corps.

Q: Well, the navy was involved, I remember, with the PBNs.

Adm. J.: The PBN?

Q: Manufactured in Philadelphia.

Adm. J.: We should have given them every one that we had, without charging them! It was a dog.

Q: They did. I think we had twenty-five and they gave them to them.

Adm. J.: They couldn't even copy a PBY up there, and I guess that kind of sounded the death knell of the old factory up there, even though in the early days of Tommy Sprague, Del Farney, and some of those people they probably served a very good purpose.

I can't remember except the PBN, selling any equipment to the navy. Of course, they sent thousands of airplanes over there, through Canada, Alaska, and over the transSiberian route. I read a report by an army air force officer who said he had no trouble following this route because it was strewn with wrecks. That's how careless they were in the ferrying of these airplanes. You see, beyond a certain point, they wouldn't trust anybody to ferry the planes. They had to take them themselves, and they were very difficult to even get to read the manual, to get checked out. They didn't know how to fly the airplane, but off they would go.

I have a classmate who's a very close friend of Kemp Tolley, Chick Frankel.

Q: I know him well.

Adm. J.: Chick at that time over there was a commodore and he was in Murmansk.

Q: For four years, four long years!

Adm. J.: He was over there and he was very much involved in the routing of the convoys, the ships that were coming in there. He was kind of a port director, the unloading of these ships. And, of course, the Russians wouldn't unload the ships. They'd take the stuff after it got on the dock. You remember the armed crews we had to provide?

Q: On the merchant men?

Adm. J.: Those poor devils over there, going across, then sitting there in the harbor, subject to all these attacks almost daily by the Germans. Then they unloaded all this mass of equipment and so forth and out into the countryside it would go.

Have you ever talked to Chick about how he finally smuggled a trip close to the front lines? And the same story all over again. They would not listen to anybody to check them out in the tanks or the airplanes or anything at all, and it wouldn't work so they'd discard it. The waste. And, of course, Ernie King was very much opposed to a lot of this. He didn't want the Russians in the war.

Q: He also wanted all the supplies to go to the Pacific.

Adm. J.: Yes, or at least a good percentage of it, and here we were sending all this stuff over there. Maybe the Russians - I don't know why they would want it. I was trying to say maybe they wanted amphibious landing craft, but I don't know how they could use it. The only need for that, of course, was the priority allocation fight between the Pacific and the Normandy landing. Except for Ernie King, I think it's safe to say that we probably would not have moved as quickly as we did from Guadalcanal up through the Pacific and gone the way we did. It took an awful lot of finesse and stubbornness on the part of Nimitz, King, and other people that we stay with the central Pacific, as opposed to MacArthur's route. I guess he probably never did give in on that idea, thinking that was the right way to go.

Q: Going back to this wartime job, can you think of any specific problems you dealt with?

Adm. J.: Well, it's kind of a joke! You know, duty back there was always so frustrating, anyway. I think the only real positive thing I ever accomplished in my tour in the bureau was that I finally got a good wristwatch _free_ for aviators. I did.

Q: Tell me about that!

Adm. J.: Before that, they had to go out and buy them, and they'd go in the drink and there would go their wristwatches. I finally got three outfits, Elgin Waltham, and one other to submit watches so that we could see which one would be the most suitable for a pilot. By that time, my immediate boss in there was a fellow named Hugh Goodwin. He's relieved Dale Harris, a close friend of mine. I approached him on this problem and he said:

"No, they don't need wristwatches. Why don't you think about putting clocks in airplanes instead of that?"

Well, what the heck. I pursued the thing, anyway, and here come the three watches. Elgin's was by far the best, but they were good wristwatches. They were't cheap watches, but they were good ones. I took them in, put them on Goodwin's desk and showed them to him. I explained what I had done and that I had to select one of the three. He picked up the Elgin and said:

"I like this one. I'll keep this one," and took the watch.

Q: Really a free one!

Adm. J.: Yes, and we went out and we ordered all these watches and the pilots got wristwatches. What they do today, I don't know. Maybe they have to buy their own once again.

I think the biggest problem I was concerned with then was to try and keep up the flow of all this associated equipment that went into the airplanes that were coming off the production line like mad, all their radios, the VHF, which was new -

Q: From all over the country?

Adm. J.: Yes, from different subcontractors, and making this fit in with the production line up in Grumman or some other place, and that was a big job to do that.

Q: To coordinate it all.

Johnson #1 -65-

Adm. J.: That's right, or to see that the right people were involved in coordinating it because, otherwise it would arrive at one place and another place didn't have any.

It was a tremendous logistics operation, really. Then, of course, once we began operating out in the Pacific, you had to create this replenishment line, not only of the airplanes, but also the spare parts.

Q: And that was a major problem in itself?

Adm. J.: Oh, gee.

Q: That was shaping up in -

Adm. J.: You had airplanes that were sitting on deck, not flying because of this one part.

Q: Later on, I imagine it was, just a bit later, Towers and George Anderson were out there in Hawaii in charge of logistics, were they not, and they were on to this problem, too?

Adm. J.: Well, they were kind of a forward BuAer, really.

Q: Yes.

Adm. J.: They sent John Towers out there and he was - I guess he was AirPac.

Q: I've forgotten what his title was.

Adm. J.: He was AirPac. It wasn't NavAir Pac, they just called it ComAirPac then. Of course, Nimitz was the head honcho, he was CinCPac-CinCPOA, the Pacific Ocean Area commander then. But Towers was out there. He was a forward BuAer, that's what he was, for all that stuff needed out there, and that was the distribution center for all the stuff going out to the carrier groups from there. It was up to somebody to keep this line going from back here in the States.

Q: When you go into specialized things like radar, you must have had some additional problems because it was such a secret thing, to begin with?

Adm. J.: Well, what you were trying to do, one of these problems, everybody wanted it immediately, you see - so what you were trying to do was to adapt off-the-shelf material to an airplane instead of something designed specifically to fit in this particular airplane. A lot of times this was quite a problem, but, once again, thanks to the ingenuity of the people in the airplane business, most of the time they made it work. They actually made it work. Some of the more serious problems were never worked out completely like trying to adapt British turrets to our airplanes, particularly the carrier types. Unless you were the right-sized person, you couldn't get in the thing, anyway.

In the ordnance section of BuAer under Freddie Boone, we had a fellow named Pete Wycoff, who was really an expert in aviation ordnance and they called him the "no-go guage." In other words, if he couldn't get in the turret, then it was no good--they had to reject it.

Q: Red Schoeffel was around there, too, wasn't he?

Adm. J.: He was in aviation ordnance, yes. Fred Boone, Schoeffel Burrows and one or two others. They were in the Gun Club people, but they were in the aviation side of it. They were real experts in that. I guess Fred Boone - well, I don't know, he and Schoeff were very much involved in it. Wallace Beakley was in that, one of the great people that I worked with at that time. He could get things done, he really could.

A lot of times, you would find people who were great in the leadership role, were great with people, but they had little in the way of technical knowledge. So, any time you find a person - and Wallace Beakley was one of those - with tremendous technical knowledge and background along with knowing how to deal with people -

Q: A great combination!

Adm. J.: Yes, terrific. He knew how to work with people, not the roughshod treatment that an Ernie King or a Miles Browning would do, but he could still get things done. Of course, he had only so much patience. If he finally realized that a certain person wasn't going to do a job, the only thing to do was get rid of him. But he could still exact the most out of any one person in any given time as anybody I've known, really.

Q: That's real leadership.

Adm. J.: That's right, it's really the epitome of leadership. He had a very sad ending. The poor guy committed suicide.

Q: Did you have anything to do with Seversky and Sikorsky?

Adm. J.: At that time, not very much, because helicopters were really just being born. The only thing I remember seeing at Anacostia was an autogyro. The choppers really didn't come into the picutre until after World War II was over. They were just beginning to come in with Igor Sikorsky, Bell, and let's see, who was the other guy. He hada foreign name, too.

Q: Major Seversky.

Adm. J.: Seversky, yes, but not as much as Igor. Igor Sikorsky was the guy. He built the banana thing with the twin rotors, which Sikorsky never believed in. I believe his name was Piasecki and he was a pioneer in the helicopter business.

Q: Well, now, as I recall, the Coast Guard did take to this idea even during World War II and did something about it and was one up on the navy in this sense. The navy wasn't interested.

Adm. J.: If they did in World War II, they were up on the navy because I can't recall that the navy did very much about it until World War II was over. I'd been on the Hornet when the war was over, came back, and they sent me to the joint staff of the Joint Chiefs. I stayed there two years and then went down to the Second Fleet on Radford's staff. I can remember that was the first time that we were using helicopters, one on each carrier, to be airborne to pick pilots out of the water.

Q: Give me a summary statement of your duty there and what the bureau was trying to do.

Adm. J.: I would say that the most significant aspect of the tour of duty in BuAer was that, to start with, we were almost totally involved in providng and expediting aircraft equipment for our allies. And after, or at the time of Pearl Harbor, we had to very quickly make a transition into taking care of our own needs, while at the same time doing as much as we could to meet the critical needs of our allies.

Q: You were aided, of course, by the fact that our industries were turning out more and more stuff, so there soon became enough for both fronts.

Adm. J.: In almost everything, not everything. There never were enough landing craft to take care of North Africa, Normandy, and the Pacific theater. There never was, and that was the fight Ernie King championed.

Q: Your tour there in the bureau came to an end in May of 1943, when you went up to Quonset Point, Rhode Island. Was that to form a group or what?

Adm. J.: Air Group 2. A lot of the carrier groups were formed on the East Coast because they had the training facilities available, whereas Pensacola, of course, was completely jampacked with turning out students and the West Coast was usually pretty well occupied with basic operational units already past the training phase. So Quonset was a natural place to go. You could go up there and, after you received your new airplanes, you could take the torpedo outfit and put them down at a field we had at Charleston, Rhode Island. You put all the fighters at Atlantic City and that's where the municipal airport is now. That was a navy field then. And you could take the bombers and put them at Wildwood, New Jersey.

So you had them all in one place where they could do all their training pretty well isolated, and, if you wanted to bring them together toward the end, when they were about through with all the individual squadrons, you bring them up to Quonset and the whole group's ready to go.

That was the main job we had, putting on air group together.

Q: Was the weather a factor at all up there?

Adm. J.: In my case, it wasn't because I'd finished all of this prior to the onset of winter. I got out of there in September or October.

Q: But the boys who were training in the wintertime had another problem, I would say.

Adm. J.: Oh, sure, definitely, but except up at Quonset it wasn't too severe. You'd get bad weather now and then when you couldn't do anything. Fortunately, by that time, there were quite a few pilots who had returned from combat tours out in the Pacific and had the benefit of experience. So they would take one or two or three, as many as they could spare, and put them in these new groups.

Q: Sort of a cell?

Adm. J.: Well, to give them the benefit of their experience. That was a big help. I had Butch Voris, he'd been out there, and I had two or three of them.

We finally finished and we were ready to go.

Q: Tell me about some of the problems in organizing a new group.

Adm. J: First of all, it's just basic training, getting them proficient in the flying of the airplane and the use of their primary weapons, whether it be dive-bombing or a fixed gun for the fighters, or in torpedo work for the torpedo planes. Efficiency in the use of their primary weapons. Then, progressing from that into night flying and all-weather flying, but you never had enough time to make all of them proficient in that. The best you could hope for was that the best pilots, maybe one-fourth of them, could become proficient, and the others you just didn't have enough time to do it.

Q: No, when you talk about night fighters, this is quite a process.

Adm. J.: Yes, and to say that everybody had to be qualfieid as such - a lot of people had that idea but it just wasn't achievable, and that was one of the problems involved at the first Philippine Sea thing, when they were all caught out and it was dark. A lot of those kids had never made more than two or three landings at nighttime. Of course, you didn't have all the aids and everything that you have now. In Vietnam, it didn't make any difference whether it was at night or day.

Q: They'd reached that stage.

Adm. J.: Yes, and you had the CCA, the carrier control equipment that monitors the airplane on the radar glide path and so forth and guides them right into the deck. But you didn't have that in those days.

You never seemed to have enough time to get all the pilots qualifed to the degree that you wanted to. Now, the good ones, like at dive-bombing, they could go out for maybe four or five runs and they were OK. Some others you just had to keep working and working with them because they didn't have the same proficiency as the other pilots did.

Q: What was the process of selectivity in getting pilots?

Adm. J.: They were just ordered to you at random as they came out of the mill. It was a grist mill, a mass production of pilots, and out of Pensacola they came. You might get one who would actually be better qualfieid if he was in a bomber outfit than in a fighter, but you had to go ahead and train him, anyway. In other words, there was not any selective categorization of these pilots as they came out of Pensacola at that time. There is now.

Q: That would have been helpful, though, wouldn't it, when you were in the midst of a war?

Adm. J.: Sure. They do that now because there are some kids they'd never send to a fighter squadron. They'd send them to the ASW planes, but they didn't do that then.

Q: How many were you training at one time?

Adm. J.: Well, for an eighteen-plane squadron you had about 25 per cent more than the airplane complement. You had that many spare pilots, and you needed that many because in Air Group 2 we had to get replacement pilots after we'd been out there for a while. They had the jeep carriers doing that, providing the replacement aircraft as well as pilots. A lot of these kids had had very, very little operational training and you had to bring them aboard.

Q: What did the experienced men you had, the two or three, contribute from their experience that was useful?

Adm. J.: In a fighter squadron, for instance, the important thing was what are the tactics that the Japanese will use and have used with the Zero? What is the thing to avoid in a dogfight with a Zero? Don't try to climb with him in a loop, things like that, and what tactics, what maneuvers to use for mutual protection, at the same time to afford you the best opportunity for getting on his tail and shooting him down. Things like that. In the case of the dive-bombers, it was more straightforward. It was just a matter of picking out the target and going down, getting on it, dropping the bombs, and then getting out of there. Then evasive maneuvers after you've dropped the bomb to at least minimize your chances of being hit. And all of this from actual experience, which later on, of course, was incorporated in training handbooks. Even so, it still wasn't the same as having a man there who had actually had this experience tell you about this. So many different things along those lines.

Q: We did have access to an acual Zero, didn't we?

Adm. J.: Yes, I think the first one that we ever had, that we actually flew, was the one they got up in Alaska, when they captured one out on the chain up there.

As time went on, your tactics were changing all the time. You were modifying the way you did things, the same as they were, even though the Japanese tended to always come in and do something the same way all the time. They could never improvise too well.

Q: Really? That's interesting. They weren's innovative?

Adm. J.: No, they couldn't adjust to change, like they said they were coming in to Midway, OK, they're coming in, and here is what they encountered. They should have gotten out of there long before they did, but they were still going to go according to the plan.

Q: How did they achieve such a remarkable plane as the Zero with that attitude?

Adm. J.: Well, that was in the basic design of the airplane. The Japanese Zero was a tinderbox. Man, you put a burst of .50 caliber in there and the thing would explode because it had no armor protection and no self-sealing tanks.

Q: Yes.

Adm. J.: But, of course, it was a very-lightweight airplane and highly maneuverable. It could outmaneuver anything we had by far, and that's why Thach and these people devised the weave for mutual protection. Never go out and try to fight by yourself.

Q: That's surprising, though, that they couldn't change and couldn't adjust, they were inflexible, and yet they had a pretty formidable war machine.

Adm. J.: Well, they did, yes. They weren't nearly as stupid and inefficient as we first thought they were. They were good pilots. They were daring pilots, there's no question about that. They had to be to take any part in the kamikaze course. It hard's to imagine.

Q: Well, now, in training your group, how much actual demonstration did you engage in?

Adm. J.: You mean myself personally?

Q: Yes.

Adm. J.: Well, I would go out and, as the air group commander, I was flying a fighter. I wasn't going to fly any torpedo plane. I was coordinating the overall training effort. Then, as necessary, pulling together, as we would all go out as a group, the torpedo planes, the dive-bombers, and the fighters coordinate that sort of training. But otherwise giving them the time schedule we were working with, that was enough for each squadron to do its own training because it was different for each one.

Then, of course, I had to worry about all the administrative problems and their welfare, the families. The families, that's a big concern. And then putting together all the ancillary things that go with the navy, like the air intelligence officer. He's the guy who did the identification, flashed those things up there so that you'd recognize them in a flash, the photographic officer, and all those people. I being the air group commander, they were part of my staff.

Q: And the photo interpretation?

Adm. J.: Photo interpretation, but usually, particularly later on, that was on the ship - they did that on the ship, in the photo lab there. The photographic officer that I had was the guy who supervised the camera installation, the kind of films to put in there, and so forth. We did a lot of that for Steichen and the fighter planes and aviators that I had on the Hornet took the first colored movie film of dog fights, and a lot of that is what you see in "The Fighting Lady."

Q: What carrier facilities did you have up there at Quonset?

Adm. J.: None. They were all operating. You would get the castoffs. They had one old carrier, the Block Island or somethin that operated in Chesapeake Bay so it wouldn't be subject to the submarine threat. I mean it was a small deck and that's what you qualified on.

Q: So that was a busy six months you were engaged in?

Adm. J.: Oh, yes, you had to compress a lot into six months of time. But these kids had come out of Pensacola and they still had a lot of basic training because, even then - well, there was no carrier qualification down there like you have now. But, even so, they did get some fixed gunnery and they did get some bombings. The biggest things they had to adjust to was the new, different kind of airplane and the new different kind of weapons that they had to use.

And pretty soon, they began to add additional weapons. They had to learn the business of aiming and firing rockets.

Q: Yes.

Adm. J.: They had rockets on everything, which wasn't any great big problem but it was something else that they had to learn.

Q: And all of this was being done under the duress of war, and that was an incentive in itself, I suppose?

Adm. J.: Oh, yes, sure, because they knew that they were getting ready to start shooting. Before that, it was well, I'll do the best I can, and the chances are I'll never have to fire this thing in anger. It's a different picture, you have to take it more seriously, and they did.

The greatest frustration was trying to get them qualified for the night work, because there just wasn't enough time in the period allocated to you really to qualify these kids, particularly with the equipment you had then. And all-weather that was just out. You just didn't have that kind of an airplane to engage in all-weather operations.

Q: At that stage, night fighters operated from the same carriers as day fighters?

Adm. J.: We had a night fighter unit of four planes, and these were specialists. They slept during the daytime. They never flew an airplane during the daytime.

Q: But they used the same deck?

Adm. J.: Oh, yes.

This is what Bill Martin was involved in. They finally realized the importance of night operations. They took the Enterprise and, as I remember, the Independence, for specialized night operations.

Q: The Independence, yes.

Adm J.: Bill Martin had the group on the Enterprise, and I've forgotten who had the other one. They were completely specialized in night work torpedo planes and fighters.

Q: Yes, that was their shift.

Adm. J.: Yes, that's all they did. Eddie Ewing was skipper of the Enterprise, which Bill Martin was on. Even today, I think he still has the largest number of night carrier landings of anybody. I think I read that not too long ago. So that was a specialized unit then. But, even so, each carrier like the Hornet, the Essex-class anyway, not the smaller carriers, still had the four night-fighter planes on them, because usually the night carriers operated separately. You might be in a carrier task group so located that you couldn't get any assistance from them, so you had to provide your own night-fighter coverage.

Q: They were independent of the group?

Adm. J.: Yes. Sometimes they'd be mixed up but most of the time they wouldn't be, because you got close to a place like Okinawa, Iwo Jima, or someplace, and, as a rule you could always expect something in the way of Japanese planes coming out at night.

Q: Yes. After all, they were the enemy!

Adm. J.: Yes, the Bettys and the Francis' out of Formosa. Gad, two night in a row, we were up all night long with attacks, all night long.

So, we got out to the West Coast, and I was supposed to go aboard the Essex. The skipper of the Essex was Ralph Ofstie. Then they said: All right, you're here at Santa Rosa, we're going to ship you on out to Pearl, and you wait to go aboard the Essex. We hadn't been on the West Coast more than a month - all the families had gone out there, and they had to pull up roots. Of course, they stayed, they didn't go to Pearl. That was as far as they could go.

So they put us all on the Cabot, the whole air group, and shipped us out to Pearl. First of all, they sent us over to Hilo, a new naval air station over there, which really wasn't suited for what I wanted to do because it rained every night on that side of the mountains and you couldn't fly at night. That's what I needed. I didn't need the daytime stuff. I finally got them to move us to Barber's Point.

Q: Whom did you have to work on to get this?

Johnson #1 -81-

Adm. J.: The people on Admiral Radford's staff then, he was out there.

So we went to Barber's Point, and it was always clear there at night. We were down on the beach one Saturday afternoon having a big beer bust and relaxing, when this fellow comes in and says:

"Admiral Radford wants to see you immediately." Well, what's up now? I went up there and here was Admiral Radford, and a couple of other people, and Captain Browning, the skipper of the Hornet, which had just come in.

Q: Miles Browning?

Adm. J.: Yes. Admiral Radford said:

"I assume that your air group's ready to go into combat." I said, "Yes, we were ready when we came out here."

He said: "Well, the skipper of the Hornet, Captain Browning here, says that he will not take the air group he has, Air Group 15, into combat. They're not ready. So we're putting you on the Hornet. Furthermore, going aboard the Hornet, you've got to shift from the SBDs you've been flying to the SB2C, and you've got one week to do it."

Well, the SB2C at that point, they called it the beast and for good reason. All the maintenance problems, all the hydraulic problems, and these airplanes looked horrible, anyway, the usage they'd gotten. So we had to go out and on that ship we had to shift from the SBD, which was a good reliable airplane,

Johnson #1 -82-

and all those bomber pilots had to transition into the SB2C in that time. Then, off we went, west.

Q: It must have been a tremendous handicap, wasn't it?

Adm. J.: Yes, and Browning was a rather impatient, intolerant sort of personality, anyway, and here we were trying to qualify these kids, and naturally they were having trouble, and he was just raising hell because they were having that much difficulty, "You came out here and said you were ready, and you can't even land."

Q: Had you ever flown one of these planes?

Adm. J.: SB2C?

Q: Yes.

Adm. J.: No. I'd checked out in one of them, and it was a horrible-looking thing to fly because, the way the thing was built, you had neutral stability, which is not very good in flying an airplane because you move the stick and you can't feel anything happening. In order to overcome that and give it something in the way of positive stability, you could look down and, here, about this long, was this arm with this great big lead weight on it, an artificial thing on the control stick to give you that feeling. That couldn't be a very good design when they've got to do that.

There were just all kinds of problems with this plane. It was just a horrible headache.

Q: And there was no possibility of shifting to the others?

Adm. J.: No. The reason he gave was, "We can't let you go aboard the Hornet with the SBDs because we have all the storerooms and everything off, there's nothing but SB2C spare parts. No SBD spare parts, and we don't want to change."

So we went aboard and there was a problem with Miles Browning from the time we went on there. I didn't have too much trouble with him after we finally got the kids to the point where they could land. The problem was between Jocko and Miles - Jocko Clark, he was the admiral on board -

Q: And Miles Browning was the captain?

Adm. J.: Yes. Jocko was the carrier task group commander. Apparently, they had never cared too much for each other from the days they were midshipmen. They were classmates, and that's another bad situation, right there. You could tell that there was not very much good feeling between these two, which didn't lend itself to making for a very happy ship.

Q: No, I guess not!

Adm. J.: I was kind of in the middle, and Admiral Mitscher, who was in command of all the carrier groups, had three of them by then and four later on. There were a lot of carriers out there then.

Q: And Arleigh was with him at that point, wasn't he?

Johnson #1 -84-

Adm. J.: He was his chief of staff.

Prior to this, Miles Browning had been in Southeast Asia. Halsey was down there, that's when they sent Halsey to take over from Ghormley, you know. Ghormley was about to lose the whole war, and King sent Halsey down there and Browning was his chief of staff.

Well, Pete Mitscher at this time was down there and he was in command of all the aircraft we had, the PBYs and the landbased Liberators that I mentioned before.

Halsey apparently gave Miles Browning pretty much free reign and he could be pretty overpowering and ruthless with people in his position, including Admiral Mitscher. So that started sort of a feud between those two.

This is all personal. I guess it's all right to mention it, isn't it?

Q: Sure.

Adm. J.: This carried over to the time when Browning came aboard as captain. Jocko had never cared for him and neither had Pete Mitscher. So, I was kind of caught in the middle of it.

Q: Yes, not knowing this background?

Adm. J.: I knew some of it, it was pretty obvious.

We were going along and we'd been on a couple of raids already. We'd been in to Truk one time - I've forgotten the other place - but, anyway, this one evening all the carriers were anchored in Kwajalein, I guess. We'd moved to Kwajalein from Majuro, that's right. Everybody was at the movies. Out there, going to the movies was a great thing, and here in the front row were Admiral Clark, Miles Browning, the skipper, and I was sitting up there, and in the back was all the crew and everybody else and all these airplanes back there. Somebody accidentally tripped a fire extinguisher off the bulkhead - this was on the hangar deck - and when he did that thing took off on that steel deck like a rocket, and you can imagine the noise it was making. Somebody, I suppose thinking it was funny, said:

"Look out, it's a plane loose and here he comes."

Well, if you've ever seen mass hysteria, that was it. There was a surge of humanity forward and I ended up in the elevator well. I was pushed in there. Pretty soon, somebody yelled "Man overboard." They knew some people had been pushed over the side, so they fished three people out of the drink - I think it was three. They turned the searchlights on and looked and didn't see anybody else, so they assumed nobody else had been pushed over the side.

I must say to Browning's credit, he did ask if he could just forget about the movies and hold a muster to make sure nobody else was missing. Admiral Clark said, no, let's go on with the movie. Well, Browning did get up and pretty well chastised the crew for their behavior, which he should have, because it wasn't very commendable. Nobody heard anything more about it until the next day, about noon, a body comes floating to the surface, by the gangway. They probably couldn't have saved him if they'd known he'd fallen over because he probably drowned right away. At that point, Browning convened an investigation to look into it. I think he had Admiral Baker.

The gist of their findings was that, unfortunate as it was and it wasn't exactly exemplary conduct on the part of the Hornet's crew, it was something that could happen in wartime conditions and so forth and didn't thereby hold anybody culpable. That got to Clark and to Mitscher and they said no, that's not acceptable, and they convened another one. I've forgotten who was head of this one. Browning named Jocko Clark as an interested party and, in turn, Clark named Browning as an interested party in the investigation. This time, I think they knew that they'd better do a little different than the other board, so they pretty well put down Browning on this, and the long and the short of it was that he was relieved about ten days later, left the ship. That's when Captain Sample, Bill Sample, came on board and took over. And I must say that it was a different ship after that, even though you still had to contend with Jocko Clark. He was a fighter, I must say. He was part Cherokee Indian, you know.

Q: Yes, he was difficult, too!

Adm. J.: Yes, at times.

I was there with the air group and we'd done very well. We'd shot down a lot of airplanes, we'd sunk quite a few ships, and we had a pretty good record by then and were thinking the combat tour was about over. They would gauge how long you could stay out there by how many losses you had and what the temperament and morale of your pilots were, and the kind of battles they'd been in. You had to gauge that.

Q: And you'd gauge that day by day?

Adm. J.: Not day by day, but week by week, almost. So we had a good suspicion that, after we'd been down to Hollandia to help General MacArthur - he claimed that he needed carriers down there to help them, that the air group was going to go back. We went down there, stayed in Manus, a great big base, it was monster and never used.

Anyway, before that, Clark called me down one time and said:

"What are you planning to do?"

I said: "Well, I'm still with the air group and, when we finish, go back, rehabilitate, and then come back and finish the war."

He said: "No. Tomorrow morning you're the air officer. I'm firing the guy we've got now because he can't do the job, and if you don't do the job I'll have to fire you, too."

So, sure enough, the next morning, I was the air officer, just like that.

Q: You weren't very happy at this, were you?

Adm. J.: No! I knew what his unhappiness was. A classmate of ours who was the air officer, a likeable guy but he wasn't very aggressive and he wouldn't take advantage of things that he knew were being done on other carriers that had been out there, like having tow bars. When you first came out there, you had tow bars to tow the airplanes forward but none to tow them aft for the respot, and that's where you save the time, because if you had to shove those things by hand and with the schedule you had, launching around the clock, you'd get way behind. So the thing to do was to manufacture these tow bars that you could fit on the tail wheel and tow these planes back. But he wouldn't do that.

I made some changes like that and pretty soon it was much smoother working.

Q: So Jocko didn't fire you!

Adm. J.: No. But he would do some things that simply weren't understandable. Admiral Sample - he became admiral - they took them off and Artie Doyle came on, a great man. What a great guy he was. He would always say:

OK, I know what the BuAer manual says, 160 feet for the F-6 with this load. Give them a little more and I'll give them 5 knots of wind extra.

So here Jocko would come up and "move them forward, move them up, move them up, you can launch faster."

Well, the fallacy of that was you couldn't. You'd launch faster if you gave them enough run and you had the people back there so they would break the wings fast and get them into the launch spot. But he couldn't see it that way. So you always had to worry about things like that with Jocko. Artie Doyle could handle him.

Q: I bet you did, too!

Adm. J.: Not as air officer so much. You had to kind of walk a tight wire rope with that guy.

Q: Your pilots, did you have any losses during the time they were operating on board the Hornet?

Adm. J.: Oh, yes, sure. Jack, I've forgotten now. We made a raid on Palau and we lost three dive-bomber pilots shot down in one raid. Let's see - I would say we lost about ten pilots out of that fighter squadron.

Q: Gosh, that's quite a - what was the state of morale?

Adm. J.: It was still good.

Q: In spite of the losses?

Adm. J.: Yes. A couple of them were operational, crashed in the water. We lost two bomber crews. They were just milling around in a circle off Hollandia, with nothing to do, and they collided. All the pilots and the crewmen were lost out of those two, and the torpedo planes - oh, when we first started out, Browning was the guy, every launch we made was at night, and he was the guy who didn't give you but 25 knots of wind. That's all he'd give you, and these planes were going off the bow and going in the water.

Q: And he wouldn't mend his ways?

Adm. J.: No, even though you'd go up and tell him. The first launch we ever made, one morning, dark of the moon, we lost two torpedo-plane pilots that way, they just went in the drink, not shot down or anything. That was the horrible thing. To be lost to enemy action is one thing, as opposed to an operational loss. They lost four or five pilots. One fellow and his crew were hit and they came back and landed in the water. They saw them in a life raft, then never saw them again, even though they sent out search planes.

Another time, a dive-bomber pilot went in the drink on takeoff. We saw him in a raft, waving to us, and he went by the port side, but we never saw him again. It's hard to imagine—

Q: How do you explain that?

Adm. J.: I don't know.

Q: The wake of the ship or something?

Adm. J.: It was broad daylight and it wasn't too rough. That thing really would upset you, to lose somebody like that.

Anyway, I was air officer for Jocko and Artie. And, oh, gee, we'd been out there over a year by now, I guess. One morning we were replenishing, and the marine orderly came down and said:

"The captain wants to see you on the bridge."

So I went up there, and I was trying to get some sleep. We were making an approach on this tanker, so Artie Doyle said:

"OK, you're the new exec. We're approaching the tanker, we're not a thousand yards astern, and you've got it."

Q: You have to be pretty flexible to deal with something like that, don't you?

Adm. J.: I wished I'd watched a little bit closer to how they'd done this before, but I said:

You have got to go up and do it, you can't flinch now."
That's the way he was. He'd test you. I stayed on that ship until we were finally involved in the second typhoon. We were involved in two typhoons in that ship. The first one was when the destroyers capsized, which was a needless thing.

Q: Jocko got criticized for all of this, didn't he?

Adm. J.: For the second one, not the first one, because, really, in both of them it was pretty much Halsey's fault. Nimitz as much as said so, but he wasn't going to be too critical of Halsey.

Q: Halsey was too much of a hero.

Adm. J.: Yes, right.

In the first one, he took us right into the eye of the thing. The second one - McCain had relieved Mitscher, that's what had happened then, and Jocko was still onboard - and we were due to make a strike on Kyushu, the mainland of Japan.

They knew this typhoon was coming up from the south, so in the early afternoon - I'll never forget it - they changed course to 110, headed south-eastward, and I said, well, we're heading away from this thing, that's good, not to worry. I turned in and pretty soon I felt the ship pitching and rolling. I mean it was rough. I thought I'd better get up and go and see how the airplanes were doing. I was still air officer then.

I got up on the bridge and I mean we were in a storm. I looked in the radar and you could see this typhoon. We were headed right for the center, and we were on course 330. We'd changed course, to go back up. McCain thought we could get across the eye and get on the other side of it, be in safe water over there, and be able to launch the next morning. Well, we didn't make it. There was all this water coming in on the hangar deck, and Jocko, of course, still wanted us to keep going as much as we could and as fast as we could to close in with the other carriers. Well, of course, actually it was the responsibility of the commanding officer of the ship and if he thought we were being endangered, he should have slowed down himself.

Anyway, pretty soon, just about first daybreak, we hit this mountain of water. Gad, it must have been ten times as high as this house, and the impact of all of that, when it came down on the flight deck, carried away everything. The edges of the flight deck were down like this, all the anntenae were gone, all the catwalks, some airplanes over the side.

We were in bad shape. Well, we slowed down about then.

Q: Did you lose any personnel like that?

Adm. J.: No, luckily we didn't because we alerted people to stay away from the side.

The next morning, of course, the question was could we operate airplanes, and Jocko said yes. Well, you could see that, with the edges of the flight deck down like this, you were bound to get turbulence. So, we launched - we had F4-Us out there then - one F4-U - the first one off, and he hit that turbulence and he just landed in the water upside down.

Q: Pancaked?

Adm. J.: No, upside down, he went into the drink. Luckily the pilot got out, but I said, "We can't launch with this, it's nonsense." So he said:

"OK, I agree. Now, what to do is to get those blow torches and cut those edges off."

Well, it's protective armored steel on that flight deck, but the captain said, "OK, break them out." and they were out there all the rest of that day and all night, and they cut about that much of it. It was obvious you weren't going to cut that stuff off.

Q: How thick was it?

Adm. J.: It was protective armor.

Q: A couple of inches?

Adm. J.: Yes, at least that.

The guy never gave up. He said:

"All right, try to find us a way of launching airplanes." So, for the first time in the war, and I think the only time in the war with an Essex-class carrier, we launched airplanes with the ship going full speed astern and the airplanes going off the stern, and, of course, we recovered them in the normal way. Well, you can't do that for very long. The engineer was about to go nuts, using his power plant that way! We operated that way for two days, and finally we went into Leyte - this was just after the Leyte-Samar operation. We went in there, and the Bennington was in the same shape that we were in.

By that time, the Hornet had been west of Pearl for well over a year. So, in view of that, they said, "All right, try to repair the Bennington here but send the Hornet back to the States." So we were going back to the States then.

Q: Why was it necessary to operate with the ship in that condition?

Adm. J.: He wanted you to operate to kill Japs. He always wanted to operate, and there was no excuse for not being able to.

It's interesting how he treats some of these subjects in his book.

Q: We take up the story when you returned in October 1945 to Washington.

Johnson #1 -95-

Adm. J.: To Washington, eventually to the Joint Staff.

Q: Yes. What kind of duty were they giving you there?

Adm. J.: At that time, the composition of the joint Chiefs of Staff, compared with what it is today, was almost unbelievab. You had the joint logistics planners, of course, and then you had the joint war plans outfit, and in the war-planning outfit there were four teams, red, white, blue and rainbow teams. On each team, you had army and navy, army air force, which later on became U.S. Air Force after they became independent and, in some cases a marine. I was on the red team together with Page Smith. We were the navy people on this red team and, at that time, practically all your planning had to do with postwar problems. For instance, the matter of allocation of amphibious shipping to get Chiang Kai-shek's people out of, off the mainland. Admiral Cook, you know, was involved in that.

Q: Yes.

Adm. J.: All postwar problems, because the war was over and nobody was thinking about planning for any other wars at that time.

Q: You weren't involved in demobilization, because that already had been planned and was taking place?

Adm. J.: Well, there was some, a little bit, maybe, in the way of allocation of shipping because there were still an awful lot of people being returned from overseas and released from active duty. There was an awful lot of that, but the Joint Chiefs didn't have to get themselves mixed up in very much of that.

Q: Were they concerned about personnel, however, in the future?

Adm. J.: That's right. They had to make some determination as to how far they were going to demobilize, down to what level, and, of course, that had to be cranked in and integrated with your budget planning because it always takes money to support people. That was done by the personnel planners over on the Joint Chiefs, not by the outfit I was in.

Q: Since you were concerned about transporting Chiang's people from the mainland, were you also concerned with that problem of the Japanese prisoners of war, of the Russians farther north in Manchuria, the army that they had taken over?

Adm. J.: No, I don't recall any involvement in that at all. There was quite a bit of logistics planning, shipping allocations, and so forth, having to do with the Japanese coming out of other places that we had overrun. Quite a bit, but that didn't present any real problem because it was only a matter of getting them aboard ship and taking them back to the homeland.

No, I don't recall that anything was ever done about those people, as a matter of fact.

Q: No. I think they just disappeared.

Adm. J.: That's right. That was the end of them.

Actually, at that time, I think the more serious and difficult planning was being done at sort of a State-military level. That's when Dennison was a member of what they called the SWNCC Committee, the old "Swink" Committee, State, War, Navy Coordinating Committee, because there were so many political problems over in Europe, many different problems, as you can well imagine. Also, what to do about trying to reestablish something in the way of stability over in Europe, and also to ensure that the security of our allies, or potential allies, was preserved, in the face of what we knew at that time the Russians had in mind. That was the big problem over there, and from that came the Marshall Plan.

Q: The danger of the whole area going communist?

Adm. J.: Yes. The only problem in the Far East, of course, was to produce something in the way of guidelines that were acceptable to the great supreme commander, who had moved to Tokyo by that time, General MacArthur. He was the overlord of the whole business there. I guess, in retrospect, that he did quite a job there. The Japanese people had a very high respect for the man, I suppose. There wasn't much change in their form of government, really.

Q: No.

Adm. J.: They still had the emperor as the figurehead, they still had the Diet. So there was no change there. Most of their problem was to pull themselves up by their bootstraps and recover, which they did in remarkable fashion.

Q: Getting a peace treaty signed and all that.

Adm. J.: Right.

Q: Over Russian opposition.

Adm. J.: Not really.

Interview No. 2 with Admiral Roy L. Johnson, U.S. Navy (Retired)

Place: His home in Virginia Beach, Virginia

Date: Friday morning, 5 December 1980

Subject: Biography

By: John T. Mason, Jr.

Q: This morning, I think, we're ready to go to Norfolk in July of 1947, when you became air operations officer for the commander of the Second Task Fleet.

Adm. J.: Yes. It's known as the Second Fleet now. I think at that time it was the Second Task Fleet. The Pacific and Atlantic fleets were organized into different task fleets, I guess, even though I don't recall that the Sixth Fleet was known as a task fleet.

Anyway, Admiral Radford asked me to go down and be operations officer. So we went to Norfolk -

Q: He was in command, was he?

Adm. J.: Yes. I reported there only about two months after he'd taken over. We were scheduled for fleet exercises and conducted them as best we could with the ships that we could pull together, which weren't too many, because that was in a very austere period. You had ships that were pretty much fully manned, but they didn't operate due to the lack of budget money for fuel.

Q: If it wasn't personnel, it was fuel!

Adm. J.: Yes. So we'd go out and have a fleet exercise, and we had trouble getting two carriers. That wasn't too exciting, not at that time.

Anyway, in less than a year, Admiral Radford was detached. He went up to be vice CNO for Denfeld, I think. And, of course, Raddy never gave up. A lot of people said, "Well, he's through, he's cut his throat on the unification thing." And, of course, he was the target of many of the remarks made by Bradley, you know, about being fancy Dans and so forth, but he never gave up. Of course, he was a brilliant man. He was a tough taskmaster, very demanding but fair. He would give you responsibility and, if you turned in a job, OK, then he'd turn you loose pretty much on your own. He didn't have too much patience with poor performance and he didn't hesitate to be really ruthless with people who turned in a bad job.

Q: Well, isn't that a characteristics of top commanders, though, in the navy?

Adm. J.: Some more so than others. You don't have to be a martinet and really be completely unreasonable, which he wasn't. He was, you might say, a pretty compassionate person. I don't think you could ever say that about Ernie King, because he treated people like machines. Either the machine was working and producing what it was designed to or it wasn't, and if it wasn't get rid of it. Raddy wasn't quite that extreme, but he was sure demanding. He set a heck of a high standard to go by and that was it.

He was relieved by Wu Duncan, and there were two completely different personalities.

Q: Exactly. I knew both of them.

Adm. J.; I learned quite a bit, serving with the two of them. Of course, with Wu, the ship availabilities situation began to improve a little bit. In other words, we had more ships available and we could begin to do something that was worthy of the name of a fleet exercise.

One of the more interesting things we did was to take two carriers, th Essex and the FDR, on a cold-weather exercise. I remember we were headed up there over Thanksgiving, the last of November.

Q: Up in the North Atlantic?

Adm. J.: No, we were going up in the Davis Straits west of Greenland. We were riding the Pocono, the flagship. Ballentine was the carrier task group commander. We stripped the two carriers down to the number of aircraft that they could put on the hangar deck because we knew there was going to be bad weather up there.

Q: There isn't anything worse than the Davis Strait!

Adm. J.: We had special cold-weather clothing for the flight crews and for the pilots. We had special snow-remover equipment to clear the flight decks, and we had these special heaters that you could attach to the engines of the airplanes to get them warmed up before they got started. Otherwise, you'd never get those things started with an inertial starter.

So, off we went, and we actually went sixty-one miles north of the Arctic circle, and I mean it was cold.

Q: What were you trying to prove? Endurance?

Adm. J.: Feasibility and an understanding of some of the problems involved in operating in a cold climate because, in World War II, you know, a lot of operations were around Iceland and Greenland. It was a test exercise.

Of course, the thing up there is that the weather can change just like that, in a matter of half an hour. We were operating airplanes one day and the wind shifted into the northwest and picked up to about 70 knots, and we had airplanes in the air. So, of course, we brought them all aboard and here you had -

Q: Did you have any problem getting them aboard?

Adm. J.: Yes, because at times an AD would come in to land and he'd just be hanging there and he wasn't moving up the deck at all. He's have to keep giving it the gun to get enough forward motion to land. And the carrier was only making steerageway about 10 knots.

So, the reason we turned around and headed south was that the destroyers began to pick up a lot of ice and got topheavy. It was getting dangerous. Furthermore, they were getting low on fuel. They got down to 30 percent and they couldn't refuel- They got down to 20 percent and we still couldn't refuel. It was too rough, 70 knots of wind. We tried refueling going downwind and everything. They actually tried to hook up and, of course, we had lifeguard helicopters near, in case anybody fell overboard.

Q: How did they function in that wind?

Adm. J.: Once you got them started and you you could get out of the high winds - of course, in those days, the helicopters you had, if you tried to start the rotor in any wind on the deck over 30 knots, the blades would cone. That was the problem there.

Anyway, there were three destroyers alongside the carriers and an oiler, and right at the same time this tremendous wave came and four people went over the side. The helicopters went after them and, out of the four, they picked up two.

Q: You can't stand more than five or ten minutes, can you?

Adm. J.: Not in water of that temperature. One of them died after they brought him on board and one of them survived, that quick. So we were in a fix there. We stopped. As a matter of fact, most of the lines were severed and we had to stop, anyway.

But Wu Duncan finally - he was always thinking, you know, a dour Scotsman - said "Look into the feasibility of going into Belle Isle Strait. There should be calm water there. See if it's deep enough and wide enough." So that's where we went and fueled these destroyers and got back.

That was the end of the cold-weather exercise.

Q: What about communications under those circumstances?

Adm. J.: That was all right, no problem, except that you got your antennas, and with your radar, you got your radar antennas coated with ice. That made a difference, but I don't recall any problem with communications.

That was an interesting exercise.

Q: I would think it was an unforgettable one!

Adm. J.: Then, we were given a directive to make a special cruise. We were to go to the Mediterranean with a special task force and just make ports of call and refuel there. Then go through the Suez Canal and go to the Persian Gulf for a whole month for a combination of goodwill visits. That was kind of a guise. We were to go in there, collect intelligence, and survey the area because the charts that we were using and the charts that the old Middle East Force that had been stationed there, they were using charts that dated back to Lord Nelson.

We started out with two destroyers, the Siboney, which was a CVE, the Pocono, that was our flagship, and two specially configured APDs that were going to be used for this surveying, the contour surveying plus on a carrier a lot of trimet photography that, in proper water conditions, could give you the contour of the shoreline and the gradients and so forth.

So we started out with that force, went to the Med, and then through the Suez Canal, and into the Persian Gulf, and, mind you, this was in the month of July!

Q: The heat was comparable with the Davis Strait's cold!

Adm. J.: Yes. We didn't do too well with that because we didn't have any special provisions for the hot one. We had a lot for the cold-weather cruise, but over there none. We had special double awnings, and, of course, you took white shorts and you wore elephant hats and things like that.

Q: Did you have air-conditioning?

Adm. J.: Not on very many ships, no. They tried to put in as much as they could. And, of course, all the other ships - the British had ships in there then - were all painted white.

Q: They were more accustomed to it.

Adm. J.: Painted white, special awnings, and air-conditioning.

Anyway, we went over there. We went to Bahrein, to Kuwait, Ras Tanura, we visited all those places, and I went with Wu Duncan to Jiddah, that's where we called on Ibn Saud - I think it was Ibn Saud, anyway, the head guy.

In the course of moving around in this surveying, two destroyers actually went aground on some reef. It wasn't their fault.

Q: How did the British operate with -

Adm. J.: They knew, they had a chart of their own in their own mind, and knew about some of these dangerous shoals and so forth but there was nothing on any chart, or maybe they had charts that were marked up or something, but they certainly didn't show up on the ones that we had.

I remember that the APD, the *Carpelotti*, was doing about 15 knots and went over a shoal, no sign of it, no indication at all, and he lost his screw. I've forgotten how he got it fixed, but he got it fixed some place where the British fixed things.

Q: When something like that happened, what's the responsibility of the skipper?

Adm. J.: Well, there were so many mitigating circumstances there. They had to have an investigation, but he was exonerated You can't blame a fellow for something that doesn't show. If you have a chart and it says here there are only four fathoms of water or here's a pinnacle, and you run into it, you've culpable. But not in this case. They didn't give him a letter or anything.

We stayed over there and we collected a lot of information, and I daresay that your hydrographic charts updated today are based on a lot of that information we collected. And, of course, it was goodwill. We made contact right away with the Aramco people, the big oil outfit.

Q: In Dhahran, yes.

Adm. J.: That's right, in Ras Tanura. In Bahrein and Kuwait was the Anglo-Iranian oil interest, which has since been changed. I don't know what it all is now. But this conglomerate, Aramco, I think the Saudis pretty well absorbed all of that.

Q: They have, yes.

Adm. J.: So that passed out of the picture, too, but they were a powerful outfit over there then. They were almost like a bunch of rug merchants, those guys. But they were hardy characters. They were required to spend only one year over there, unless they volunteered for a second, whereby they had double pay. They threw a couple of great big parties on the beach, all these guys with their rugs and all this stuff to sell. No matter what kind of a car it was, if it lasted one year you were doing good.

Q: Because of the heat?

Adm. J.: The sand, heat and sand.
    That was an interesting cruise, too.

Q: Tell me about your visit in Jiddah.

Adm. J.: Well, it was a very formal thing. We were briefed by people from the embassy about how to behave and things not to mention, not to talk about. But he was a very friendly person and, of course, he offered you coffee and food, and you were supposed to eat with your right hand because your left hand was used for something else personal, you know - all these funny customs. The ambassador made a great big fetish of this. Well, I don't think they would pay that much attention to you, really.

Of course, I wasn't with the admiral when he went in to see the head sheik. I was with him, though, when he called on the Sheik in Kuwait, and he's the fellow who had a yacht that had been given to him by Gulf Oil, I think. Its railings were gold-plated, actually gold-plated. We got ready to call on the sheik - I've forgotten his name - and, of course, the thing to do is have something in the way of unusual gifts because you knew that they were going to give you something. It might have been nothing more than a live goat or something, but you were expected to give him something.

Q: It's a very important thing, this exchange of gifts.

Adm. J.: Oh, yes. So the admiral got the best pair of new binoculars he could find and took those along, and, gee, this fellow was simply delighted because he didn't have any binoculars. I was amazed.

Anyway, we arrived, stepped out of the boat, and, as you approached the palace, here were, I would say sixty to a hundred of these black Senegalese who looked as though they were about seven feet tall and weighed about three hundred pounds, in their fancy dress, you know, with their spears and things.

Q: They were the palace guard, I suppose.

Adm. J.: They were, but I don't know why he chose them. Anyway, we went in and we were royally received, and coffee and little tidbits of food and stuff. I didn't know what I was eating, but out of courtesy, I went ahead and ate it anyway.

He was quite friendly. I was very much, really more impressed with him than I was with the fellow in Jiddah, actually, even though he didn't have the influence and the power in the gulf that Saudi had. He was a very wealthy man and at that time from every barrel of oil produced and exported, he was receiving, I think, twenty cents. That's all he got. But in those days twenty cents means a lot more -

Q: A barrel of oil was only three or four dollars, wasn't it?

Adm. J.: It was that much.

Q: It wasn't that much?

Adm. J.: No, it wasn't that much. He would sell it when it came out of the ground. You'd see these big tankers out there, and they'd drill these wells. They'd go down 2,000 feet, that's all, 1,000 feet maybe. No pumps, such high pressure it is fed through the valves right out to the ships. At that time, the

Johnson #2 -110-

only big refinery was in Bahrein, a great big one there, and they were building one in Ras Tanura. The Aramco people actually set up a big school there to train the natives to operate the refineries. They did a good job over there, those people.

So, that was our Persian Gulf cruise. We came back -

Q: It was an educational one, too, wasn't it, as well as a profitable one?

Adm. J.: Yes, it was.

Q: It's a different part of the world. Did you come back with any gifts, any rugs, or anything of that sort?

Adm. J.; We bought some rugs over there. I bought one that at one time had been a very valuable rug. I don't know whether I'd had too much beer or what, but, anyway, I brought it back and the thing was in such dirty condition, full of sand and so forth, that we had to send it to the cleaners. Well, he called up and said he wanted to charge about three hundred dollars to clean it, so we just left it there. I guess we should have gotten it, really.

Q: You certainly should!

Adm. J.: It was a great big rug.

Q: He cleaned it and -

Adm. J.: He was ripping us off, I think. It was about a 12 x 16 rug. A lot of people brought back a couple of small ones.

While we were in the Med, going over there, we went in to Izmir, Turkey, and for every officer in the ship on the staff this barge came out and brought a carton of Turkish cigarettes and a bottle of raki, which is a very strong liqueur. I'll never forget, we went to this one party with the Turks there and this officer said, "One raki like this, two raki no good." What you do is you take it in a little glass and you pour a little water in it and it turns milky white. So every officer had a bottle of that, a carton of cigarettes, plus a bottle of some kind of Turkish wine.

We also went to Crete and there they gave a big party for us, and had all the mutton and meat and everything, and the wines, and there they gave everybody a bottle of ouzo. Ouzo is potent stuff, I tell you.

We came back and the customs people wouldn't let us in.

Q: They wouldn't let you bring it in.

Adm. J.: No. In the first place, raki is an aphrodisiac.

Q: Oh.

Adm. J.: You're not allowed to land that. So, we gave it up.

I finally went ashore, went to the officers' club at Little Creek, right here, and the customs people agreed that if we turned over every bottle we had on there to the officers' club and let them dispense it at their bar, that was OK, so we gave it to them. For a long time, one of the favorite drinks at the officers' club at Little Creek was a raki cocktail. We kept the cigarettes -

Q: I don't see how that complied with the law!

Adm. J.: A liberal interpretation! We had a problem what to do with it. The ouzo, of coure, I could never take that. I remember the first day I went ashore, I saw these two bluejackets out. I didn't know what had happened to them, and I said, "What's wrong with those guys? They look in bad shape to me."

"Well, they got a bottle of ouzo and drank it all, and that's what it'll do to you.

Q: It's a wonder it didn't kill them. It sounds like pisco. Do you know pisco in Peru?

Adm. J.: No, I've never been there.

So, we came back and I shortly thereafter left the staff because about that time Artie Doyle pulled me out and said he wanted me to come to Glenview to be a training officer at the Naval Air Reserve Training Command, so that's where I went. But I always remember being with Admiral Duncan. He was always very nice to me, very considerate. Any time I needed anything, I could always call on him. There are many, many stories about him. He was a completely different person. You've heard a lot of the stories.

Q: I knew him over a period of two or three years, I guess.

Adm. J.: He was just placid, outwardly he was.

Q: A very meticulous man.

Adm. J.: He was, and deliberate, you know. He moved at one speed and, like they say, we were out at sea doing something and he was conning the ship, and he said:

"Right standard rudder."

About that time, the officer of the deck said:

"Captain, there's a fire on the hangar deck." He said:

"Rudder amidships."

"Captain, there's a fire on the hangar deck."

He said, "Put it out."

Q: You know he was a brother-in-law of Harry Hopkins?

Adm. J.: Yes, he and Ralph Davidson married sisters. After Wu duncan's wife had passed on he went down to Penscaola and married again while I was there. He either stayed with the Davidsons or saw a lot of them. He was actually on the porch one evening talking, and Mrs. Davidson was inside, doing something, and that's when the house caught on fire and she burned to death.

Q: I didn't know that.

Adm. J.: Oh, yes. From there he moved in to the San Carlos Hotel and remarried.

I sent him a Christmas card, and I remember the last one I ever got, he said:

"Maybe my time is approaching. I'm not going to worry about it. When it does, don't bother too much, just put me in a hole over at Fort Barancas." That's a military cemetary, and that's where he's buried.

Q: We had a diversion. We were talking about Wu Duncan and about the plans for the air attack on Tokyo, the surprise attack from the Hornet. Tell me the -

Adm. J.: Well, he was air planner more or less for King at that time. He called me up - I was still in BuAer - and said:

"I want you to find out for me in no more than twenty minutes the shortest distance that a B-25 can take off."

Naturally, I went to the air force characters and they gave me the statistics, the distance in a 20-knot wind over a 50-foot obstacle, and gee, that turned out to be 4,000 or 5,000 feet. I didn't know what he wanted it for, and he said:

"No, go back. That isn't the information I want. What I want to find out is the shortest distance that a B-25 has ever been able to take off in a 25-knot wind."

Well, the air force had never tried anything like that. If I'd known what he had in mind, I would have approached in differently but he -

Q: Wouldn't tell you?

Adm. J.: No, it was so secret. Anyway, BuAir finally borrowed a B-25 and went right down here to Norfolk, to old Chambers Field, and there they actually tested the thing and determined the distance in which it could take off, which was compatible with putting it on the Hornet, and loaded it with two 500-pound bombs.

Johnson #2 -115-

Of course, he never told me a thing. I didn't know a thing about it until the thing had happened. Of course, Hank Miller, can give you chapter and verse.

Q: Hank Miller told me all about going down to Eglin Field.

Adm. J.: Yes, he and Jimmy Doolittle.

Q: Well, you came back and you were -

Adm. J.: I was detached and went out to Glenview.

Q: Was this something that you welcomed?

Adm. J.: Not at the time because I could think of some other places I'd rather go for duty rather than Glenview. That was a training command. But, I must say it was a valuable experience and about that time more emphasis was being put on the ready reserve, anyway.

Q: Yes, you went out in January of 1950?

Adm. J.: Yes, and shortly thereafter there was a directive from the secretary of the navy that every officer at some time in some part of his career must spend at least one year with the reserves. That was the importance they attached to the reserves then.

We went out there and, of course, at that time we had twenty-eight air reserve stations throughout the country, all over the country: one here, one at Anacostia, Willow Grove, New York, Squantum, the midwest, on the West Coast. They weren't flying the same kind of airplanes the fleet was flying because we didn't have them to give.

Q: They were flying old, beat-up planes, were they?

Adm. J.: Yes, they were, they were overhauled airplanes, and they were known as the weekend warriors. This was the air reserve, not the surface reserve. We had no surface reserve headquarters, as such then.

Q: How many were there approximately?

Adm. J.: I've forgotten how many thousand there were but in that many stations and that many squadrons, there were several thousand, and they had enlisted mechanics, also.

The point I wanted to make was that a very large percentage of these kids had been in combat in World War II. They'd been in combat, so this flying meant nothing to them. They'd come out one weekend a month.

Q: They just wanted to keep up their -

Adm. J: Well, they got paid for it. They were paid well for that - one weekend per month plus a concentrated two-week training period in the summer. All of them got that, and they kept their proficiency up pretty well.

Well, along comes Korea and all of a sudden we're in a police action - no one would ever call it a war then, and a tremendously increased requirement for pilots and squadrons on the carriers. I'll never forget Artie Doyle, when I said:

"You've got the so-called ready reserve, can we use those people?"

He said: "Certainly, how many do you want?"

So, on a selective basis, we went out and we got, as I remember six fighter squadrons, two VS squadrons, and two VP squadrons, called them to active duty. We kept them on their home base for a month, so they could get straightened out with their family affairs, which was a considerable thing, you see.

Q: Yes, it's quite a wrench.

Adm. J.: To make arrangements, and we had to help them a lot of times with the airlines. A lot of them were airline pilots. To get released and see that their equity and so forth wouldn't be jeopardized, and things like that.

They were flown to the West Coast. Well, at first AirPac took a dim view of this whole thing.

Q: Why?

Adm. J.: He really didn't think they could cut the mustard. The biggest problem, of course, was that they had to transition to a fleet airplane and, in most cases, the fighters were jets.

Q: And they had not flown them?

Adm. J.: No, they'd been flying F4Us. Olathe had some jets but it was about the only station, I think.

We sent them out there, and each squadron - of course, we had to put an ACI officer, that's the intelligence officer, and an administrator. That's all we put in there. Otherwise they were on their own. In a matter of two or three months, they were ready to go, they went out aboard the carriers, and performed just as well as any fleet squadron.

I was in command of the Badoeng Strait over in the Yellow Sea and had a reserve VS squadron, and they were just as good as any other.

So that was the ready reserve.

Q: Well, they had an unusual background as reservists.

Adm. J.: We don't have that now. In the reserve today, and it's still worthy of the name of a standby or ready reserve, an awful lot of those kids have had very limited fleet experience But some of them are still good and it's a worthwhile thing to have a fall back on in an emergency.

Q: It's almost a necessary thing, isn't it?

Adm. J.: Yes, right. Of course, the VP squadrons went to Whidbey. I had to go up there and talk to Admiral Jack Perry and his staff. He was head of the patrol wings, and he wanted nothing to do with them. You know how tought he could be, but I finally convinced him. I said:

"Admiral, give them a chance. They'll be all right, I can guarantee you that because the airplanes they've been flying aren't too different from what they're going to get here. There's no problem."

And they didn't have any problem at all.

Q: What was Doyle's job at that time?

Adm. J.: He was chief of naval air reserve training. John Dale Price was chief of air training down at Pensacola, having relieved Blackjack Reeves, I guess. John Dale Price, Artie Doyle, Oscar Bryce, who at Glenview was head of the marine air reserve, and that was quite a combination - Bryce, Doyle, and Price. You just don't see people like that any more. They were the days when you had characters in the navy, I mean real characters. I don't think we'll ever see the like of people like that again.

Q: How do you account for that?

Adm. J.: They were people who were brought up in aviation and the ones who survived it, came through it, had to be that way, their makeup had to be that way - the Jerry Bogans, Raddy, Doyle, Sample, Switzer, those people. They were the great guys who came up. In the war, they were the ones who - well, they didn't by themselves win the war, but they were very instrumental out in the Pacific.

Q: Jimmy Thach swore by the marine reservists whom he had on board out there in Korea.

Adm. J.: Well, you see, what happened was that he and Blackie Regan rode the ship. By that time Jimmy had left his ship and he was with Regan, the CarDiv commander of the jeeps out there as his chief of staff.

So, what you do, you go out there and, for your six-month deployment, you would spend two months operating out of Yoko, on that side of Japan, with an ASW squadron, antisubmarine warfare. Then you would go all the way round to Sasebo, on the other side of Japan, and there you would relieve maybe an Australian carrier, or usually an American carrier, take the ASW outfit off and bring aboard a marine fighter squadron. At that time, and the same was the case with Jimmy, I had a marine air reserve squadron with checker boards, and those guys were good. From there, of course, you'd go all the way out into the Yellow Sea and you'd operate I guess three weeks at a time and then one week in Sasebo, and you'd be relieved by another carrier, usually the Sydney, the Australian carrier. Admiral Dyer was the task group commander, a very difficult person at times.

Q: George Dyer was difficult?

Adm. J.: Oh, gee, he could be. I was skipper of the Badoeng Strait, the big thing, and I had the destroyers with me and I was a task unit commander. Back in Sasebo, the task force commander was Admiral Scott-Moncrieff, the Britisher, aboard Ladybird, which never moved. She was a very palatial ship but never moved. You see, this was a UN force.

Q: Yes, I remember that.

Adm. J.: That's why Scott-Moncrieff was the task force commander. I'd go up there and I would have the Badoeng Strait; I would have one Canadian destroyer, the Athabaskan; I had a Dutch destroyer, the Van Galen - I always had trouble with her skipper because of his guttural talk; one British destroyer; and two American destroyers. That was the force. That was the UN force. We'd go up there during the daytime, send the marines off, and try to hit the North Koreans where they were located. Admiral Dyer could never understand why we'd send all these marine planes in there to bomb, rocket, strafe, and everything, then at night they'd open fire on the American cruisers.

Well, we took pictures and I told him what they were doing. In the daytimne, they'd hitch up their oxen and haul these things off someplace and hide them, and then bring them up at night and start shooting.

Q: They had tunnels up there?

Adm. J.: Sure, all underground. You couldn't find those things in the daytime. But he never seemed to understand that.

Q: He was very unhappy that Raddy removed him on the premise that he was not a flyer.

Adm. J.: Raddy didn't remove him for that reason. He may have had it in his mind, but I'm sure there were other reasons, because Raddy was not parochial in that sense at all. I never knew of anything like that. Is that what he thinks?

Q: That's what he thinks.

Adm. J.: Today, really?

Well, of course, Raddy removed some people. You remember - well, it is Radford Field now, Cubi Point.

Q: Yes.

Adm. J.: Where they cut the side of a mountain away. Well, Thomas Sprague, and he was the first squadron commander I ever had and I had a great deal of respect for him, he said cutting away the side of a mountain to make an airfield was utter folly. Raddy, of course, went ahead and did it and that was the end of Tommy Sprague as NWAirPac.

Q: Raddy's Folly!

Adm. J.: Yes, and it's a good thing we had that field, I tell you, a great thing. Of course, they did have to move an awful lot of dirt, but we were in trouble unless it proved absolutely right. So I would say something else was the reason for that. The way he handled things in the Yellow Sea was, in my opinion, not exactly outstanding. We'd go up to the DMZ - we never went much farther than the DMZ to make the strikes and then at night we'd retire, so, north of the DMZ the Shantung Peninsula is only about sixty-five miles away at the most, so there were occasions, depending on the atmospheric conditions, when you could pick up by radar all the tremendous fishing fleets. Well, this one night, Admiral Dyer became alarmed that the ChiComs were up to something and were concentrating a lot of navy vessels. Well, in the first place, they didn't have any kind of a navy, anyway, and I was pretty sure it was a fishing fleet, but he said:

"Send two destroyers over there to investigate, and report to me."

So I sent them over there as fast as they could go, and I said:

"As soon as you find out and can come back, get in communication with me and let me know."

Well, they waited until they came back visually and reported. I guess they should have woken me up, but they didn't find anything but a number of fishing vessels and a couple of them   . So, the next morning, I sent a report, and then I received one of the strangest invitations I've ever received, "Request your presence for luncheon promptly at twelve o'clock aboard Rochester."

Q: In other words, be there!

Adm. J.: Yes. I got in a chopper and went over and he said:

"Before lunch, I want to talk to you. Come in here in the cabin. When you're told to send a recon mission like that, you should know that as soon as you receive any information you report it to me immediately. Furthermore, it should be done as expeditiously as possible because Admiral Martin, who's over there with the Seventh Fleet, was alarmed about this."

He really chewed me out!

Q: And that's what you had for lunch!

Adm. J.: Oh no, we sat down for lunch with the skipper. I'll never forget and I often think about it. I said, "But they were just fishing vessels," and he said, "That's beside the point. You missed the point."

I wasn't going to argue with him. I'll never forget, he'd come aboard and he still wore those high-top black shoes. But he was well liked by a lot of people. In Annapolis, they think very highly of him still. He's mellowed quite a bit. Some of this, I'm sure, may have had a lot to do with what happened to him.

Q: Well, now you haven't completed what you were going to say about the training command.

Adm. J.: That was the highlight of it. We sent these squadrons off to Korea and so forth and, not too long after that, I got a call from Washington telling me I was going out to Japan to take command of the Badoeng Strait.

Q: But this did entail visiting all the training schools around the country, didn't it?

Adm. J.: Oh, gee, more traveling than I've ever done all the time I was in the navy. You made a trip once a month because there were that many to cover you had to make an annual inspectio

Q: This had to be on a weekend, did it?

Adm. J.: Yes, when they were there, always on a weekend. In order to cover twenty-eight of them, you were going every month. Then, in addition to that, there was the military inspection. That was spit and polish, you know, see that everybody -

Q: That was important.

Adm. J.: Yes. Well, anyway, Artie was making that trip and a good part of the time he wanted me to go with him. So I finally created myself two training inspection teams, my assistant was head of one of them and I was head of one of them, to kind of lighten the load because, otherwise, it was a chore, particularly when you were gone every weekend practically.

Q: What took place at these reserve air training stations during the week?

Adm. J.: Well, you had the active-duty people, the TARS, as we called them, and they had all kinds of logistics, administrative work to do, and getting ready for the training periods, the two-week training periods that your reserves were coming on board. You couldn't have them all at one time. They had to be staggered. So they would have pretty full employment all during the summer and the rest of the time they kept busy. They were hardworking people.

Q: The reserves are very special people because they also have a foot in civilian life and they have some political clout, don't they?

Adm. J.: They're very, very good ambassadors in the civilian world, they really are. A lot of them were very, very prominent business people, wealthy people, heads of airlines, and things like that. Oh, sure, they're great people. And that's the thing that Artie Doyle exploited, and then, about that time, they had to accelerate pilot-training. You could turn off pilot-training just like shutting off a spigot of water, but cranking up again is a different thing. There are too many different things involved to get it cranked up overnight. It takes a long period of time.

They finally got that going, and then, along with it, of course, you had to accelerate your NavCad recruitment. That's when Artie got Marsh Gurney to come out there and recruit the best possible quality of kids they could find for the aviation cadet program, which was a tremendous success. They really got some good people and down to Pensacola they went, out they came as pilots.

Q: How long a period was required to train them as pilots?

Adm. J.: Well, you didn't want to short-cut that too much because that would be counterproductive. It still would take them close to a year because you had to give them a lot of ground-schooling, too. These kids didn't know anything about the navy. You couldn't do it in much less than a year, you'd be kidding yourself if you tried to.

Then, again, of course, once again the Korean War ended and, zoop, like that you had to cut back your activities. That's the thing that's so disruptive.

Q: You were operating in this time in Johnson's period in DOD, weren't you? Secretary Johnson, who was -

Adm. J.: No, he was SecDef when I was with the Second Fleet.

Q: And he continued until the Korean War.

Adm. J.: Yes.

Q: And his policy was to cut down on everything.

Adm. J.: Right, He didn't want any more carriers. He didn't care too much for the navy, that's right.

Q: So this was an added handicap to the development of your program, right?

Adm. J.: Right. After that, of course, with all the other very severe budget cuts and so forth, it was a very, very good question as to what was going to happen to the reserves, who had just proved themselves. They were cut way back on the money for their training. Then they began to close the bases, close them down.

It's up and down, peak and valley, and this is really not a very good way to run a railroad in the military sense.

Q: Why can't the Congress be convinced of this?

Adm. J.: I don't know. That's a good question but it doesn't have an answer. With the exception of some few like, maybe, Mr. Stennis, they don't think that big. They just don't think that big. They think too much of their own self-interest and what's good for their constituents, rather than the country as a whole, I'm afraid to say. Some one has described them as dishonorable people put together in a conglomerate group who call themselves the Congress of the U.S.

Q: Well, anyway, you were relieved from the reservist assignment and you went out to the Badoeng Strait.

Adm. J.: Right.

Q: That must have been exhilarating.

Adm. J.: Oh, yes, over there in the Yellow Sea. You're on your own over there. You were vulnerable to all kinds of weather because we got no weather reports, none, of course, from Red China, so we had to make our own weather maps based on what we could get locally in the way of soundings and so forth, and hope that was right.

Q: That was only partially effective, then, I take it?

Adm. J.: Well, if you were 50 per cent correct, you were doing well.

Q: How did it compare with an earlier time, in World War II, when you ran into those typhoons? How did the weather service perform?

Adm. J.: It was about the same. Halsey had his weather man with him and he used to send him on local weather recon flights. But, with a typhoon, you get so many preliminary things-warnings that there should be no difficulty in diagnosing a typhoon.

But in the Yellow Sea, you get these sudden fogs, where you get a wind shift, and you get high winds and fog. Then, you're caught with airplanes over Korea and the problem is to get them back on board. You have to always keep that in mind and try to look ahead as much as you could. We were just lucky that we didn't get into any more trouble than we did.

Q: Also, I understand, that the cold winds from the north are absolutely terrific?

Adm. J.: Oh, gee, we were there in the winter and I think that was one of the bleakest Christmases I've ever spent in my life. Let's see, I relieved my good friend on the Sydney and he came in to Sascho for Christmas, and I was on the line.

Anyway, we were up there and I'll never forget Christmas Day. We were sending out strikes and here my good friend the Canadian in the Athabaskan comes along to get some fuel and ice cream. They always wanted ice cream from us. Here he is up on an open bridge, snow going, and it's horizontal. He had his great coat on and he had a mug. So I get on the telephone line and say:

"Good morning, how are you?"

He said, "I'm a little cold. Would you like a little brew here. We'll send you some over."

I've forgotten what it was, some kind of a bouillon with rum in it. It tasted pretty good, but I tell you it wasn't allowed on board. But he was a wonderful person. I got to know him pretty well, and the next time we came in to Sasebo-

Johnson #2 -130-

the regular officers' club there was just one little quonset hut, that's all they had. I went over there and he introduced his doctor. Well, he convinced me he was a doctor, he'd done an appendectomy. Do you know who the guy was? He was a famous imposter. He wasn't a doctor. He'd never been to medical school or anything. They finally caught up with the guy. He was the fellow who masqueraded over in Europe as an ambassador from Canada and three or four different things. There's a book written about the guy.

Q: I have read about him, yes.

Adm. J.: But how he could stay in the Canadian Navy that length of time and pose as a doctor I'll never know. He said he'd done an appendectomy. He was a very, very interesting guy to listen to. He could charm you like a snake-charmer.

Q: I suppose that was part of his equipment!

Adm. J.: Yes, he could convince you of anything.

I guess I spent about four months out there in the Yellow Sea. The war was dragging on. You never knew when it might end or what might happen because everything was pretty well stabilized in the DMZ by that time. There were always the critical things of Pusan, Inchon, and all that stuff. There was never any thought of moving north, it was just a question of intelligence to be sure we weren't caught once again by any movement of the Red Chinese.

North Korea - well, all of it - has always been something of an enigma to me. I've paid several visits there after that as Commander, Seventh Fleet, and CinCPacFlt and talked with Pres. Park many times in the Blue House, he called it the Blue House. I thought he was a very intelligent man. Of course, he was dictatorial and maybe that's the only way you could do things in that country over there. It's very disheartening to go out into the countryside and see how a large percentage of that population lived, it's almost peasantry, really. So, in time, you couldn't help but feel as though there'd be trouble and, of course, there always is. The background of some of the trouble they got into before.

Q: They've had a remarkable industrial development, however, just as the Japanese -

Adm. J.: Yes, they have but not equal to the Japanese, but sure they've got cheap labor and, economically, they're doing pretty well. But the benefits of that are confined to a relatively small number of the population. There really isn't any middle class there. That's part of the trouble. Either you're up there, blue collar, and you're doing real well, or you're a Kim or a Park or something like that, or else you're out in the boondocks and you're living the way they did many, many years ago. All of the niceties of modern living aren't available to those people. Maybe more of them are getting them now, but it certainly wasn't evident to me when I was there.

Q: And part of the problem is that they don't have them but they know they exist?

Adm. J.: Yes. A lot of things they make over there, all kinds of radios and TVs, but that's all exported, practically all of them. But, I guess you can say it's pretty well stabilized, which is something to be said for the situation. Most of it caused by having 45,000 troops there, except for that, and one time, you know, Carter had an idea of pulling everything back. That would have been a disaster.

Q: The country would have been overwhelmed.

Adm. J.: Oh, sure, they were just waiting for that sort of a thing, just waiting for that.

So, I came back in the Badoeng Strait -

Q: How did you function in the jeep carrier?

Adm. J.: Well, compared to some of the other carriers, not too good. Our top speed was about 17 knots, we had a single screw and a single rudder. A ship like that doesn't maneuver too well.

Q: No, of course not.

Adm. J.: You got below 5 knots and you lost steerageway, you couldn't do anything with that ship.

Q: How many planes did you carry?

Adm. J.: About thirty. We had a relatively small deck. But they were pretty efficient little ships, considering what they came from and how they were built.

Q: Did they do much with mines when you were out there?

Adm. J.: No, we were always told to be on the alert for them, particularly floating mines, but I think on two occasions, and I don't know where they came from we had a destroyer go over and sink a couple of them. I guess they were back from the days of Inchon, I suppose.

In and out of Sasebo, we were always preceded by two minesweepers right ahead of us.

Q: Because they hadn't completed the sweeping?

Adm. J.: There were still some that were floating. And you had to go through the nets. There were nets there at Yokosuka and Sasebo, which were a hell of a hazard. I don't know how many ships finally tangled up in the nets at Yoko because you usually had a cross current of about 5 or 6 knots in there, and you were told, in order not to damage the nets, not to exceed 12 knots. Well, you go through there this way, and that's no good.

Q: When did they finally clear those areas?

Adm. J.: Jack, I have no idea. I guess at the end of the Korean War, when the armistice was signed, they ceased worrying

Johnson #2 -134-

about it. I never heard anymore after that.

Q: You were telling me off tape a little gem about using former imperial Japanese naval officers for pilots.

Adm. J.: To bring the navy ships in and to go alongside the docks and to take them out. They knew the waters.

Q: They spoke English, too, didn't they?

Adm. J.: They were pretty good at English, yes. A typically Japanese version of English, but I remember going in to Kobe because we were going to shift the marine air reserve squadron under Bairoko and we had to go alongside in Kobe. So here comes the Japanese pilot, a little short fellow with a top hat on, and we had to get a box and put it up there for him to stand on so he could see out of the window of the bridge. I explained to him: this is the Badoeng Strait, and he said:

"I never handled a big ship like this."

I said: "Well, this isn't very big but you have to be very alert to one thing, namely, that below 5 knots you begin to lose steerageway on the ship. You only have one screw and one rudder.

So he started coming alongside and we had a wind and tide moving us onto the dock. He was doing about 10 knots and slowed to 5 knots, so, sure enough, he had full left rudder and his bow was going like that. Pretty soon we were headed right for the end of the pier, still doing 5 knots. He said:

"Something funny happened. I don't know what."

Then he was yelling in Japanese to the tug, belching all this black smoke, a wood-burning tug. So I said.

"OK, I'll take it," and I dropped the anchor."

Q: About the only thing you could do at that point?

Adm. J.: Yes, dropped the anchor and, fortunately, the bow hadn't gone enough to the right to get us in trouble, so we just went on it, went alongside the dock, paying out chain as we went along, you see, and used that anchor to hold us, and I could make enough turns whereby I could control the steerage of the ship. That's how we got alongside.

That was unusual because, as a rule, they were expert shiphandlers.

A very, very close friend of mine in later years out there was Admiral Isiguri, when I had the Seventh Fleet. He had one eye and he used what he called a monocle. He was head of all the Japanese naval forces in Yoko. I knew him real well. "At Midway," he said "your dive-bombers come down like this, very, very good, we could do nothing. Pretty soon I swim." He was on three different ships that were sunk and he survived all three.

Q: Where did he lose his eye?

Adm. J.: In Midway, with some of the bombs and stuff flying around. They seemed to be very sincere and dependable people.

I don't know--sometimes you wonder. The older Japanese I think you can depend on. They certainly have no desire for any altercation with the United States because that's where their security lies, particularly with the nuclear weapons and the umbrella we provided them there. And, economically, it's tremendous. But the younger people, the different societies you see, you can see them beginning to feel just like in Nazi Germany, maybe a feeling that at some point they should being to assert themselves once again as a power in this part of the world. I may be wrong on that, but I -

Q: Well, we want them to, though, don't we?

Adm. J.: Well, yes, we'd like them to be more self-sufficient and really create more in the way of delf-defense forces. But, once again, that's the way Germany started, self-defense and then a buildup that was used for something else. But at the moment they've got confidence too, because they know they have security, and at the same time they don't have to spend a lot of money on military expenditure. They can concentrate on industry and economics and so forth, and that's why they're doing so well. I think they'll have to wait a long time before they ever get the islands back from the Russians.

Q: Yes, if they're any value to the Russians, they're not going to give them up.

Adm. J.: Well, I came back to the United States, went into overhaul, and I left after a very interesting tour.

Q: And learning a lot?

Adm. J.: Oh, yes.

Q: In preparation later for the big carrier, wasn't it?

Adm. J.: Yes.

Q: But you had some preparation of quite a different kind coming up at this point?

Adm. J.: Let's see.

Q: At the National War College.

Adm. J.: It was a good school. The concept of it, of course, is to prepare you for very, very -

Q: You were a captain at that point?

Adm. J.: Yes. You come back and you mingle with people of the other services.

Q: This was in 1952?

Adm. J.: Yes. The Korean War was pretty much - well, there was an armistice, the war isn't over yet, really, it's still in a state of armistice, that's all it is.

But you mingled with people in the other services, and about an equal number were State Department people, CIA too, and there was one other outfit.

Q: Was the Treasury over there?

Adm. J.: The Treasury had one student. CIA had three, two or three, and the State Department - it was a mixed bag of people.

Q: But they were all people on their way up.

Adm. J.: They were career people, even though you kind of wondered how they'd ever make it. Some of them did real well but some of them were typical striped-pants diplomats who had little or no understanding of the real security interests of the country or of the military. They'd get up and talk but a lot of the times they didn't exactly make too much sense.

Q: Wasn't that one of the reasons for throwing them with the military?

Adm. J.: Well, it was for an exchange of ideas, for the services to get to know each other and to get to know the State Department. After all, the whole matter of the country being run and so forth is sort of a team effort, and the more there's an understanding of what each has to contend with and what the problems are, the more efficient it's going to be.

Q: And all the men at the school at that point were still young enough to absorb new ideas, and yet they were men who gave promise of advancement in their careers?

Adm. J.: And another step, of course, we had a lot of exercises, I guess you'd call them such, with the Industrial War College.

Of course, all that has been combined now as the National Defense College, or University. Anyway, bringing in the logistic part of it plus the other and State was supposed, in a sense, to prepare people for some of the more advanced, complicated, and profound kind of planning you might be involved in, like on a unified command staff or something over in the European Theater.

Q: Logistics, in one sense, has been overlooked by the military largely, hasn't it?

Adm. J.: Yes. You never gave it the importance it deserved until you were faced with it. Like in World War II when Admiral Calhoun was there, he made people realize the importance of it. You could never -

Q: It was something essential that they didn't have?

Adm. J.: Could never have done anything like that unless you had the logistics.

Q: Why, as a senior naval officer, do you think they overlooked the logistics side of it?

Adm. J.: Because there's no glamour. They think it's Supply Corps, and Supply Corps business is completely different from logistics. That's a military application. The army attaches a lot different priority to it than the navy does. Maybe the navy is doing better in that regard now. I don't know, I'm not too sure, because the Service Force, particularly the Service

Atlantic Fleet. There isn't any as such. They did away with that, and this is another Zumwalt gem. Now the Service Force has lost their idenity. That's bad. In Vietnam the Service Force, those guys were a tremendous variety of all kinds of different ships and all kinds of different supply lines to be operated and Admiral Felt insisted the Navy do it because he knew he could depend on the navy to set up supply headquarters to support activities in Saigon, Danang. That was all navy Service Force, throughout Vietnam. The army finally had to take it over in Saigon, but the Service Force are the ones who set it up and made it work.

So that's logistics the way it should be. Ed Hooper was-

Q: Ed Hooper and, before him, Bill Irwin?

Adm. J.: Yes, and Hooper has written a book that tells you this story. Then they come along and they abolish the Service Force itself. I don't understand that, because in the Service Force you had people who specialized in the thing. They were experts in it. Sure, maybe it wasn't as glamourous as being skipper of a cruiser or something like that, but if they had accorded logistics and the Service Force the recognition it deserved, they would have promoted some of those people, more of those people. Furthermore, they would have sent a lot of top-grade people, right at the top of the list, to the Service Force. But in Vietnam -

Q: So it would be a career?

Adm. J.: Sure, they could look upon it as a career and not a dead end.

Q: Yes.

Adm. J.: As I've said many times, it will take us many a year to get over a lot of these things that Zumwalt did, really. That's just one typical thing that he did.

And the amphibious people are really unhappy people.

Q: Can you assign that to the fact that here was a man who hadn't had complete experience prior to becoming CNO, hadn't had a fleet command?

Adm. J.: I don't know what to attribute it to. I think that he came in there with just one idea and he became obsessed with it almost to the point of it being a crusade, the sacred cow idea of special interests. I didn't think they might be called interests, anyway. That had to be offset. In other words, he would send anybody to command of the Sixth Fleet, to be commander of Task Force 60, with the carriers. Anybody. It doesn't have to be an aviator. He started this and, to some extent, it's being done today. In many cases, it will work. In other cases it won't work and it didn't work. Even with Stansfield Turner it wasn't too good. I haven't heard of him sending a nonsubmarine guy to a Polaris submarine, though.

Q: Well, there's another reason for that! A man named Rickover!

Adm. J.: Oh, right, he'd have to run roughshod over him.

But once again, here were two services that felt as though they were elite, and the amphibs are a very proud outfit, too, as they should be. They have a right to be. But now, I know, they're very unhappy. I think they're going to do the same thing again this year, actually force people to go into Rickover' program, and this is going to be a devastating thing. He can't get enough volunteers to meet his quota. He'll only consider the top 50 per cent. Some of those people volunteered and he turned them down.

Q: For whatever reason, he turned them down?

Adm. J.: Yes, nobody knows. Who knows?

Q: To get back to the war college -

Adm. J.: That was a good sabbatical!

Q: You had to work, however.

Adm. J.: Oh, sure you do, work on your term paper or thesis or whatever.

Q: Yes. Well, now you had to select a certain subject, didn't you?

Adm. J.: Yes.

Q: What did you select? What were you interested in?

Adm. J.: As I remember - well, your selection wasn't too large.

Johnson #2 -143-

Q: You mean the scope wasn't too large?

Adm. J.: No, they were narrow subjects and, as I remember, they were divided up into different groups and each group would have four or five subjects to select from. The one that I was more or less told to use, which I wasn't too happy about, was the role of the U.K. in the European Community -

Q: In the Common Market?

Adm. J.: It was the Community something, but it was the Common Market, that's what it was. And you'd explore the pros and cons. If they stay out, could it succeed, was it important to the British to come in, why were they not too anxious to get in.

Q: I take it that at that point they were not yet in?

Adm. J.: No, they were not, and the thing was in kind of a state of flux. They were debating about coming in but they were setting certain conditions for their entry into it, which were not acceptable to the other European countries.

Q: They wanted to protect their own farmers, as I recall.

Adm. J.: Yes.

Q: And the Commonwealth?

Adm. J.: And it affected the Commonwealth, and that had a big bearing on it. As you got more into it, it became more interesting, but nothing like some of the other subjects.

Q: You were sort of in the position of a young fellow getting out of the academy and being forced into the nuke service!

Adm. J.: Yes, well. It was hard to find any research material on it, very difficult.

Q: Because it was current.

Adm. J.: Yes. They had a good library but even so the amount of stuff you were able to dig up from that was very sparse. You had to crank up some of your own thinking on it. It was not the most electrifying thing that the student body wanted to hear.

Q: Did you force it on them, nevertheless?

Adm. J.: Yes, and the professor said, well, considering the subject he was involved in, it's all right. I would have preferred something like "Spain and NATO, Yes or no." should Spain be in it. Of course, that's a little bit more simplified.

But it was, as I said before, an enjoyable thing, and friendships are made there. You got to know people, and friendships have lasted ever since then, more in the army and the air force than the navy, really.

Q: Some of those men turned up in your later career, didn't they?

Adm. J.: Rivets Rivero.

Q: Was he in that class?

Adm. J.: In that class, that's right. Ed Hooper was in that class.

Q: Two bright lads, I must say, they are.

Adm. J.: In the air force, there was, gee - in the army Johnny Johnson, he was chief of staff of the army. I don't remember any of the air force names. For some reason or other, there were more of the people in the army and the navy who moved on up to flag and generals rank than in the air force.

Q: That's surprising.

Adm. J.: Yes. Quite a few of them made BG and that's as far as they went.

Q: Were you in a carpool?

Adm. J.: Yes, I was in a carpool with a fellow named Stevens out of CIA and an air force colonel, whose name I've forgotten now - Tocan I believe. He became a BG and later on was head of the Tactical Air Command at Langley Field here.

Q: That usually worked out as an experience where you could exchange ideas.

Adm. J.: Sure. The informal exchange was much more beneficial and really interesting than the pure academic part of it, a lot of it telling sea stories and things.

Q: What tour did you take?

Adm. J.: Let's see. We had a choice of South American, northern Europe, or southern Europe. I took northern Europe. We went to Paris, then to Weisbaden, Frankfurt, Heidelberg, Copenhagen, Oslo, and then London.

Q: And you had an opportunity to talk with government leaders?

Adm. J.: Oh, yes, we had briefings in all these places, first of all by the embassy people then by people from the country, and the attitudes in all of them varied very greatly because even then Denmark and Norway were very, very reticent to have any close dealings with you. That's why, in those two countries, we had to wear civilian clothes.

Q: Why did they have that?

Adm. J.: They didn't want that kind of open presence there. They're afraid of the Russians, or had some apprehension about them. At that time, you may recall, I think a MIG had defected to Denmark someplace, so, of course, they were getting a lot of pressure from the Soviets, as you can well imagine, and they were debating whether or not to return this airplane and the pilot, too. I'll never forget, this embassy guy came by and said, "Now, for goodness sakes, when you go in there to briefings and all this, don't mention about the MIG." Somebody must have been asleep or out someplace or something, and about the third question he said:

"Sir, may I ask you what are your plans for disposition of the MIG?"

Well, a curtain just fell over the whole place and that, for all practical purposes, ended the briefing. They were just very sensitive on that.

Q: They've been somewhat sensitive all along as NATO members, haven't they?

Adm. J.: Yes. Of course, the thing they (the Danes) were not very sensitive about was their hatred for the Germans, more than the Norwegians.

Q: More than Quisling himself?

Adm. J.: Yes, the Norwegians are still that way, but it's still more ingrained in the Danes. We were in Heidelberg. We went to see the Red Ox, the famous beer-drinking party, where they carved all the names in the table, a list of all the duelers, and everything. There were four of us, and we sat down and ordered beer, and we met two charming Danish couples, man and wife, very charming people. They lived in Copenhagen and said:

"When you get to Copenhagen, be sure to look us up and we'll go on out to Tivoli Gardens and have an evening and we'll show you the town."

About that time, this German officer, straight as a ramrod, clicked his heels, and said:

"Excuse me, you're American military men. May I sit down and join you?"

Nobody wanted to be rude to the guy, so they said, "Sure, sit down," and at that moment all the Danes got up and left. That's the last we ever saw of them.

This fellow sat down, and he was interesting, I'll tell you that. He'd been with Guderian, the tank commander. Of course, he didn't address his remarks to me, they were more to my two army colleagues. He said:

"One reason I wanted to talk - I know you're here to enjoy yourselves and not to talk business, but, I would suggest, and we're very familiar with your tanks, but we consider them to be very, very much inferior to the Russian tanks that they have now, and we don't think you would fare too well against them."

He just volunteered this information. Well, of course, the other guys said, "What proof do you have of this?" But this guy had been in combat with Guderian and he knew a little bit about tanks, and, based on new designs and so forth, they are coming out with tanks with a lot more fire power and so forth to compete with the Tiger tank than the Soviets have.

So much for Copenhagen. Oslo, once you get to know the people there they're friendly but it's very difficult to break through their initial reluctance to talk to people. They go down the street looking down at the sidewalk, they don't look up and speak to you.

Q: Well, that's a general Scandinavian trait?

Adm. J.: They were more reserved than I realized. I'd never been there before.

Q: That sabbatical year, which involved some work and some pleasure, came to an end in 1953?

Adm. J.: Right.

Q: And you were coming up the ladder. You went in as head of the Air Weapons Systems Analysis.

Adm. J.: Yes.

Q: Tell me about that.

Adm. J.: That was in Op-05, and at that time Ralph Ofstie was head of 05. 05W was a relatively new outfit created in 05, working directly for the head of 05. It was supposed to analyze current weapon systems as well as possible, based on what operational reports you could get, what OpTevFor introduced, and so forth, and come up and see that perhaps we had the right mix of all of the weapon components for an ASW group, for instance. You take the ASW group and study that. We did more of that rather than saying OK, how effective is the Mark-48 torpedo, because that's more for the technical bureaus.

I remember one of the studies we made, which goes back to what we were talking about yesterday, which got me in a little bit of trouble. The future of the seaplane in the navy as a weapon system. At that time, there was all this enthusiasm for the Seamaster and for a seaplane fighter, the Dart made by Convair. You remember the one that when they were demonstrating the plane and it disintegrated in midair.

Q: Yes.

Adm. J.: You had the Seamaster and Leslie Stephens and other people were talking about we wanted people who put together maps and marked out all these different landing places all over the globe where these seaplanes could operate. We looked into it and finally came up that, considering the logistics and the operational difficulties, it just wasn't a very good thing to be involved with, cost-effectively, it wouldn't pay off.

Admiral Ofstie had to go up and give this report to Admiral Carney, Mick Carney -

Q: Who was CNO at that time.

Adm. J.: Yes. He picked a bad time to go because he'd been out and had a heavy lunch and so forth. He didn't understand the seaplane thing very much and I don't think was very much interested in it. Ofstie said, "Well, you put him to sleep"!

Q: I'm surprised because he was usually pretty alert.

Adm. J.: Yes. Everybody thought we'd gone to extremes in doing a great disservice to give the seaplane that kind of a bad name, but, as it turned out, particularly going and spending all this money for Seamaster and the Dart, it just wasn't worth the money.

Q: But it took about five more years before it was actually cut off, didn't it?

Adm. J.: Oh, sure. It took a lot of convincing because once you get involved in that sort of a thing, it picks up a lot of momentum and it's pretty far along the road before you can turn it around, just like the nuclear-powered airplane. This fellow Richardson, who had been at the aircraft factory, he became hepped on that subject. So if he could make that pay off cost-effectivewise, in terms of payload, economics, and range; but by the time he got through putting all this lead-shielding and everything in it, you couldn't carry anything. They kept that thing alive for I don't know how many years, spent a lot of money on it.

Q: What were some of the other things you -?

Adm. J.: They're about the only two I can remember right now. I'm sure there were others.

Q: But you were involved with OpTevFor?

Adm. J.: Well, to the extent that we had the benefit of their operational test reports, like on the 3Ts. We were looking into those at that time, the surface-to-air missiles that were just beginning to come in in a big way, the Terrior, the Tartar, and the Talos. Did you want a ship that was all-missile or did you want some guns on it or not? I guess there's still divided opinion on that, except people are coming around based on experience in Vietnam. That was pretty good to have some kind of guns on the ship.

We were a little bit astray, a little bit out of our field, because that was really more the surface people, Eli Reich and those guys. But anyway we thought it worthwhile to take a look into it because we wanted to take a look at what was involved in integrating your missile defenses in with your aircraft defenses, the fire control and the mutual interference problems, and so forth.

Q: Were you involved with WSEG?

Adm. J.: No, we didn't get involved with WSEG, except a couple of times they asked for some special information that they wanted to use as the base for setting up some test. I didn't get involved with WSEG until later on, when I was a carrier division commander. They were working at a higher level, with the Joint Chiefs, and they could have done a lot of good, I think, if it had been prosecuted properly. I never felt that we accomplished an awful lot, even though I thought it was a very worthwhile office to have.

Q: Did it continue?

Adm. J.: For a long time after that, whether it's still in existence today, I don't know.

Q: How large an outfit was it?

Adm. J.: It was relatively small, and purposely so. We had an expert in carrier aviation, ASW, and patrol planes, and missiles. Of course, like any study group like that, whether it's current studies or long-range, you always have to contend with other officers who have their own, you might say, sacred cows that they are proud of. They're the ones who know about that, so don't be making studies that are critical of what we know most about ourselves.

Q: I imagine BuOrd was somewhat sensitive in this area, wasn't it?

Adm. J.: Yes, they always were and always have been. Of course, later on, they became BuWeps, which was a monster.

Q: That wasn't until about 1960?

Adm. J.: Yes, that was later--P. D. Stroop and Pirie.

Q: Was the Sidewinder in being when you were there?

Adm. J.: Not at that time. The Sidewinder was just coming in about that time, as I remember.

Q: That was BuOrd, wasn't it?

Adm. J.: Yes, because, you see, at one time anything, whether it was the guns or the armor even or the bomb racks, anything on an airplane that had to do with fire power was BuOrd. No cognizance for that went into BuAer. The only thing that BuAer ever was able to get was the gun sight! The turrets, that was all BuOrd and with all the cutting and fitting they had to do and, except for the pressure of the Vietnam War, we'd probably have been in more disagreements and controversies than we were.

Q: What about Ships' Characteristics, were you involved with them?

Adm. J.: No, we weren't involved. That's the area of the Ships' Characteristics Board.

Q: But they were also concerned with ordnance of all sorts?

Adm. J.: Well, they were concerned with the armament suits, the guns and so forth that you had on there, yes, but they would call in different people -

Q: You said, off tape, that there were certain people in the navy who were not actually convinced of the value of this particular group and its efforts.

Adm. J.: In 05, they were not convinced that there was a need for it, because, once again, whether it be in Op-51, in the missiles, Op-55, in the airplanes, or some other place, the equipment, they held this over our head all the time, in expertise they needed a man to analyze what they had and so forth.

Q: There was overlapping, wasn't there?

Adm. J.: To some extent there was, but the point they missed is that in many instances they got themselves all wrapped up and involved in nuts and bolts. Too much so, whereas actually BuAer was supposed to do that. So a lot of times, they couldn't see the forest for the trees, and that was the big value of having an 05W, a so-called objective analysis outfit, to take a pretty much neutral approach to the thing and let the chips fall where they may, even though you knew you were going to step on somebody's toes. It's always good to have an outfit like that.

Q: And to change personnel even in that outfit?

Adm. J.: Oh, sure.

Q: So you don't begin to think of it as your empire.

Adm. J.: That's right.

Q: That's bureaucracy all the time!

Adm. J.: Yes. It's been around many years and we'll probably always have it.

Q: The only time that it seemed to work effectively was when Raborn was given such power as Special Project officer for Polaris missile that he could -

Adm. J.: Well, he was given a blank check to expedite the thing, which was kind of unusual. I guess it paid off.

Q: It certainly did, in terms of results.

Adm. J.: As I said before, apparently there was almost resentment of 05W. There were certain people on occasions who, when there were certain developments or things coming along, seemed to deliberately withhold information from us. Of course, it wasn't any particular business of ours, but at that time there was a big, big argument going on as to whether the fighter of the future should be two-seat or single-seat. And there are still some people today who go for the single seat. And, of course the Vought people lost out with their airplane with a single seat against the McDonnel-Douglas, who had the F4-U, which is the two-seater, with the radar operator, which was proven to be the best way to go.

Q: Such arguments are useful, however.

Adm. J.: Yes.

Q: In discovering the various facets of the problem.

Adm. J.: A lot of times, of course, it's kind of risky to make those decisions based on a paper study, because in a lot cases you were never really able to resolve this except with an actual flight vehicle in actual flight test, a tactical test of it. Mistakes have been made by doing this sort of thing.

Q: Yes.

Adm. J.: Although not too many.

Q: You must have been a pretty good person to have in this section at that time because you have the kind of personality that can disarm those who object.

Adm. J.: Well, you had to be persuasive as you could, and not be autocratic. In other words, always listen to the other fellow.

Q: That's what I mean.

Adm. J.: In that way, at times you can disarm some of these real, real dyed-in-the-wool thinkers, you know, who won't give an inch. They begin to see the light, and, of course, we had in 05W, as you would expect, a bit of dealings with the research outfit, Chick Hayward -

Q: Oh, yes.

Adm. J.: He didn't have it then. I've forgotten who did have it. Of course, all the black boxes and all that stuff, super secret decisions locked up over here.

Q: Maybe this is an opportune moment to ask you to comment on this super secrecy in the service, the good points and the detriments in having this. It withholds information that's essential.

Adm. J.: Well, of course, it all depends what kind of a project it is and the nature of the secrecy. In other words, I would say that in the case of Manhattan it was primarily conducted in exactly the right manner, because that had such far reaching implications that it had to be closely held. There were people working on components who had no idea what they were doing, even though Chick will tell you that he knew exactly what was going on and everything, and all he had was the radio altimeter. I still have some doubt that, until much later on, he knew what he was going into.

Now, as opposed to that, and there are probably more exampl of overdoing secrecy that on the other side, and, of course, the more recent being the rescue over in Iran. So secret and everything that the people, if they had been in on the know, could have detected some of the possible pitfalls, either in the training or the equipment, the concept, and so forth, and might have made the thing successful, as opposed to the fiasco that it was. I think they very greatly overdid the secrecy on that. Up to a point, it had to be secret, sure, because you didn't want the other guys to know that you were going to pull this thing off, very true.

A lot of times, they go to extremes of secrecy which hurts the proejct when, actually, a lot of the information that they're trying to withhold has already gotten out, anyway. I can remembe the Torch Operation, when we went into North Africa.

Q: So can I!

Adm. J.: This was supposed to be a great big secret and so forth. Well, I don't think there were very many people who didn't realize exactly what was going on then, because here, down in Norfolk, when you see two or three hundred air force fighters come down with all this desert camouflage and being loaded onto ships headed east in the Atlantic, why I think you could put two and two together and get four out of that pretty easily.

The Nauseword Hotel burned a couple of weeks ago, that's where all the original planning took place for Torch, right here at Ocean View.

Q: Oh, really?

Adm. J.: Yes, with the British and Americans.

No, I think on many occasions we overdo the secrecy thing. In the Bay of Pigs it was overdone. Of course, the whole concept of the operation was faulty there. An operation that big should never be given to CIA. I think I said that yesterday.

Q: We learned a lesson at that point.

Adm. J.: I hope so.

Q: Are other services quite as secretive?

Adm. J.: The army, I think, is about the same as we are. SAC is worse than any of them. I guess they feel as though, since they're the real protectors of the A-bomb and so forth, they've got to have super super security and secrecy as well as for their plan, the great big integrated plan that they have and so forth.

Q: Yes, they're in possession of the ultimate weapon.

Adm. J.: Oh, yes, so I guess they're probably justified in most of it, even though some of it, I think, in the final analysis they would find out if they ever had to implement the plan, that if the people down in the lower operating echelons knew more about what they were doing and how they were doing it, instead of going off blind, they would do a better job.

Johnson #2 -160-

Q: That's why I think it's sometimes a bit of a detriment.

Adm. J.: There's a gray area in there. Sometimes it isn't too hard to cite, but I think that can be overdone to the extent that it is a detriment, yes.

Q: Well, in 1955 you got a very delightful big assignment?

Adm. J.: Oh, yes.

Q: This was a great fillip to you.

Adm. J.: Yes. There had been a lot of talk about it, and a couple of people were absolutely certain they were going to get the job, so I didn't really expect it.

Q: There weren't too many jobs of that sort, were there?

Adm. J.: No, and a classmate of mine was absolutely certain, so I had no idea. Admiral Bill Rees, who was deputy 05, called me in and said:

"Here's a piece of paper that I think you will be delighted to read."

It was a thing from Jimmy Holloway, who was chief of BuPers, and they had gone through all this business of comments and so forth, recommendations, as to who should be the commanding officer. In one place there, there was a D and I knew it was Wu Duncan, who was the vice chief, and it said:

"What we need for this job is not a PIO expert but someone who knows how to deal with people and has an appreciation of the operational requirements of a carrier. I therefore submit the name of Johnson."

Coming from the vice chief, I guess that helped me quite a bit!

Q: I'm sure it did.

Adm. J.: So, Jimmy Holloway called me over, had me come in his office, gave me coffee, shook my hand, and said:

"I'm sure all your contemporaries are very happy with this choice," and I said:

"Well, I kind of doubt that!"

Some of them were bitter for a long time on account of this.

Q: Blamed you!

Adm. J.: For making some kind of an end run, you see. I never talked to anybody about it, never even mentioned it. What I wanted was to leave 05 and go out to sea and get command of something, sure. But they really made too much of it. It became almost a navy political football, the way they kicked it around. There were a lot of people who had their favorites who were really pushing.

Q: No doubt.

Well, the Forrestal was the first of the class.

Adm. J.: Oh, yes, a ship that big and people say, "My God, it's too big."

Q: 50,000 tons.

Adm. J.: More than that.

Q: How many planes complement?

Adm. J.: 110 to 130, depending on the mix that you had.

It was quite a job for any ship, to go down and take a crew like that and put it together, get them trained and the engineering department organized. Part of the nucleus crew were the engineering people.

Q: You were there six months before she was commissioned?

Adm. J.: About four months. I stayed in the Chamberlain Hotel and back and forth to Newport News. Of course, Newport News Shipbuilding with Mr. Bill Blewett and those people were an absolutely wonderful corporation, helping you to get things ready and even making last-minute changes which had not been and never were approved by BuShips, but which we knew we should be on the ship.

We had this nucleus down there so that when we went out on the shakedown trails, part of my crew had as much to do with operating the engineering plant as the Newport News people did. So they had a good break in there.

Q: Was this before Newport News became Tenneco?

Adm. J.: Oh, yes, long before that. This was in the days of Mr. Bill Blewett and those people. It was still an independent outfit, no union, no strike problems, no labor problems, nothing of that sort.

And, of course, you had to get your flight-deck crews on there, all those people, your steam catapults, arresting gear, the CIC people and all this, put all of this together—

Q: Quite an administrative job!

Adm. J.: Oh, gee, and hopefully you'd have access to enough schools for radar operators. You'd put as many as you could on other ships that had steam catapults, even though the Mark that we had was different. Of course, a lot of them had had a lot of experience because I could pretty well have the pick of the people I wanted.

Q: Yes, it was like a special project, wasn't it?

Adm. J.: Yes, in some respects.

So, I was commissioned and then we had the outfitting in Portsmouth, and then you go off on the shakedown. Then you come to the moment of truth, how well you're going to do with this crew on there. Of course, before that, really almost a night mare was putting together the program, the ceremonies, for the commissioning.

Q: That gets into the realm of the political.

Adm. J.; Oh, you can't imagine! All the different people who wanted to get in the act.

I went up to Admiral Duncan and said, "I've got a problem as to who the main speaker should be." He said:

"First of all, you'd better go and see Mr. Thomas," he was the secretary of the navy. So I went to see him. Andy Jackson was his aide. He took me in and Thomas said:

"Thank you very much. I'd be delighted, I'd consider it an honor."

So, I went back and began to put together the program and so forth, the other people I would have. About a week later Andy Jackson called and said:

"The secretary doesn't think he should do it because he was the speaker at the launching, but he wants Jimmie Smith, who is the assistant secretary of the navy for air, to be the speaker."

He didn't leave me any choice –

Q: He's already made the selection himself.

Adm. J.: Yes. So I went up to see Arleigh Burke and he was ready to hit the ceiling. He said:

"I won't even go to your damned ceremony. If he couldn't be the speaker, you should have come to me."

I tried to explain to him I didn't have a chance. So the time dragged on and, of course, I sent out invitations and I had to make up the program and everything and he still hadn't decided whether he was going to come down. So I went in one day and finally asked him. I said:

"Admiral, you know, we've got to have you down here. It would be a great honor, and people would like to see you down there."

He said, "OK, but I won't make any speech."

Then I went in to see Radford, who was chairman then. Yes, he would come down, but he said:

"For God's sake, who was stupid enough to make the uniform white service?"

I said, "Well, the commandant is in charge of all this and he prescribes the uniform. It's October 5th and you don't change the uniform until October 15th."

Well, gee there I go again.

Well, the day of the commissioning, this front came through, it rained, people were wet, and I mean it was cold. Admiral Radford was there with his umbrella with Mrs. Radford and, boy, did he give me a nasty look.

We had all kinds of dignitaries. You can't imagine the people who wanted to come to this thing.

Q: Except the ones you wanted to come!

Adm. J.: Up on the main platform, I had two or three former secretaries, including Mr. Sullivan, who had been a great supporter of the carrier. We began to introduce these people, introduced Admiral Burke, and all of a sudden, he goes up to the podium.

Q: He's going to speak, anyway!

Adm. J.: Yes. He said:

"I'm not going to make a speech but I just have to have a few minutes with you," and he pulled out a piece of paper.

He said:

"What I have to say is not addressed to anybody except the crew. I'm talking to the crew of this ship, nobody else. Here's a great ship produced by a great shipbuilding concern with the benefit of all the modern technology you can think of at the moment in terms of what is needed for operational aircraft, a floating airport, if you will, but it's nothing but a bucket of bolts and a bunch of steel, cold steel, depending on what you people of the crew make it. You're the life blood in this ship, and it's up to you to make it something that really operates the way it should and be not only a good ship, but a great ship. That's all."

I'll never forget that as long as I live, what he said. In other words, he was talking to the men, the people.

Q: What was the complement, by the way?

Adm. J.: With the air group on there, you had between 4,000 and 5,000 people.

Q: A regular little city!

Adm. J. Oh, sure, we had evertying that goes with a city. We had a lot of different innovations, too. The habitability of the ship, which has been steadily increasing all the time, which is a good thing. In other words, we'd long since given up hammocks, but there the enlisted people had real good, comfortable bunks, they had good lighting in the spaces where they slept, they had a completely different and much better arrangement to be sure they got hot food at the canteens. Before, there were the old messdecks and you had a mess cook and he's throw the stuff down, you didn't know whether it was going to be hot or not. You go through the line, you have a selection of food, a completely different concept, and of course, even opposed to that, many improvements have been made on that aboard ships for the comfort of the people.

Q: What were some of the contributions you made prior to the commissioning of the ship, the feed in from your experience, that were then incorporated by the builders?

Adm. J.: Once again, it's a matter of people, people who have had quite a bit of experience in carriers. So I wanted to make sure that I had as department heads in the air part of it people who had carrier experience and knew carrier operations, and therefore would know the kind of people, the chiefs and those people, the key people, to get on board to work the thing. The supply department and engineering, I wanted to be sure I had good people. I didn't know as much about that from experience, but the air side of it is, after all, why you have a ship that operates airplanes, to make sure that you had at least the best that you could accomplish, the kind of real qualified, competent people to do the job.

The squadrons were already formed. You had to take that. Fortunately, they were good people and they had a good commander by the name of Ralph Werner. He was a tremendous leader, a good pilot.

So, we go off on the shakedown, and we immediately became a showboat. Here, you'd go out of Gitmo every morning and come in every evening. I don't know why the ship couldn't stay out but the riders from the Training Command wanted to be home with their wives, I guess.

So, weekends, here are sixty congressmen coming down, coming down with the secretary and Admiral Burke. One time, a bunch of people came down, we had to get under way Sunday morning with Tom Gates, and go out and operate to show off to these people.

Q: You didn't have the president come down, however?

Adm. J.: No, we never had the president come down. A lot of senators and congressmen, though.

Q: Well, that's an educational thing, and it's an opportunity, isn't it, to get support for the navy?

Adm. J.: It paid off, I'm sure. They'd come down, some of them, particularly the congressmen, come on board on all ships but on the carriers there were a very large number of them. They had these reflector lights on the deck which would reflect light and guide you for walking or for placing the airplanes, pushing the airplanes, or something. When a congressman saw these, he'd say, "I'd like about forty of those for my driveway." Another one comes up and says "I was down looking through the supply spaces and I saw these wonderful hams and I asked him if I could have two or three of them." You start this sort of a thing with these guys and there's no end to it!

But Symington was a very astute visitor, I'll tell you that.

Q: Symington was?

Adm. J.: Oh, yes. His questions, and some of them pretty tough questions. He wanted to know everything he could find out about what increased capabilities you had, vulnerability, and so forth. Of course, as we'd said all along, with this large a carrier, with its length and with a closed-in bow, you would be able to operate that ship with a steady platform in sea conditions in which other carriers wouldn't be able to operate, and we proved it very shortly after this, because, coming back from the shakedown, Bob Pirie, who was Commander, Second Fleet, said:

"OK, I want the Forrestal in the fleet exercises."

The other CVA was the Midway. We operated, we did all right. We kept right up with the Midway, even though we were a brand-new ship and everything. On the last day of the exercise we were to launch all of the airplanes and send them in to Oceana. Well, the Midway said, "No, it's too rough, we're not going to launch," and they were taking water and so forth. We went ahead and launched and had no problem at all.

Q: Proud to show off your ability!

Adm. J.: That proved the increased capability of the ship in rough weather. Of course, that didn't mean there weren't some conditions in which you wouldn't be able to operate, but certainl the main thing is that it has a much better capability than the Essex class or even the Midway.

We finally finished the shakedown and came back on the fleet exercise, and then came in for the post-shakedown check to correct all the things that went wrong. Even in the shakedown the ship had a lot of problems. The thrust bearings. For years and years, the navy had used a type of thrust bearing partly lubricated mechanically and partly electrical with one standby-I've forgotten, but anyway, BuShips decided to change that.

Q: For the Forrestal?

Adm. J.: For the Forrestal, the first time. There were objection but they were overidden.

So here, we go out on the shakedown and, to make a long story short, we find, though the ship finally limped back in on one shaft with tugs standing by to tow her in. The others got so hot, even with hoses pouring water on them, that they couldn't keep them cooled down and had to lock them, had to shut down the turbines. So they went back to the old system after that.

Q: What's the wisdom of inaugurating something new like that?

Adm. J.: Somebody always thinks he's innovative and he's making progress. Admiral Duncan used to have a sign that said: "Never be the last to accept a proven new idea or the first to throw away a proven idea" - or something like that. If you have something that's working and no problems, why change?

Then they go out on the shakedown - of course, Newport News is doing all this, Mr. Edwards, the wonderful pilot they had was at the conn on the ship. They'd go up to full speed, 25 1/2 knots, then, all of a sudden, all engines back full. Oh, man, that's a severe test.

Q: I would think so.

Adm. J.: Then, at the same speed, you do right full rudder and then reverse and do left full rudder. Well, on shakedown, it wouldn't go full, it went only about two-thirds of the way over. Didn't have enough power in the hydraulic steering somehow or other to do that. So it had to be accepted conditionally, and that had to be fixed later on.

Then they go out in I forget how many fathoms of water, anyway it was pretty deep, and they'd say, "Let go the anchor." Of course, you had this tremendous anchor and each length weighed 160 pounds. You let go, free fall, and you're supposed to catch it with the electric brake. Well, this thing started out and there are all these people up there in the fo'c'sle with that chain coming out of there, it sounds like two freight trains. They yelled to the bo'sun to brake it. He tried to brake it and a lot of blue smoke came out and, boy, that chain just kept going. Fortunately, we were in a depth of water that the anchor hit bottom.

Q: Hit bottom!

Adm. J.: And then fortunately he was able to stop it. Otherwise, it would have gone out to the bitter end.

In the case of the Saratoga, which came after that and was built by New York Shipbuilding, they lost the anchor chain and everything that way.

Q: It just went right on down?

Adm. J.: And I think it killed two people up on the fo'c's'le. You can imagine that bitter end coming undone, whizzing around. We were lucky, but, anyway they had to redesign the brake. Those are some of the things you have to do.

Q: The rudder problem, then, wasn't taken care of until you had a -

Adm. J.: No. That was a major job, you see. They couldn't do that until we had a refit. They had to make a lot of changes on that. The Inspection and Survey Board were on board of course, on board during the trials. The fellow in charge called his boss and unfortunately, he came back and said, "No, we're not going to accept the ship.

I said, "The commissioning is only a week away and I've got 20,000 invitations out, all the arrangements made and everything. You can't say you're not going to accept the ship now. It's not that bad."

He said, "No, we refuse to accept the ship."

I finally got on the radio telephone and got Admiral Duncan. He was still vice chief, and I explained to him, and he said:

"Tell him to accept the ship." That's all he said. And he did, conditionally, of course. Newport News accepted that. They knew they had to fix it. There was no problem. So that was the shakedown.

Those were the days when Newport News used to really put on an elaborate trial cruise. They took practically all the hired help out of the Chamberlain Hotel. They took waiters over there with their white jackets and everything, they came on board. And they had all kinds of visitors there. They had a bar set up in both wardrooms. They had about one hundred dozen oysters, all kinds of seafood and everything, and for the four days it was really something. I don't imagine they'd ever be able to do that again, but it was really something in those days.

Anyway, we came back from the shakedown and the fleet exercise, and everybody was very pleased with the way the ship performed, and then we went into the yard for the post-shakedown.

Even before the ship was ever commissioned, the selection board came up. So, here, I hadn't even commissioned the ship, turned it over, and I was on the selection board for flag rank. Of course, I wanted to keep the ship a while, so once again I had to go to Admiral Duncan, and he said:

"All right, don't worry, you'll keep the ship a year, anyway", which I did.

Q: You didn't put on your stripes?

Adm. J.: No.

Q: That must have given you a lot of assurance, however?

Adm. J.: Oh, yes.

Q: The fact that you'd been selected.

Adm. J.: Yes.

I was relieved by Bill Ellis and shortly thereafter he took the ship over to the Med. I was sorry I missed the Med deployment because it would have been interesting.

Q: Tell me about the balance of your operation on there.

Adm. J.: It was in fleet exercises and different things, special exercises. Of course, we had to spend much longer than I thought we would have in the yard, fixing things like the steering machinery. We stayed there much longer than I thought we would.

Q: How do you keep the men occupied, a crew like that?

Adm. J.: Well, coming into the yard, of course, that's a good time to give them as much leave as you can because you can spare a lot of them. On the other hand, in a yard like that you have two different sets of job orders. One to be done by the ship yard and the others by the crew. This is decided in a joint conference with the ship yard - there are some of them that won't do. In other words, they'd say, "That's the ship's force who should do that." So you had all kinds of projects that the ship's force had to do. So they keep pretty busy, but, all in all, it's a pretty dull period, a pretty unhappy period, being in a ship yard. It's hard to keep the ship clean. It's impossible, as a matter of fact. You've got all the workmen coming on board and going off, there are a lot of things being torn apart and scattered around. The ship really gets dirty. It's a bad time, but it always had to be done.

Q: Before you commissioned here, when you were assembling the original crew, how many different schools did you have to send them to?

Adm. J: Oh, there are all kinds of schools available.

Q: All along the East Coast?

Adm. J.: Yes, and at that time, once again, there were other changes to be made. At that time, we had the Training Command, and part of the Training Command were those people down in Gitmo. The ship's riders there, the ones who went out to sea, would help you with any problems down in engineering, on the flight deck, and places like that. The Training Command had the firefighters school, they had Dam Neck for CIC, fighter direction, and any number of different places where you could send people for their schooling. It was a very good setup.

They still have Dam Neck, but I never hear anything of the Training Command any more. I don't know what happened to it. They must have something the equivalent of it. At one time, this was a separate command in itself under CinCLantFlt, with an admiral at the head of it. With a lot of new ships coming out, that was a very important command.

So, there were all kinds of schools you could go to, including quite a few at the manufacturers' plant. You could send them there to learn about different equipment you had on board.

Q: Did you have to go to shiphandling school?

Adm. J.: No, but before the Badoeng Strait I went to shiphandling school, firefighter schools, CIC school, which was a requirement for all commanding officers the first time. That was a very helpful thing. They had a duplicate setup on the West Coast of what they had here.

Q: This brings up a question. There is a difference, isn't there, between the two coasts in some schools, the necessity for training that applies particularly to the Atlantic or to the Pacific?

Adm. J.: No, not really. As long as it's basic training, it's pretty much the same. There's no difference really. You could send a man to either one of them and when he came out of it you'd never know the difference.

Q: Well, you were down in Gitmo?

Adm. J.: In Gitmo. It was Saturday afternoon and we had a lull period for a change, so I was out flying around, getting in some flight time. I came back aboard, went to my cabin, and found out that Admiral "Cat" Brown had paid me a visit. He'd come down there for some reason or other and had come aboard. I wasn't aboard, so he left a note that said:

"I'm very curious, now that you've been selected for flag rank, what is to be your fate when you leave this harbor and this big ship here goes aground over on the port side of the channel?"

Q: That's an interesting question to pose!

Adm. J.: Yes, but not very enjoyable. That's Cat Brown, you know, he's always pulling your leg.

Q: What would be the result of such a thing?

Adm. J.: You're through, just like Captain Brown on the Missouri. He was considered one of the top-notch people by this time, when the Missouri ran aground out here in the fishnets. That was the end for him. No, there's no recourse from that sort of thing. I don't think there should be, but now things seem to have changed, the thinking seems to have changed a little bit, particularly since we now have the JAG Corps. For example, the skipper of the Belknap, a cruiser alongside a carrier at night, and he's down in the wardroom watching movies. And he's alongside a carrier, and you remember the horrible collision they had, cleaned the topside off and they lost several people. She was just put back in commission very recently. I don't know whether he's in the navy any longer, but from the investigation nothing serious happened to him. I think he received a letter of censure or something like that.

Q: In the case of, as Brown posed the question, a man who'd been selected but hasn't actually become -

Adm. J.: Well, it would be academic. He'd be through.

Q: As a captain, or what?

Adm. J.: Well, it all depends how long he stayed in because you don't make your number right away, particularly in my case because I was pretty junior. This was two years before most of my class were coming up, so it would have been quite a while, anyway, before I made my number. It would all hinge on that.

Q: But that selection wouldn't be taken away from you, would it?

Adm. J.: For all practical purposes, it wouldn't make any difference. At the time you left the navy, if you hadn't made your number, you would not be retired for pay purposes with that rank.

Q: That's what I was getting at.

Adm. J.: No.

Q: Because that does make a difference.

Adm. J.: Yes, it sure does.

Q: You were talking off-tape about this technique of using planes at the corners of the flight deck.

Adm. J.: They call it pinwheel operation.

Q: Tell me again.

Adm. J.: Well, it's very simple. You'd have four or six airplanes on each side, on the stern, and in the bow, and control them from the bridge. Like a pilot, the captain could control them, and he'd tell unit 1, 2, 3, or 4 to turn, depending on which way he wanted to turn the ship. With this much twisting momentum given by the thrust of these engines, you could start turning that ship in no time at all. This became a pretty favorite way of maneuvering a ship out of tight places, particularly in places where there were inadequate tugs or there were no tugs at all. But it was soon stopped for the simple reason that they were beginning to wear out the engines on the airplanes.

Q: An expensive way of doing it!

Adm. J.: Yes, right, but as an expedient it was a great thing for a while.

Q: Well, in 1956 you, I imagine regretfully left the Forrestal?

Adm. J.: Oh, yes, you always hate to leave command of a ship because I've always told junior officers "the best job you'll ever have in the navy is commanding officer of a ship because your authority is absolute and your responsibilities are just as absolute as your authority, and all this with your accountability." Of course, as I alluded to earlier, accountability seems to be a thing that they have become a little wishy-washy about. For example, the Belknap, where he got off and I thought it a very, very culpable thing to be - anybody sitting down in the wardroom watching a movie when his ship's alongside a carrier.

Q: Maybe this is an appropriate time to ask you to comment on the element of a good command. I mean what's involved?

Adm. J.: Command at sea -

Q: This being command of a combatant ship?

Adm. J.: Of a combatant ship, particularly a combatant ship, your authority is more direct even though you still are in a chain of command. That's very true, but you have under you, depending on the size of the ship and so forth, a number of people and, first of all, you're responsibility for their welfare, for their safety; you're responsible for the efficiency of fighting the ship, and you're to be held accountable for anything that happens to that ship. To be held accountable and responsible in this manner, of course, as set forth in Navy Regs, your authority must be absolute within the ship.

It had to be absolute. Otherwise, there's no way you can exercise the various elements of leadership required for a good ship or to have the required discipline that goes with leadership.

Once again, the most successful people in command, and I think this is a very, very important ingredient of leadership and the exercise of command, is the ability, in an intelligent way, to delegate responsibility and authority within the ship, if it's that sort of a command or in the staff, if it's something bigger than that. A lot of people simply do not have this faculty. They don't know how to do that. I've known people and there are many examples of people who literally wore themselves out by being afraid to delegate responsibility and authority. They stayed on the bridge twenty-four hours out of the day and the result - a collision. And the board of investigation found that he was completely fatigued.

Q: He's lost his effectiveness?

Adm. J.: That's right. You can't stay up there continually and expect to function normally. There's no way of doing it.

Q: Normally, a man who does not have that ability to delegate doesn't advance up the ladder too far, does he?

Adm. J.: Sooner or later, it's going to catch up with him. He may be lucky and get away with it, particularly in a time of lower tempo of operations, peacetime, and so forth, where you're not involved in anything of a very critical nature. But any time you're involved, first of all, in combat or a situation like in the Indian Ocean or the thing going on right now in the Mediterranean, this sort of thing, as I said before, is going to catch up with you.

Q: Well, too, you can differentiate, can't you, between a command in peacetime and a command in wartime? It requires different characteristics?

Adm. J.: Well, it's more severe, but you still have responsibility, of course, in peacetime but the environment you are operating in is completely different. It's bound to be more severe in times of combat, and one thing that should always be remembered is that in time of combat you're liable to be confronted with very critical situations which demand a very, very important decision to be made immediately. In other words, you can't get on the TBS or something and go to a superior and say, "I'm in this situation. Request instructions." That's no good.

There's been a tendency lately, with improved communications and so forth, even starting at the national levels, that here people overseas, the ambassador and other people, are not allowed to exercise the initiative that they were permitted to at one time. That's at the diplomatic level. Carrying this on to the military, there has been a tendency to go too far in this direction and almost to a dangerous extent, because, first of all, it's not the most effective way to engage in combat or to get the most out of your fighting units, and, secondly, it tends to destroy initiative on the part of the more junior people in command, which is a very bad thing in itself. You see that happening, at least I have seen it happening, more and more and I think this is a very dangerous trend. It started, I suppose, back in the days of the missile crisis, when SecDef McNamara insisted that he have a patch-in whereby he could talk directly to the ships on station, as Dennison told you, I'm sure.

Q: Yes, indeed. As Anderson will tell me.

Adm. J.: Yes, and the same thing in the Gulf of Tonkin incident on the Maddox. Here, people in Honolulu were calling me, telling me to get busy and patch in the skipper of the Maddox direct to SecDef. He wanted to be able to talk to him and appraise the situation minute by minute, and then he would decide what he was going to tell him to do. In other words, he circumvented the military in the normal chain of command. You see examples of where people have become very reluctant and hesitatnt to go ahead and make decisions on their own. Along with that comes the other thing, they don't speak out like they did at one time. They're afraid to speak out.

In the case of the Gulf of Tonkin thing, the skipper of the Maddox was undoubtedly under attack by the PT boats and, at that moment, I happened to be in the flagship at Yokosuka, and Secretary Nitze was coming in to the Tokyo International Airport. So, Peg, my wife, and I were going down the hill in the car to get in the helicopter and go over to the airport to meet Secretary and Mrs. Nitze. Here comes a car up the hill, blowing its horn, all excited. I got out and here was an urgent priorty message from the skipper of the Maddox.

Here he is in the Gulf of Tonkin on patrol. I'm up in Yoko, and he says:

"Under attack by enemy PT boats. Request instructions."

Well, this is really a very, very bad thing to be confronted with because anyone should know with certainty you are entitled to and actually required to defend yourself when attacked. If it's one of those borderline things, it may be a little understandable why he would request instructions, but in this case completely nonunderstandable. Of course, he proved to be incapable of carrying out the job as skipper of that destroyer particularly when it came to crisis situations such as this. He did shoot back long before I could get any word to him, and then what he did was head south at flank speed.

Q: He ran away from it?

Adm. J.: Yes, so Tom Moorer and I, long before Tom Moorer got on the horn with me, I finally got him and I said:

"Reverse course, get on station, and remain on station." But he was getting out of there. He wasn't going to stay. That's the overall net effect in that sort of thing, what it does to the thinking of people in the more junior positions of responsibility. That's a very, very bad trend. Maybe it'll turn around. I don't know.

Q: Hasn't it been augmented, too, by the recent attention to minorities on board ship and their access directly to the CNO?

Adm. J.: Well, sure, that's something that started under Zumwalt. As Tom Moorer and others have pointed out, here was a big carrier tied up at San Diego and they had in effect what I would consider without any question, mutiny. Here this minority group on the dock refused to come back on board and do what they were supposed to. That's as close to mutiny as I can think of. And, once again, the skipper's thinking was, gee, you've got to handle this with kid gloves, you can't go too far, got to think of the repercussions because this is a minority group, and so forth. What he should have done was deal with it very firmly and if that wasn't adequate - they disagreed with it -- as Stockdale said, "OK, you can have my suit."

Those are all the things involved in command and, as I said before, here are some of the essential elements of command that seem to have been watered down or distorted to the point that there's now doubt in the minds of a lot of junior officers as to exactly what they're supposed to do. You can talk to a lot of them and that's one of their concerns, and one of their disappointments, that here I'm expected to exercise leadership in order to be a good naval officer, to make my way up the ladder, and so forth. I'm supposed to demonstrate qualities of leadership and exercise same. How can I do it in this sort of environment?

Q: And, I suppose, in a sense, it does reflect an attitude that seems to prevail in the populace in general. I mean an unwillingness to assume - to bite the bullet.

Adm. J.: There's been quite a bit of that, yes. In other words - and I've written things to the paper here-what it amounts to insofar as national will is concerned, and this is what we're talking about in the ultimate sense we have by demonstrating this perception of weakness pretty much lost our guts. A perception of weakness by hesitance to do things at the time when they should be done and the wishy-washy way we go about doing them, and this is not exactly a show of confidence in the minds of your friends, first. That's bad enough, but, secondly, in the mind of potential enemy and by virtue of such, as has been demonstrated many times, he is tempted more than ever to go ahead and do things that otherwise he would not do.

Q: Actually, this was a factor in the recent presidential election?

Adm. J.: Sure. If we assert ourselves very strongly and demonstrate willingness to do the things required, no matter what grave risks are involved, that's the only thing the enemy's going to pay any attention to.

Those are all the things involved, some of them, of course, pretty much abstract. Aside from the professional things like engineering, seamanship, and those things, a lot of this you can get out of a book. You can read a lot about leadership, and some of the better writings on leadership came from Douglas Southall Freeman. Some of his lectures are classic and he was very frank to admit that he was partial. About the great Robert E. Lee and Stonewall Jackson.

But, in talking about leadership, once again he stresses those things that are most important in the exercise of leadership, the first one being know your men, take care of your men - those two things, and then have courage and be sure of what you're doing. That's one of the most famous speeches he ever made to the Naval War College.

Q: I've seen one pretty good one, too, delivered by Jerry Miller.

Adm. J.: I guess I missed that one.

Q: That was not at the war college, that was down at the Armed Services, a very effective speech.

Well, now we're going to leave the Forrestal as in 1956 you became director of the Long-Range Objectives Group in the CNO.

Adm. J.: Right, that was Op-93.

Q: Op-93, was it?

Adm. J.: Yes, the Long-Range Objectives Group, which is no longer in existence.

Q: Did you succeed Rivero?

Adm. J.: No, Rivets succeeded me. Don Griffin was the first one. He formed it, and it grew out of what was recognized as a need for some sort of long-range shipbuilding program. In other words, considering the money involved at the time, spent on the design of a ship and building of it, we should have some better way of approaching what our needs are, rather than a sort of hand-to-mouth thing, budget year-to-budget year, in order to have some prospect of coming up with the right sort of mix and the right numbers. The Ships' Characterist Board, they never got anywhere with that. All they had to do was the qualitative side, nothing on the quantitative or the mix sides. That was the origin or the birth of the Long-Range Objectives Group. It was called the Long-Range Shipbuilding Program.

Q: Was this for ten years? You didn't go beyond that?

Adm. J.: For ten years. We didn't go beyond that, no, you can't do it beyond that. Arleigh Burke used to tell me:

"Don't give me this thing. You can't see beyond three or four years, and I can do that. So I don't know what you people are trying to do."

He had misgiving about Op-93, not completely but some. But, once again, as I've said before, we cut across lines and when you're working directly for the vice CNO you begin to step on toes of other people, and don't bother this weapon system of mine, this is sacred, you go to somebody else and take it out of their hide, not mine.

So, that was the origin of it, projecting ten years hence, including any ideas for perhaps a new design of ship, be it a frigate or something that's a little different from a destroyer, with a different armament suit on it or something. We'd come up with ideas like that. That's the way this started out and that was the first product that came out of Op-93. Following that, as sort of an evolutionary thing this ten-year plan began to include other things in it, things other than just the ships. But that was the essence of it, the main thing was the ships.

Q: You began to consider economic factors, too?

Adm. J.: Well, yes, sure you did.

Q: Inflation and all that?

Adm. J.: Long-range objectives, you see now, because here are the things that you honestly, objectively think the navy needs. But that doesn't mean the feasibility of accomplishment, depending on what the budget would be. Maybe we would have two or three different options for the different levels of money. In other words, cutting and fitting. But, once again, the way to start on this without being greedy and going to extremes, is to put down what you think the navy really needs, really honestly needs. Looking ahead, for the long term, for the navy to carry out its -

Q: For the defense of the nation?

Adm. J.: Yes, control of the sea, projection of power, and the rest of it. That's what Op-93 was all about.

Q: Now it gets into the realm of real politics. I mean what does the navy need ten years hence and what is the state of our enemy ten years hence.

Adm. J.: What is the world situation, what is the nature of the threat. You can't begin to fill in these blanks down below that until you address yourself to them, and some of that, of course, becomes educated guesswork. The same in developing any plan, you can always do pretty well on capabilities. In other words, you can enumerate what he has. He has this many divisions or he has this many ships, this many carriers.

Q: What the enemy has?

Adm. J.: Sure. OK. That isn't determining what your threat happens to be that your navy can fight it with, because in some way you've got to try to figure out as best you can what are his intentions. And that's the sticky thing right now. They know what the capabilities of the Russians or the Poles are, but what he intends to do, you can't read his mind to that extent, and he's not going to tell you. That becomes a very difficult thing, but there's no use trying to push it under the rug. You've got to address yourself to it as best you can, and then, from that, and separating that to one side, what part does the navy play in this along with the other forces. What kind of a navy will you need. That's what the LRO Plan would do as best we could, and we had a hell of a time selling it.

Q: Yes, because there'd be so many -

Adm. J.: He always said, "Oh, no, you can't take this away from us." You'd go to Rickover and he'd say:

"No, it doesn't make any sense. All these ships should be nuclear-powered." Well, at that time, of course, the state of the art didn't permit going that far with nuclear power. It was too expensive. Later on, they came along, sure in certain types of ships that should be nuclear-powered, I quite agree. That was a pretty sticky thing we had to address in the long-range planning, how far to go with nuclear power in what types of ships.

That's what the Long-Range Objectives Group was put in there to do.

Q: You had to be right on top of what R & D was doing, didn't you?

Adm. J.: Oh, sure. We worked very closely with them. What could you expect from the state of the art as you knew it then and as projected into the future what they could project, what they could give you as advanced weapon systems and other things, making some of them probably obsolete. We got in trouble in this. We were cirticized by people because, once again, as with their sacred cows, they insisted on the worth of and necessity for what they were talking about, and they received agreement on it, including building a lot of DEs, escort destroyers, that had practically no air-defnese armament. None, just ASW, single-mission ships, and ships cost too much money to be building single-purpose ships. True, you can go too far in trying to make a ship do too many things, multi-multi-purpose, but, at the same time, you've got to realize that if you are escorting a convoy, it's not good enough just to be able to counter a submarine, ASW. You've got to recognize that part of your threat may be from the air. And, to have a ship that's completely naked in air defense doesn't make very much sense. They got these DEs and they're really a hybrid ship.

Q: Were they related in any way to the World War II frigates?

Adm. J.: No, this was a brainchild of Charlie Weakley and Charlie Martell, both of whom are dead, God rest their souls. They were the ASW czars and they had their way with Arleigh Burke and some other people and convinced them the DE was the economic way to go, you could produce large numbers of them because they were cheap, and that's what you need for the convoy concept. That was the beginning, that you agree the convoy concept is the way to go. They may be right, but convoy, that's another question, but you can't neglect the air-defense part of it. They were saying, OK, if you're worried about the air threat, you've got to send a carrier along. Well, that's putting the carrier in a completely defensive role and, at least initially, you're not going to have enough carriers to divert to the purely defensive air-defense role. We no longer have any of the old Essex class. They had been mothballed and then sold for scrap. We don't have those, and have to depend for ASW on something else, which, of course, was a very, very hard decision because the economics and the budget limitations we were faced with made it pretty obvious that we couldn't build any more Essex carriers just for ASW, even though I do think some of them could have continued service for a long time, much longer.

Q: Another ten years?

Adm. J.: Yes, with a little modernization.

Q: A FRAM program for carriers?

Adm. J.: Yes. So, instead of that, they said, OK, the ASW carrier has to go. The rationale for that was that on the big carriers they have such a big deck and so much space, we're going to put ASW helicopters on them. We're going to put S-2 and S-3 aircraft all mixed in with these other airplanes, which really created one of the worst nightmares known to man in terms of what an air officer has to contend with on the ship, because it was all the mixture and everything in terms of a real combat situation, he's got a mess on his hands - how to control all these airplanes for the different missions, and think of what you have to have in the way of spare parts for all these different planes.

Q: You'd have to have an auxiliary ship with spare parts!

Adm. J.: No, but close to it. So, what are these units going to do. I guess they would be useful because they can provide the ASW protection for the carrier battle group, that's what they call it now. And, in some areas, of course, that could be considerable. The submarine threat is going to be pretty severe. So that much can be said in favor of putting the units on there as long as you cannot have a separate ASW carrier or you cannot depend completely on destroyers for ASW defense, which at the moment, you cannot, even though they have sonar, they have towed sonar, they have the LAMPS helicopter, they have the Mark-48 torpedo, they have Hedgehog, and all these other weapons. But, first of all, you've got to detect something. Sonar says you've got something under you, maybe it's a school of fish. Anyway, then you've got to identify, classify, is it a submarine or not. After you've done that, then you have a fire-control problem. In other words, wait that out and destruct as soon as you can, and the problem is compounded by the fact that you're going to have the deep-diving, fast, nuclear submarines. And he can go underwater just about as fast as the carrier force. This presents a problem, and along with this, at times, it seemed as though one dilemma creates another one because here we have, and I noticed in the paper yesteday or maybe today they just authorized money for two more attack submarines. Well, you can use an attack submarine in a variety of useful ways like the GIUK barrier lines, a bunch of submarines coming through there. They could probably, waiting on station, detect them but, once he begins to move at any speed, the ambient noise is going to destroy pretty much any detection. He can lay in wait, detect a submarine, identify, and so forth, and work out the fire-control problem and close with destroyer.

But the idea of using an attack submarine in company with a carrier, with the carrier force, and with all the associated noise levels from all the ships, this presents a problem to the attack submarine. Furthermore, if you have destroyers and at the moment there's no reliable way of communicating from a surface ship to a submarine submerged - they may some day arrive at that, but it wouldn't be very good if he confused this U.S. submarine to be enemy and made an attack on it. That's the problem. It almost precludes using an attack submarine in close company with carrier forces. So you have to depend on the destroyers or the units aboard the carriers.

Well, we've digressed.

Q: That was a very interesting digression, however, and a valuable one.

Adm. J.: All these things had to be taken into consideration when you went through this very involved, deliberative process of working up the LRO.

Q: Would you talk about the input that came from intelligence and how valuable that was in your projections?

Adm. J.: Well, once again, when you try to set down and enumerate pretty much what the world situation would be like, looking that far ahead, then the kind of threat you'd be confronted with, you had to go to intelligence and get the best you could, the very best you could. A lot of times the people in intelligence don't want to look too far ahead because they're not sure of it. In other words, they don't want to go out on a limb. Current intelligence, oh, yes, they can give you reams and reams of that, what the current situation is, and, once again, they love to concentrate on capabilities. Sure, they

Johnson #2 -196-

can give you that A to Z, but what are you going to do with it, where would you use it or when would you use it. Well, that's pretty well down to the dark alley.

Q: It puts their profession in jeopardy, doesn't it?

Adm. J.: Well, they've made so many mistakes, I guess you can't really blame them in some ways for being gun-shy. They've guessed wrong so many times and missed.

Q: In a category with weather-forecasting!

Adm. J.: Yes, it's not an exact science.

Q: But then what other branches of government did you call upon -?

Adm. J.: This was just within the navy. We didn't go outside the navy.

Q: You didn't?

Adm. J.: No, because in ONI - of course, ONI had a pretty good exchange with DIA - CIA wasn't involved in it too much because this was pretty much of a national political palaver. But DIA, Defense Intelligence Agency, that was another matter. We got a lot of useful information from them that we could use..

Q: But I wonder how capable they were in economic forecasting?

Adm. J.: The DIA people?

Q: ONI.

Adm. J.: I don't know how accurate they were. There were as good as CIA, I know that.

No, that's a pretty hazardous thing. I guess on the economic side, it's even more so than maybe the military or political. Who knows when you're going to have a depression or monetary crisis in South America?

Q: Or a drought somewhere!

Adm. J.: Yes. You just have to make the best educated guess you can and hope that it's presented in such a way that there's room for error. When you use that and integrate it in any other type of planning, the margin for error.

Q: When you look at this picture and the problem you had to deal with, all the facets to it, and all the inputs that were necessary in order to come to some kind of a conclusion, it just boils down to the fact that the personnel involved were terribly important.

Adm. J.: Oh, sure. You had to have the very best that you could find and capable of sound, mature judgment and able to express it.

Q: Did you select your personnel personally?

Adm. J.: Well, when I took over they were already there. I had to get rid of one person because he didn't fit. How he ever got in there, I don't know, and I guessed right in his case.

He was a likeable person, married to a very lovely girl. She had a lot of money. He finally came to me and said:

"Will you sign this? I have a hardship case," and that's the only way he could get out. He couldn't just openly resign. He had just made captain, so you knew he was all right then. His hardship was that her family was in St. Louis, and her father was ill, so she worried about him so that she couldn't sleep. That was his hardship!

I went ahead and signed it because I was going to get rid of him and have him sent to some other place, because he was no use to me. He just couldn't handle this sort of thing. You had to be able to sit down and be innovative in your thinking and relate some of the material that we collected to something that you could imagine some way in the future. You had, of course, the very parochial guys who came in there with set minds. In other words, they were convinced that the only thing that would ever be worth anything at all for any mission was a submarine, whether it be for logistics or what. So I got rid of him. He had a wonderful war record in submarines but he was so single-minded that I couldn't use him.

Q: He was wearing blinders!

Adm. J.: Yes.

You had to hope that you would get a person with a sort of unique ability in that sort of a job.

Q: How rare is a person like that?

Adm. J.: There are more of them than you would think, but they tend to be in the minority, I would say, very definitely. Just like you don't always find a person completely adaptable to being on a joint staff. When you come in with a contingency plan, you've got to have this ready in the morning, so you've got to have a pretty sharp guy to be mixed up in something like that.

Q: And to work under pressure?

Adm. J.: Oh, right. So many times, they try to be as selective as they can but they don't always hit it, the kind of people they sent in there. They were good naval officers in some other field but not in that. Like intelligence, I wouldn't be any good in intelligence.

Q: How understanding was BuPers in filling slots in a group like that?

Adm. J.: In years past, way back, it was very poor, but as the years went on I think they've been pretty good. They do a very good job, considering the problems they have in trying to catalogue and characterize and have a computer bank, something in the way of just what capabilities this person has. Or, perhaps more important, for this particular unique capability, what names are under that. That's more important than getting all these names and listing what they're capable of or not capable of.

Q: Being in command of a shop like that, the requirements on you were somewhat different from what they were when you were in command of the Forrestal?

Adm. J.: Oh, sure, completely different. The responsibility wasn't the same, and your authority was shorter. It could be measured. It was pretty important, but nothing comparable to what it would be in command of a ship, I don't think. I'm not trying to water down the importance of the planning committee but I just don't think you could say that the reasponsibility would be the same as in a ship. Maybe the difference wouldn't be too great, or as great, in peacetime as it would be in wartime. Certainly, it wouldn't.

Q: Of course, that was not particularly a wartime job, anyway.

Adm. J.: No. When you become involved in war, a lot of these plans and things come out of the Joint Chiefs. That's a completely different matter, and, in the Vietnam War, I must confess I could never quite figure out just exactly what plan came out of the Chiefs as opposed to the Whiz Kids, Dr. Enthoven and others. I don't know. Somebody knows, I guess, but at times I couldn't tell where they came from.

Q: You can bet most of them came from the Whiz Kids by way of the Joint Chiefs!

Adm. J.: Undoubtedly some did. We had planes going on missions over Vietnam, jets, high-performance airplanes, that were using fat bombs. That's not very good for a high-performance airplane. The production lines had not been geared up or increased at that time because people like Enthoven would come out there, twirl his pencil, and say:

" Our inventory shows that you have adequate bombs, 500-, 1,000-, 2,000-pounds, even with increased sorties per month on Vietnam."

Furthermore, in terms of not the fat bombs but the streamlined bombs, here we had a tremendous stockpile in the Atlantic Fleet. So, of course, Admiral Sharp, who was CinCPac goes to Admiral Smith, CinCLant, and says:

"We need these bombs." And he says:

"These are NATO stockpiles. I can't touch them," and actually he couldn't. So here we didn't have any bombs and this guy was telling us on paper the inventory showed that we had them, but it doesn't do any good if they're not available.

Q: Then, of course, they would always have in mind the str cture of the secretary, would they not, that when the war was over you didn't have any bombs left? You used up your last bomb."

Adm. J.: The last bomb had been dropped. They didn't need any replacement aircraft. That's the way these guys figured. In other words, running it just like the Ford motor plant, you did not want any large inventory. That's bad business. Well, you can't run a military outfit like that. I heard them say that so many times, we can't afford a big inventory.

That's the danger of over control by civilians. You must have civilian control, there's no question about it, I'm not going to argue with that, but it can be carried to such ridiculous extremes and can be a very, very dangerous and disastrous thing. In the overall organization, overall general planning and so forth, the SecDef exercises that authority and control. But then when it comes down to the strictly military operational implementation, carrying it out and the exercise of initiative at the tactical level and so forth, you cannot have people who have no knowledge of military operations who are that distant telling you how to do it. That's the worst possible thing you could ever do.

Q: In this Long-Range Planning Group, Op-93, it must have been somewhat discouraging at times. Your results, your plans, as you developed them were not fully accepted always -

Adm. J.: No, you couldn't be discouraged. That was something you had to accept, that you were going to run into opposition from the different elements. You had to have a pretty thick skin, go ahead with what you thought was right, and present it. And even though, hopefully, it was not accepted in toto, there would be enough out of it that would be accepted as guidance that you would be a lot better off than if you had no objectives plan at all. That's about the approach you had to take.

So, here, Mr. Gates is secretary of the navy, and he was continually giving me a bad time because what we need is a Navy Rand.

Q: Rand?

Adm. J.: You know, the Rand Corporation.

Q: Oh, yes.

Adm. J.: A navy Rand, something comprable to that. He said:
"My aide here Captain Guyler, he comes in and gives me more ideas than you people do, and they make more sense."

I said: "Well, Mr. Secretary, in case you don't know it, Noel Guyler comes down to our place about once a week, milks our brains, gets these ideas, and takes them back to you as though they came from him."

He said, "Oh, well, you're just jealous of Guyler, his ability, and so forth. Here's what I think of him," so he pulls out a fitness report he's making out and recommended the guy be promoted to vice admiral, not to rear admiral, to vice admiral!

Well, anyway, we produced "the Navy of 1980," ten years hence - or whatever it amounted to, and we had the thing completed to the extent we were going to go. We weren't going any farther if we were to be realistic and objective. It listed what the navy would look like in terms of ships and carriers, and we projected twelve Forrestal-class carriers. That's all, twelve, even though some people were saying eighteen. Well, I guess we missed it a little bit because with the Indian Ocean thing, I doubt we can do it with twelve.

Anyway, we had this thing ready to go to press, and Don Felt called me late one afternoon - I was about ready to go home. He came in there and, boy, I could tell he was all excited. He said:

"If Mr. Gates calls you in some kind of conference on something and he says part of the trouble with the navy is they have no plan, they don't know what they're doing. They're charging off in all directions and what you need is something produced like the Rand Corporation does."

I said, "Admiral, look, we've been working on this, we've been telling you about this. I've briefed you on it and so forth."

He said, "Oh, yes. Well, where is it?"

I said, "It's in the process of being printed."

He said, "Get it printed up in one hour."

So we went back and got it, and here it came out with a nice little blue cover on it and so forth –"

Q: In an hour!

Adm. J.: We had one copy for him, yes, and he took it up to Mr. Gates and he was satisfied. He thought that was great, Don Felt did. But Mr. Gates wasn't satisfied.

Q: Gates had been around long enough in the navy.

Adm. J.: Oh, but he was never too understanding, really. In some personal ways, I liked Tom Gates. In other ways, he was not exactly the sharpest secretary we ever had.

That was my final deliverance in Op-93, producing that, and I turned it over to Rivets and said, "Good luck to you because you're going to need it."

There was a recent article in the Institute Proceedings about how Op-93 started and came to an end, and it showed pictures of the people, Don Griffin, and myself, Rivets, Tom Moorer.

Q: And J. B. Colwell was over there, too, finally, wasn't he?

Adm. J.: I think he came there –

Q: He was toward the end.

Adm. J.: I think he was there about the time of its demise.

Q: Yes, he was. He told me the story and he ran into great difficulties.

Adm. J.: Oh, gee, at times you wondered if you had any friends left. If you just gave in and put all of this stuff in there, you would have a navy that cost five times the budget you expected to get, if you tried to please everybody.

Any planning is a sort of hazardous process.

Q: But necessary.

Adm. J.: Very necessary, yes. There are different ways of going about it, some more orderly than others, depending on the kind of planning you're involved in.

Q: And I suppose a lot of the plans that are made by the people who organize them know full well that they'll never be used.

Adm. J.: I don't know what they do today. I'm sure they must have, I would hope they have a long-range shipbuilding program because it would be pretty sad if they didn't.

Q: You say that with delivery of the plan, the paper, that was printed within a hour to Don Felt, you at least got an accolade from him.

Adm. J.: Well, I'm not sure. I had the feeling that maybe he thought that I had finally produced something to show for all the time we'd spent and earned my wages.

Q: This was in the year 1958, and you were about to take over another very interesting assignment.

Adm. J.: I must say in some ways I was glad to get out of there.

Q: I would think so.

Adm. J.: You can't stand a situation like that too long. You're doing your best and trying to be really honest about what you're doing and so forth, and then to see it chopped up and disregarded isn't very good for morale, as a rule. Even Stu Barber with a piece of paper that put down what you felt were some of the long-range implications of Sputnik - Sputnik had just occurred and was making all the headlines and everything -

Q: And the military, especially, were quite upset by it.

Adm. J.: Yes, they didn't know how to figure on just what the implications were. Of course, some of them were far beyond anything anybody could come up with, but it was really a major turning point, probably more so even than the fact that the Russians were building a nuclear bomb. Of course, there was no secret about that, either. As long as you've got the resources and the material, you can build an A-bomb, but delivery of it is a different thing. A long-range missile, that's a different capability.

Q: And that was the essence of the jolt?

Adm. J.: Yes, true. In other words, what kind of defenses do they have? People began searching around - what kind do they have, are they any good at all? What can we construct that would be of any effectiveness? We were talking about building 10- and 20-foot concrete things, you know. At that time, civilian defense was a more popular thing than it is now. Now you rarely hear about it at all.

Q: In that day, of course, you had Nelson Rockefeller in New York State building shelters and all that sort of thing, and people hoarding food.

Adm. J.: Oh, yes, a lot of states were building shelters.

Q: It had one good effect, did it not, in that we turned our attention to the talented young people in universities in certain areas, engineering, electronics, and so forth?

Adm. J.: Well, yes, I suppose you'd say that was a spin-off, but I was glad to walk out and say, OK, and salute, good luck! And, once again, relieved Don Griffin. That was the third time I relieved Don Griffin, went aboard in Barcelona, Spain. I relieved him in the squadron of the Enterprise, in Op-93, and then in CarDiv 4.

Q: CarDiv 4 was stationed in the Med, was it, when you took over?

Adm. J.: It was deployed at that time, the Forrestal and the Randolph. Peg and I went over in the Constitution, had a wonderful trip, and arrived in Barcelona about the time of Thanksgiving, I guess. We checked into our hotel. I couldn't find my trunk with my uniform. The morning of the change of command, I went aboard the Forrestal, and there was Don Griffin, and he had about 180 people lined up, two rows, to greet me, plankowners of the Forrestal when I put the ship in commission.

Q: How interesting!

Adm. J.: Yes. I remembered quite a few of them, not all of them. Gosh, that many people, you couldn't remember all of them, but a couple of the old chiefs, I remembered them. These were enlisted, there were no officers, of course, from the tour of duty I spent.

So, I went aboard, the staff was there, and almost immediately over in the Med at that time of the year you begin to run into trouble because, much as I respected people over there during operations, to insist over there in the Med that every type of plane aboard a carrier be qualified and checked out for night flying, you're going to get in trouble, because some of them were not equipped to fly at night. The A-4 had a bad gyro. Swede Ekstrom was then the commander of the Sixth Fleet and he said, "Look, you've got to do something about this, we're losing too many people." They were losing pilots every week.

Q: You mean killed?

Adm. J.: Yes, going in. So I said:

"OK, we're going to concentrate on the all-weather fighter and the AD."

The AD, they don't care whether it's daylight or dark. It didn't make any difference to the old prop airplanes, and forget about the others. We can't do it over here. The F-4D even though they say it's all weather, it's not all-weather. The thing is too-short-legged. You've got to cycle the thing fifty minutes, and you know what that means?

Q: Yes.

Adm. J.: From launch to landing, with any reserve at all, the longest it can stay in the air is fifty minutes. What good is that?

So, that was the first policy I enunciated there, we'd concentrate on the airplanes that were suited for night flying and have a sensible potential for it instead of a blanket thing that said everybody qualify.

Q: Isn't that an illustration of what you were talking about earlier, leadership, the ability to make a decision like that?

Adm. J.: Well, it's a combination of that plus exercising common horse-sense judgment, together with knowledge of airplane operations and what's involved. And, once again, thinking about people, the pilots, you see, because Peg and I went - I'll never forget, after the first week we went into El Sombrero, in Naples, went up to the bar in civilian clothes, and these two kids came in. I knew they were pilots. They were drinking, and one said to the other, "Well, I wonder who's going to be dusted next, who's going to go in." And it turned out, this one little kid was taking off in an F4D and, God, that thing went off and something happened to the launcher and he went in just like that, anyway, and he was killed.

Right then I said more attention had to be given to peacetime operations purely concerned with increased readiness and so forth. You just don't go out and kill people when it's unnecessary.

Q: When it can be avoided?

Adm. J.: Sure.

That was the first thing I ran into. Of course, in the wintertime a lot of people don't realize how horrible the weather can get in the Med. It really can, the mistral coming in. We'd go in to Barcelona, we'd go in to Naples, we'd go in to Livorno, and the wind would be so high and the seas so heavy that you couldn't send any liberty boats in, no liberty, many times. And you get these horrible rainstorms and things. There's no use trying to fly in them. Unless there's a military necessity for it, forget it.

Things began to kind of stabilize and level out a little bit, and a completely different attitude on the part of a lot of people, I tell you. Stop killing people. A lot of people, as long as you give them a fifty-fifty chance, don't worry too much about getting killed in a war, but in peacetime they don't like that.

Q: That's a wasted life?

Adm. J.: Yes, and it's a different situation.

Q: You found there was a difference in morale in the fleet?

Adm. J.: Oh, sure.

Well, as I say, things began to taper off, level off. CarDiv 4's deployemnt was about half over when I got there.

Q: What did it cover? Six months?

Adm. J.: Six months. Terminal to terminal, it was about seven months.

Q: Did you have one carrier in both ends of the Mediterranean?

Adm. J.: Sometimes we would spread them this way. I never liked to do that, unless some higher authority said to do it, because you get three times the mutual support by having two together and the supporting ships than you have with one here and one here, that is, counting the defensive forces one has. You put them together and you get so much more mutual support.

Q: But there was a political factor, wasn't there?

Adm. J.: That's why if it came from higher up we would do it. Just like several times I wanted to take one carrier out and send it up to the Barents Sea, somewhere up north. In other words, let those people know there was naval power around some place. NATO said no way will you ever be allowed to decrease the carrier force in the Med to less than two.

Q: Even for a brief period?

Adm. J.: That's right. Only rather recently, in the last year, with Tom Hayward, were they able to get a change in that, and with some difficulty in order to put one in the Indian Ocean. There's only one in there right now.

Q: Of course, that was a compelling -

Adm. J.: Yes, but it still took the Joint Chiefs and SecDef and maybe someone ever higher up to overrule NATO on that, because they wouldn't give -

Q: What about the substitution of a British carrier?

Adm. J.: They don't have any now. The French have the Clemenceau and the Foch but they, of course, are not committed to NATO.

Q: No.

Adm. J.: I don't know where they are, as a matter of fact.

Q: Did you have any diplomatic missions while you were there with the carriers?

Adm. J.: No. I would say maybe quasi. At that time, you see, the French were still in NATO. I went to Marseilles and Toulon a couple of times and did some joint planning with them, whereby we operated in a joint exercise which involved French land-based air, French Navy land-based air, and French ships - convoy exercise and ASW. We did quite a bit of that. They were very good. I made some very good friends with those guys in Toulon, but, of course, after that they pulled out of NATO.

It was the Italians mostly we socialized with. They're great people. I went up to the Italian naval academy and met some wonderful people up there.

Q: Where's that, Spezia?

Adm. J.: No, Spezia is where they have their ASW research center. The naval academy is at Livorno, Leghorn. I went up there and made a little speech, got to know those people. Most of the contacts I had were with civilians, much of that was Sixth Fleet and CinCSouth. The people in Naples yes. Of course, we spent a lot of time in Naples, the mayor of Naples and those people, I got to know a lot of them. But, as I say, that was completely social.

Malta, we didn't have too much to do with Malta. Poor Malta was on about its last legs. The British were about to pull out.

Q: Mintoff was in the ascendancy?

Adm. J.: Oh, yes, very much so, and a tremendous feeling of anti-Americanism and anti-British over there. The east end of the Med was relative quiet then.

Q: Amazing!

Adm. J.: There was nothing kicking up in Lebanon. The Arabs were pretty quiet. They didn't have anything in mind at that time.

Q: And the Spanish?

Adm. J.: They always welcomed us, even though we had a touchy situation with Rota from time to time because at one point, they wanted twenty-four hours' notification of just one carrier airplane coming in to Rota.

Q: That was just an impediment they were building up, wasn't it?

Adm. J.: Yes, they just wanted to make sure that they were controlling. After all, we let you build this base and put your aircraft there, but we still control it.

Q: What about North Africa? Were you barred from North Africa at that time?

Adm. J.: They had made some request about going in to Tripoli or some other place, and they were turned down. They didn't go. The same in Egypt, it was turned down.

Q: Were you barred from Wheelus?

Adm. J.: Yes. The Libyans, they're pretty nasty. We didn't have any access to that. By that time we were pretty much gone from Lyautey in Morocco. At one time, that was a big navy base and quite a communications station. But we were phasing down there. They told us we had to get out of there.

So, a good part of the Second Fleet with Admiral Austin, he came over, but they were relieving units. We had a big joint exercise together. We were relieved by the incoming outfit, and we headed back.

Q: That was a great problem in logistics, getting the families back, wasn't it?

Adm. J.: Not particularly. They were on their own. Quite a few went over, quite a few didn't go over. But they were on their own, you see. They had to pay their way, find a place to live, and everything.

We got back and I guess we didn't have much of anything to do for quite a little while. Then, we became involved in some real intensified workup and planning for a WSEG exercise, called Wexval 9, 10, and 11.

Q: Wexval?

Adm. J.: Wexval, WSEG group evaluation. The concept involved here was to evaluate how effective or how vulnerable a fast carrier task force is against attack by land-based bombers in an ECM environment, and this was to take place over a period

Johnson #2 -216-

of two weeks, and we were to be at least 200 miles at sea.

Q: Off Norfolk?

Adm. J.: Yes, 200 miles, which meant we were beyond bingo distance - bingo distance being a measure of the fuel you can burn down in your normal jet cycle, still bingo them and have enough fuel to come in and land at Oceana. We were beyond that. All we had as a ready deck was the old FDR, so if the deck on the Forrestal was fouled up, we could at least try to land them on the FDR. All operations at night, nothing in daytime.

Q: It was necessary to be out that far?

Adm. J.: Well, they insisted you be out that far so you could be rid of any interference from the land, and also to present some kind of a search problem for the air force. The air force bombers were the ones doing this, B-47s, I guess they were, twin-engine bombers.

Q: Who was Second Fleet?

Adm. J.: Smeddy was Second Fleet then.

Q: I'm beginning to suspect this might have been the operation he told me about.

Adm. J.: It probably was because he was much involved, he and Mason Freeman, who was operations officer.

We began to work up for this and, of course, they were going to need all the jamming devices they could think of - putting up chaff, dropping all this "window," and all the electronic jamming. And, unless we could see through that and direct the fighter planes, we were in trouble, really in trouble. First of all, we had the CC, the carrier control approach - that's the glide pattern I mentioned yesterday. We didn't have any fear about the ability of the pilots to get back on board. Fortunately, we were able to dismiss that as opposed to the trouble we had in the Med. We took a lot of the attack planes off and really beefed up the fighters. We really had a deckload of fighters.

We had about three months to get ready for this - maybe two months. We sent all these CC crews out to Dam Neck. They received specialized training out there, how to burn through, to see through, all this jamming on the radarscope and to recognize it. Then how to get it out of there and see around it or through it, and still recognize where your planes were and where the incoming planes were, and make the intercept. It was a remarkable thing that they did, I tell you. I never expected to see anything like this.

So, here came the first night, once again dark out there and all this stuff coming down. It was a mess on the radar, clutter and everything. These operators down there under the direction of this one little guy, Presson, the CIC officer, intercepted every one that came in and flew alongside of them to make sure that he knew he'd been intercepted. And out of

Johnson #2 -218-

the whole gang intercepted - they must have sent thirty or forty airplanes out, I don't think more than maybe two or three ever even got over the carrier before they were intercepted. That went on for two weeks. The same thing every night, with a layoff on Sunday.

Q: How did the Air Force feel about this?

Adm. J.: They thought they had us where the hair was short, they really did. They couldn't figure it out. They just tried all kinds of deceptive measures, airplanes from different directions and different stuff. They were trying to get new things from all over the country, but we could keep up with what they were doing.

I sent a report in every morning to Smeddy - this many came in, what the weather was, how many intercepted, and so forth. Then we got back and wrote the report up, and it was hard to believe, really. He had a little trouble believing we'd do that well because he was a little bit skeptical of it, but his understanding of carrier operations - there was no reason why he should have any great understanding of them. What he wanted to do was to put the Northampton, that was his flagship - she was fitted up with the most sophisticated electronic gear of any ship in the navy, so much so that they designated her as a national command post. But it still didn't have a lot of equipment that the carrier had in order to monitor the operations of the airplanes. Furthermore, to be perfectly frank and blunt with you, you don't have a staff that has the understanding of carrier operations. Unless you're on this carrier, right there on the spot and at night in this kind of operation, if anything's going to happen, it's going to be very, very fast, and, unless you react very fast, you're going to loose somebody.

Mason Freeman, his operations officer, said:

"Oh, we war-gamed this up at Newport." I said:

"I don't give a damn where you war-gamed it, I'm giving you the realistic facts of life and you'd better get off of this tack because it's not going to work."

Well, they still weren't convinced, and I think - George Anderson was CarDiv 5 then - he talked to Smeddy and, after thinking it over and talking to Smeddy's air operations officer, Dan Smith, he finally said:

"OK, you got them, I'm not going to bother you."

At least he did that. A lot of people wouldn't do that, and he often said, "That was the right deicision, and I'm sure glad I did."

But it was an amazing thing and it proved that, if you could concentrate with the proper training facilities to make the people available, starting out with pretty good basic skills, you can raise its efficiency to where they are good. What happened? When the thing was over, these people were ordered away, dispersed, and we lost the whole team effectiveness, almost. We still retained some because we had a nucleus, but nothing like what we had before. Unless you have some means of continuing this, you're going to lose it. That's the trouble with the very rapid, continual turnover of personnel.

Q: The rotation, yes. The idea was presented to me one time that the navy should try to develop some system wherein men who perfected certain skills at sea should stay at sea for a much longer period of time. This came from Charley Duncan.

Adm. J.: Well, the idea in itself is good, but, of course, you can't make them stay at sea too long because it's counter-productive. Of course, right now in port you see some of this because long performance, long time at sea, they're getting out. They're losing so many people, the skilled people, and the ones you don't want to lose are the ones who are getting out. So you've got to be careful how far you go in that direction.

The ideal situation, like on the Hornet, we went out to the West Coast and went west, and, except for extreme emergency, everybody stayed on board. You really had a team going then, and you kept it intact. But peacetime is a different thing. I just don't know all the answers how to overcome that. That part of it was contained in a separate report we did send in to the navy, some of the lessons learned from the Wexval exercise: the value of concentrated training, that it's a team effort, and, unless you have continuity, it in time will become weak.

Q: Yes, even for the participatants because they're dispersed.

Adm. J.: Yes.

Q: And as individuals, they lose the team spirit.

Adm. J.: At one time, in the air, and all had to come back aboard the Forrestal.

During all this time, except on the morning that we were all through and were sending the planes home, in broad daylight two of them collided. Other than that, there was not even a blown tire. Here, you know, they'd relaxed, they were going home, and both of them were lost. That was the only aircraft accident we had in the whole thing.

Q: Remarkable!

Adm. J.: It was. I've still got somewhere the message and a letter of commendation I got from Smeddy about the whole thing.

That was about the end of any real excitement that I had with CarDiv 4 in the Med and in this Wexval. Of course, we'd been involved in some concentrated training in flying for a rather extended period of time. So, my year was beginning to be about up, anyway.

Q: You felt that was perhaps more productive than the long-range planning?

Adm. J.: Oh, heck, yes, you could put your finger on something that you'd accomplished and knew was constructive. Hopefully, it would be constructive if people applied the lessons that came out of it, all of which weren't, of course. We expected too much, but I'm sure it was valuable in many ways if people kept it in the back of their head and remembered it.

Q: Would this sort of thing find its way to one of the war colleges as a part of teaching, instruction?

Adm. J.: As a rule, no. Most of the stuff you see at the Naval War College is something they cranked up in their own war games. They don't even refight the Battle of Midway there.

No, they don't like the idea of war-gaming this thing up there before we did it, to see if we could get any ideas from it, but I don't think the machines up there were capable of that, anyway, particularly the ECM part. They couldn't crank that in.

Q: Well, I would think a discussion might be useful, cross-fertilization kind of thing?

Adm. J.: Well, to my knowledge it never was. I was never asked to go any place and give a presentation on what happened. I think they wanted to dampen the thing down, because we would have had to go beyond CNO. It's too bad that it wasn't given better, not to use the word publicity, but that it wasn't disseminated a little bit wider than it was so that people could, perhaps, glean something in the way of knowledge about things.

Q: In that sense, it's a waste?

Adm. A lot of it was. I feel that way very strongly. I think, in that regard, that WSEG probably read it with interest and filed it away, and, of course, no wonder that WSEG was finally eliminated. That's what they would do with about every test and exercise that they had conducted. So what's the use of the operation? The man at the head of it was a wonderful person, I thought, and we briefed him on everything, Gavin.

Q: General Gavin?

Adm. J.: Yes, he was head of it. I guess they probably briefed the Joint Chiefs, they had to, because they had to get their approval before they could conduct it, and that's as far as it ever went. And there was about as realistic a war game as you could get, much better than on a machine, even though they do pretty well on these war-games machines these days.

Q: I've heard of another experiment that came out of Dam Neck with Admiral Fahrion was there.

Adm. J.: Admiral Fahrion, that was way back.

Q: Yes, it was.

You were there with CarDiv 4 for a longer period than a year, weren't you?

Adm. J.: Not much more than that.

Q: It was 1958 to 1960.

I take it you were kind of a favored, white-haired lad in having this assignment?

Adm. J.: Not necessarily. I just happened to fall into being in the right job at the right time and conduct the Wexval thing. Of course, there were quite a few CarDivs and anybody who showed any potential at all in carrier command would go to at least some kind of a carrier division. Of course, at that time, they still had the Essex class. I think the Bodoeng Straits and all those were gone. We did have the Essex for ASW.

Q: That was 5, which Anderson had, wasn't it?

Adm. J.: Yes. He was riding in the <u>Saratoga</u>. Johnny Hyland was the skipper of her.

George was feeling pretty good about everything because it was certain he was going to the Sixth Fleet and, unless he stubbed his toe, he knew he had a very good chance to be CNO, which was a lot different from what his outlook was at one time. Of course, being with Ike didn't hurt him at all. He was over in Paris with Ike.

Q: That was a very valuable experience for him, not only the contacts -

Adm. J.: Oh, yes, and he was a very valuable asset over there, and the General realized it and put a lot of faith in things that he delegated to Anderson, many of which were a little bit outside of what the senior naval officer was wont to do.

Q: Yes, it got into the realm of the diplomatic.

Adm. J.: Or the political side, much more than Dave McDonald. Dave, of course, is a wonderful guy, but he's going to do exactly what he thinks he has to do and that's where it stops. He does whatever he does well, of course.

Q: In 1960 you came back again to Washington.

Adm. J.: I came back to Washington.

Q: You were seesawing all the time now.

Adm. J.: Yes. I did have some other so-called shore duty other than Washington, but not very much. I had many times indicated a preference for duty at the Naval Academy but I never even came close to that.

Q: You mean to teach over there?

Adm. J.: In some capacity. I just thought I'd enjoy being around the Naval Academy. Never even came close.

Q: Well, but, as it happened, weren't these Washington assignments beneficial in terms of career?

Adm. J.: Certainly, some of them, I guess so, but you don't have to have that many. I think everybody should be exposed to Washington duty. As a matter of fact, it's a rare thing to hear of anybody selected for flag rank who hasn't been exposed, very true, but I don't think it should be carried to the point where they'd consider anybody indispensable to Washington duty. But, you see, to be caught in that sort of a circuit by virtue of having been there and knowing the ropes and so forth, you usually come up somewhere near the top of the pile for being a likely candidate to go back.

Q: If there's some senior person —

Adm. J.: Who knows you and you know him. Here, I went to 06B.

Q: Yes.

Adm. J.: With Oley Sharp.

Q: That was a lively period, in 1960, in Plans and Policy.

Adm. J.: That's always been a lively place to be. Vietnam was just beginning to boil. We were actually doing what we called the Sheep Dip operation in Laos. Sheep Dip meant we contracted with Air American and they were doing clandestine operations and air recce to see what the communists were doing over there.

Q: Was this Rolling Thunder?

Adm. J.: No, this was before Rolling Thunder, and they called it Sheep Dip because these people were sent over there in disguised uniforms, you know, you've been dipped so they couldn't be recognized as Americans under contract to the Defense Department. I think General Lansdale was pretty much behind organizing and putting this on.

About that time, of course, we weren't accomplishing too much in Laos, really. You could do some recce but the rules were so strict that they weren't getting much information, even later on, when we started doing it with carrier airplanes. But, about that time, the French were beginning to have trouble - no, then they were out of South Vietnam.

Q: Yes, they were out by that time.

Adm. J.: They were out, and this is when Diem had pretty well taken over from Bao Dai. Bao Dai had gone, and Diem, the Catholic, was the guy throwing his weight around with Madame Nu.

Q: Very much Madame Nu!

Adm. J.: Yes, and the situation was really deteriorating pretty fast. Nolting was the ambassador there. I remember we used to see all the messages "for the eyes of So and So only." It was a rapidly deteriorating situation, even though Diem inherently, in himself, was a very capable, intelligent man trained by the French government, and there weren't too many of those people around. He was down there and, of course, thousands and thousands of refugees had come down there - we brought them there from the north. People tried to tell him, "Look, you've got to institute reform, you've got to bring in the Buddhists." Well, of course, the Buddhists probably wouldn't do much because Cao Dai and the Hoa Hoa, and all of the other religious regimes over there, and have, you might say, a coalition government. But the main thing was land reform, pacify the people, make them happy, and, that way, you would overcome the influence of the VC, which was really beginning to operate then in the countryside at night, into the hamlets, and really scared these people to death. If you didn't accede to what they wanted, that was the end of you.

Q: The end, yes.

Adm. J.: Nolting was relieved. I guess Harkins was the MACV out there. They relieved Nolting and sent Henry Cabot Lodge down there, and he was told by Big Minh that things were getting so bad that the generals were going to do something about it.

So the big question was what to do, and the instructions were the U.S. cannot come out publicly and condemn Diem on this, but we will not oppose what they plan to do. So of course, one coup aborted, then they did put on the other one, and the only thing, I think, that Lodge ever told them was, "For God's sake, don't kill that guy." But that got out of hand. Diem and his brother Nu escaped underground, you know, and some other people caught them and that was the end of them. They finished them off.

Well, Big Minh, now, he's the guy, like they say, strong as a bull and about one-third as smart.

Q: He was a general, wasn't he?

Adm. J.: Oh, yes, General Minh, Big Minh, greatly respected in the army, but having no civil, government ability at all. He didn't know anything about it. He wasn't going to last very long, he couldn't there was no way he could. So, that's when, who was it, Khan took over? Another coup and Khan took over. In those days you didn't know how long you were going to go before you had another coup, and in the meantime the VC were capitalizing on this, exerting themselves more, becoming more aggressive, more open, and increasing in numbers, and, of course, we began to send an increased number of people over there and increase the latitude of what they could do. It was up to 25,000 or so about this time, then they increased that and even put people at the battalion level, U.S. army people, as instructors with the RVN, the Vietnamese Army, which, of course, was not very effective.

Q: The problems of identification were great, too?

Adm. J.: Oh yes, because at night you'd go into some of those villages and you didn't know whether you were going to run into the VC or not and by the time you knew it you'd have a knife in your back.

The situation just deteriorated more and more, and that's when there was a gradual buildup of army forces in South Vietnam. About that time, Felt was relieved by Sharp, and I left as deputy to Sharp and went out and relieved Moorer in the Seventh Fleet.

Q: How did this development and all the political implications out there in Saigon devolve on Plans and Policy?

Adm. J.: Well, there were a lot of papers being generated in the JCS by the Joint Staff, and Plans and Policy, depending on what area it was, and, of course, for Southeast Asia we had two desks that did nothing but concentrate on that. They were the ones who would study the papers and work up the navy positions for Oley Sharp to take to Plans at a level below the Joint Chiefs, hoping that they could dispense with a lot of the papers and they wouldn't have to consider all of them because there were just too many of them. They would consider the papers and decide what to do with it, pass on them for action, or buck them up to the Joint Chiefs, and, depending on the seriousness of it, they would send it up there, many of them having to do with Vietnam. To what extent shall we increase the army forces out there? Harkins has now recommended 10,000 more men, he wants to increase the scope of their activities, shall we go along with him? Well, of course, then they had to get into the matter of liaison with the State Department, because they would have the final judgment on some of those things.

They were just involved in a mass of stuff regarding Vietnam, day to day. You were lucky if you got home by nine o'clock at night. Plus, by then, all the MAAG supplies, all the logistic support for the army out there. There was practically no navy yet.

Q: No.

Adm. J.: It wasn't operating down there.

Well, about that time, I was send to Omaha. That's where I was, before I went out to Honolulu.

Q: When you were still with Plans and Policy, was Krulak operating in Washington?

Adm. J.: Yes, he was operating in the Defense Department. That's when he got to know McNamara so well.

Q: Yes.

Adm. J.: He was sent out there with the State Department. Of course, Lansdale had been out there. Lansdale was probably the most knowledgeable man on counterinsurgency operations and guerilla warfare.

Q: Yes, and Krulak was heavily involved in that, wasn't he?

Adm. J.: Yes, he was, but he didn't have the background or the moxie that Lansdale had. Anyway, he was sent out there by McNamara after he began to get so many conflicting reports, how well we're doing, how poorly we're doing. Kennedy was still president then.

Q: Yes, he was still president.

Adm. J.: All right, so Krulak goes out there, and he did go out in the countryside and visit the hamlets and the chiefs of whatever they call them, not countries. All the hamlets, the chiefs, the people who were supposed to exercise power in the countryside.

Q: The countryside was divided into areas.

Adm. J.: Yes, but I forgot what they call them - provinces I think.

He talked with all these people and pretty soon got a good feel that in a lot of the areas the VC controlled it almost at will, even the marketplace, even in the marketplaces. They looked pretty peaceful in daytime, but at night it was a different matter.

Now, the State Department guy only went to places like Danang, Hue, Saigon, so he comes back and says, after talking to Harkins and these people, the situation is improving, we're doing all right. Krulak, sitting right with him in the same room, gave exactly the opposite report. That's when Kennedy said:

"Gentlemen, are you sure you two people visited the same country?"

And it kind of sounded that way. Of course, the State Department guy was way off base.

About that time, I think, they sent - I don't know whether Westmoreland had gone out there or not - anyway, I think McNamara went out himself and took a look at it, and he began to see that things weren't going too well. About that time, there was another coup and Thieu took over from Khanh but he wasn't much of an improvement. Ky eventually took over.

While all of this was going on, I was still in Omaha with the JSTPS.

Q: When did the hamlet program begin, the so-called hamlet program of McNamara?

Adm. J.: The pacification program, the hamlet program?

Adm. J.: Yes, doing things in these villages to sort of bolster -

Adm. J.: It was pacification.

Q: It was a social welfare program as much as anything, wasn't it?

Adm. J.: Well, the idea was to go in there and, first of all, organize local militia as security, day and night, to instill confidence in these people that they were not going to be assassinated by the VC at night. Then, in view of that, to disassociate themselves from the Viet Cong, not to let any of their young boys join the VC, and to gradually expand the hamlet program, whereby you had more pacified areas that were stabilized and under control of the RVM, the hamlet chief, and the province chief. In that way, you would pacify the countryside. This was based on the experience of Thompson, the Britisher, and this is how he won the guerrilla war in Malaya, by the same tactic.

Well, either we didn't have enough people doing this or the VC knew how to counter it, because, for a certain period of time, a certain area would be pacified, and then all of a sudden it would change and the VC would be in control of it again.

Q: Probably they were pacifying the VC while they were out there!

Adm. J.: Then they said, all right, the thing to do is to get the RVN to search and destroy, go after these guys. You knew they were there, you knew they'd been there, but it was worse than a needle in a haystack. You couldn't find any of them, except the next thing you knew you were ambushed. So there was this searching for more and more ways to get the country under control and stabilized, and again to really neutralize the VC. And, as Thompson told them to do this, if you think the VC have 10,000 men, you've got to have ten times that many if you're going to do anything in this kind of guerrilla war in the jungle.

Q: He struggled for how many years?

Adm. J: That was his ratio in Malaya.

About that time, I left Omaha and went out. Oley Sharp had me come out as his deputy. I think it was about then that Westmoreland went out and relieved Harkins.

Q: Then you had a MACV?

Adm. J.: Yes, and then about that time I think Taylor went o and relieved, maybe a little bit later, Lodge as the ambassador.

Well, between Max Taylor and Westy, they evidently conceived the idea that they were going to fight another Battle of the Bulge. All these divisions, the mobile division, sent out there and located at different places, along with all this air support, helicopters and stuff, and really go after them from these protected enclaves, the conclave concept. In other words, they would be in there so they would be safe from the VC at night. Except for specialized patrols, they'd keep everybody in there and then in the daytime, they'd go out, fan out, and comb the countryside, root these guys out, and get rid of them. That was the concept. So, it grew to 100,000, to 200,000, and they were still requesting more and more people. By then the Marines had one division up in the I Corps, at Chu Lai and Danang.

About this time is when the Maddox incident happened. The Maddox was up there in the Gulf of Tonkin.

By that time, I had been sent out to relieve Moorer so he could come back and relieve Sharp, and Sharp relieve Felt. Felt was retiring. So we established the DeSoto patrol, and we had special electronic receiving equipment on there with Vietnamese interpreters. They maintained electronic silence, but they could listen to what they were saying. Every two months they were supposed to make a transit up - I've forgotten how far, but not all the way to Haiphong, short of that, but pretty well up there, stay well out, at least twelve miles out -

Q: Beyond the DMZ, though?

Adm. J.: Oh, yes. Oh, heck, yes, because you wouldn't collect anything down below. They had other means of doing that. Above the DMZ and I would say a little more than halfway up the coast to Haiphong, and staying out at twelve miles even though we recognized a limit of three miles. We just had the Maddox then, just one destroyer.

Before that, they had come up with a concept - I think Lansdale had come up with this concept - of what the Norwegians had done with what they called their Nasty boats, very, very fast patrol boats -

Q Very special boats!

Adm. J.: Oh, yes. We got some of these. I think the Germans built some, and they brought them over.

Q: We got about a dozen, didn't we?

Adm. J.: Yes, and the concept at one time was to hire mercenaries, hire Germans, to man them. That was turned down. Then they said, "OK, we'll put Vietnamese on them." The idea was to go up there and do raiding operations against the coastline and destroy power plants and a lot of other things and be a general nuisance, which they were, they were like hornets. They weren't too successful at first because since they weren't getting any reaction from the Vietnamese you knew they weren't doing anything. And, mind you, these guys were getting, I think, either fifty dollars or a hundred dollars per hour bonus for every hour they were north of the DMZ. OK. What a lot of them were doing was going up and circling, circling -

Q: Until there was no danger!

Adm. J.: Four hours and come back. That's when they put American people in the crews. Spec Ops, they were called, A Spec Op.

Q: Did we begin to develop an American version, an American boat, that was comparable?

Adm. J.: The Swift boat?

Q: Yes.

Adm. J.: Well, the Swift wasn't as fast as these boats. These things could really take off. The Swift boats were coastal surveillance boats that was used along the South Vietnamese coastline. It wasn't the equivalent of the other boat at all.

Anyway, they put Americans in the crews to really keep these guys honest. I knew the operations were going on. Westmoreland would never give me any kind of a schedule, even what day of the month they were to go up there. I said:

"Well, we've got to know the patrol schedules in order to avoid mutual interference; we've got to know when these boats are going up there."

I never did get any.

Q: And the reasoning back of that?

Adm. J.: Secrecy once again. There you go again.

Q: This involved the commander of a sister service?

Adm. J.: Yes, overdoing secrecy to your own disadvantage.

Of course, they went up and they were beginning to stir up the Vietnamese. They were getting worried about it and getting very touchy about it. Every time the Nasty boats came up there, they'd send out PT boats but they couldn't catch them. They were just too fast.

So, on this one occasion when the DeSoto patrol was up there, he was just starting his transit north, the Spec Ops guys had raided Hainin Island. Then, the next night, the Desoto patrol was up there, the Maddox, and the Vietnamese thought it was once again the patrol boats, our patrol boats, so they sent these three PT boats out against them. They actually launched torpedoes. The Maddox opened fire and, based on the intercepts and things they read after the whole thing was over, (in other words, comrade so and so has now gone in boat number so and so), they knew they'd sunk one and damaged the other two, that's all, even though they claimed three of them.

Of course, that brought forth a very severe warning to Hanoi that we had a right to operate in waters outside the territorial limit on the open sea, and any further attacks such as this would result in very dire action.

We told the Maddox to stay on station. He said he was getting out of there and we told him to stay on station. He had run at such high speed that he was low on fuel and I had to refuel him. I wanted to beef him up, anyway, so I sent the Turner Joy up there to join him and top him off. Tom Moorer and Oley Sharp got in the act and they were telling me to do this, and I said I'd already done it. McNamara wanted to get direct communications with the Maddox, he wanted to talk to him, and I said it couldn't be done. I lied but I told him that anyway.

So, the next night they're zipping along and the first thing you know (by that time I'd pulled the flagship out of Yoko and was headed south; I wanted to go down there and be close to the situation) we began to get these urgent messages: "I'm under attack again. We're firing at the PY boats. We don't know whether we've hit anybody or not." Then began to arrive all this flood of inquiries from Tom Moorer, Chick Clary, O Sharp and McNamara, "Confirm, confirm." You have to validate the fact that you were actually under attack because this is the thing that will decide whether a retaliatory attack is ordered. So, of course, I told Maddox, "You've got to report immediately what the hell happaned."

Well, unfortunately on the Maddox they didn't have any automatic equipment, they had to do it hand-encrypted, and, my God, it took hours and hours.

Q: They were overwhelmed, yes.

Adm. J.: And all the time the guys were driving me nuts. Every hour they were calling, "What happened? What actually happened?" I gave them what information I could. I said:

"That's all I have, and I can't tell you whether in my own opinion an attack occurred tonight or not. All I can tell you is that one did occur last night. That's all I can tell you that's certain and as soon as I get other information, I'll tell you."

Apparently Moorer and Sharp decided on their own, that there had been an attack and that's what they told McNamara, and that's when President Johnson ordered the retaliatory strike.

Q: Based on the belief there had been a second attack?

Adm. J.: Yes - the retaliatory strike against the PT boat base at Vinh.

I had to pull "Connie" out of Hong Kong at flank speed. She was there on liberty. I was told to go in and launch the retaliatory attack, to be over target precisely at 12:15, when the president would announce on the radio and TV that we'd made a retaliatory strike.

Q: It had better be exactly on time?

Adm. J.: Yes. Here was the old "Connie," boy, she went all out and she made it on station. We launched the strike, we went in - only one strike, that's all you could send in, nothing more. As I recall, we got in about twenty minutes late, so the president, as he said, got on the air and announced we were doing this. They did shoot down one airplane, Alvarez, he was the first guy shot down and captured, POW. Even to this day, people are writing books like Truth is the Only Casualty and people say, "OK, the Vietnamese were alerted to this by the president's speech and were ready for you when you came in." I said:

"Well, if they'd been alerted, they'd have shot down more than one airplane."

The pilots came back. They said they saw Alvarez on the beach, waving. I should have gone ahead and sent a plane in to pick him up, but I was turned down on doing this, so he stayed there until the war was over.

Q: The longest period for any of them!

Adm. J.: Yes, by far.

We pulled out of there. We didn't even stay in the Gulf of Tonkin then. We had the DeSoto patrol continue, but we pulled out of the Gulf of Tonkin and went south because it was a one-shot affair. Nothing happened for quite a while. Oley Sharp was all for really going after them.

The next thing that happened was when the VC - they were getting bolder all the time - pulled off a big mortar attack on the barracks at Qui Nhon and killed a lot of U.S. soldiers. Another warning, and then, of course, when they hit the second barracks, that's when they really started to use retaliatory strikes. Even then, of course, it was only a one-shot affair. Before that, the only strikes that had been authorized, I guess, were the armed recce things over the north, and they were called the Flaming Darts, and then in Vietnam, that was the first of the Rolling Thunder, very, very limited, just single strikes, and we pulled out.

I guess things began to escalate more and more with the VC attacks down in South Vietnam, and that's when they gradually began to build up more and more air strikes down there, until they finally were doing this on a pretty regular basis, except for the standdowns that you would have on occasion.

Q: Tell me, Admiral, why we were so meticulous about observing the three-mile and twelve-mile limits when we were trying to defend the South Vietnamese?

Adm. J.: Well, it's international law, and the State Department insisted we observe international law, even though the enemy violated it at every turn.

Q: Wasn't it possible to have some sort of tacit agreement with the South Vietnamese government? We were bolstering them up and supporting them?

Adm. J.: Well, inside the three-mile limit was North Vietnam. The only time you can do that is if you're actually in a state of declared war, hostilities.

Q: That was at the root of our problem, was it, the undeclared war?

Adm. J.: Well -

Q: One of the roots!

Adm. J.: We never did declare it.

Q: No, we never did.

Adm. J.: We declared open hostilities, but it was never Congress declaring war, although it did pass the Gulf of Tonkin Resolution, which gave the president the same powers as though war had been declared. He could do anything he thought was fit in order to save Vietnam from communism.

No, the three-mile thing really didn't affect the situation. The real critical thing was helping South Vietnam, and the ineffectiveness of the bombing up there was the very, very poor target system they gave us to hit and the very restricted number of times we could go against it and when we could go against it. It wasn't anything in the way of a concentrated effort. The rules of engagement were absolutely awful because, except for the specified targets, even though you saw four or five SAM sites and you photographed them, you couldn't hit them until you came back, reported them, and got authority - even though these things were shooting at you. Stupid things like that. Those were the things that were really hurting us so badly. It was not really an integrated or coordinated effort in the use of air power up north with what all these troops were doing down south. Westmoreland had his own air cover down there.

What they should have been thinking about was to reduce, minimize, or eliminate the threat posed by support of North Vietnam to the VC, choke that off, and do it in the right way up north. Then, all the troops that Westmoreland had in there, including one division of Koreans, all the RVN and all these people, could really go out and wipe out the VC, the task being easier because of a logistics problem if we had done what we could have done up north. But they never related the two together. They just said, "Well, the bombing up there is something to demoralize them and convince them they can't win, and finally they'll capitulate." They always held out that hope.

They weren't about to do that, even though they were in pretty bad shape at times. So it was just a matter of gradualism and the bombing campaign was frustrating us. First of all, the manner in which they approved the targets and all the publicity given to it, the people in North Vietnam were forewarned of it. We finally got approval to hit the POL, the power plants. Well, by that time, they'd already - I don't know where they got them, but they had hundreds and hundreds of mobile power plants, and the streets of Hanoi were lined with thousands of drums of POL. We alerted them, so what we did was too late.

I'll never forget the famous message when we hit the two big power plants in Hanoi and Haiphong, "Haiphong is dark tonight." It was. Two nights later, all lighted up. We had knocked out the main power plant, but that's how they could bounce back.

It took us so long to get permission to attack shipping in Haiphong, mine the place, and then take all restrictions off the bombing. We had what we called the doughnut, Haiphong and Hanoi. You couldn't drop anything in there, except on very select targets. I mean you weren't supposed to kill any civilians. I don't know how you can be sure of that.

About the time of the Tet offenensive, these people were really in pretty bad shape. If we'd just accelerated what we were doing, continued what we were doing, with even a build-up in the targets, they couldn't have stood it. I don't think they could have stood it, I don't care what anybody says. But we didn't do that.

Q: A tragic story!

Adm. J.: By that time, it was too late, really because the American people were sick and tired of fighting the war.

Q: This was a concomitant to the whole thing, the buildup of anti-war sentiment?

Adm. J.: The media, including TV, press and columnists they

were just as bad as the ones who finally rescinded the Tonkin Resolution, McGovern, Church, Cranston, all those guys--the doves wanted us out of there. They did that, of course after Nixon went into the Parrot's Beak in Cambodia.

So, by that time, they wanted us out of there, all of the Congress, Mansfield, Fulbright from Arkansas - bring them out, get them out, it's up to the Vietnamese, let them take the responsibility. Then the Vietnamization program started. In other words, let the RVN take over the whole thing, get all U.S. troops out of there.

Well, that was the beginning of the end. They (the ARVS) were defecting every month in big numbers. You couldn't depend on any of them for five minutes. You know many of them were infiltrated by the VC. The situation just began to collapse and cave in. That's when the North Vietnamese began to move in massive numbers of troops even after the Paris peace negotiations -

Q: Yes.

Adm. J.: They took over Hue, they came down the Street of No Joy, Route 1. They walked into Danang with no trouble. From then on, they could walk into Saigon. South Vietnam had gone by then. Totally mismanaged and mishandled.

Interview No. 3 with Admiral Roy Johnson, U.S. Navy (Retired)

Place: His home in Virginia Beach, Virginia

Date: Saturday, 6 December 1980

Subject: Biography

By: John T. Mason, Jr.

Q: I think today, Admiral, that we'd better lap back a bit -

Adm. J.: Yes, we kind of glanced over that.

Q: Yes, we did.

Adm. J.: Sometimes, I'd as soon do that.

Q: You just barely mentioned the fact that you had duty as deputy director of Joint Strategic Target Planning at Offutt Air Force Base in Nebraska, and this was during 1962 and 1963. So, would you start off by giving me some idea of your responsibilities and of the setup?

Adm. J.: I think the best way to start that is to give you some idea of the origin of the JSTPS. I don't think I did that.

Q: No, you didn't.

Adm. J.: This goes back, of course, to the very, very severe interservice fight between the navy and the air force at the time that Polaris came into the picture, because, of course, Polaris was pure and simple a strategic nuclear delivery system. That's all it was, and, as such, we felt as though it would complement SAC. They looked upon it as being in competition with SAC because nobody could do any job as well as SAC.

Q: They over-rated themselves, didn't they!

Adm. J.: They realized the future impact of Polaris as the Polaris program expanded and the effect of it on the overall strategic nuclear planning. So, they started out immediately, LeMay and his people, first of all that they were the only ones who had any expertise to do the target selection from the intelligence-gathering that they had, and then to lay down the operational part of the plan. They were the only ones who had that expertise, so they had to have control of that.

Well, in the navy we never argued that they had the best background and people trained at this. But that wasn't any reason to necessarily exclude the navy from this because we had pretty good people, too.

The second thing, and this was really the knotty thing, was that by virtue of doing all of this part of the planning, they had to have <u>operational control</u> of the Polaris force.

All you had to do was mention that to Arleigh Burke and, boy, he would just go right out the window because it was obviously totally unacceptable to the navy, because it's a matter of principle, the same as in the British Navy or the French Navy or any other navy, that no one shall ever have operational or tactical control of your combatant forces, except your own people. Of course, for a long time there was argument as to what extent they'd let the British have operational control of the American naval forces.

Q: Yes, and it worked the other way, too. The British took the same course.

Adm. J.: Yes.

So, that became a very, very difficult thing to resolve, and Mr. Gates was in the middle, telling them to put their heads together, knock off all this infighting and so forth, and come up with something. Paper after paper was produced, and finally they did compromise. The Air Force reluctantly. I'm not sure that all the Navy was completely satisfied with the outcome, but we simply had to work with SAC. There was no getting away from that. Here was involved the possibility of delivering hundreds of nuclear weapons on an enemy and to have to have two different outfits going separate ways would be rather stupid.

That was the origin of JSTPS, whereby CinCSAC would be double-hatted. He would remain as commander in chief of SAC plus being director of the JSTVS, which was to be a completely joint outfit, including even army people, even though they really had nothing to contribute. And it specified that the deputy would be navy. Originally, of course, Arleigh Burke insisted they really pick the top-notch people to serve on it, Jerry Miller, people like that. They were really "hot shots," and butch Parker was the first deputy.

They started out and this, of course, was to create the SIOP, the Single Integrated Operational Plan, in the event the president presses the button to set off a nuclear war, presumably, of course, in response to what somebody else did. He wouldn't ever initiate a strike first. You had what was called the NSTL, and that was developed by the intelligence people, the master National Strategic Target List worldwide. They were to select all these different targets that they thought were of the greatest primary interest to survival of the Soviet Union, that's who we're talking about. They were in maybe three or four different categories. You had the cities, of course, first; number two, you had the industrial targets; and three the military. Then, having come up with your target lists, in order of priority, of course, according to the importance of all these targets, then you begin to fit into that the operational aspects of it. In other words, what airplanes would deliver what, what missiles would be used, what would Polaris do, and what weight of effort is required on any one target to destroy it, how many options do you want. Do you want cities alone, do you want a combination of industrial and military, or do you want military alone? That's the famous counterforce, counterstrike. You never had any preemptive strike option because we'd never strike first.

Q: Isn't this the thing that was turned upside down six months ago?

Adm. J.: Yes.

Q: Changed from the cities to the military?

Adm. J.: Yes, and some industrial, too.

Q: A very significant change.

Adm. J.: Yes. It started out that way, but somehow or other the cities targeting got into it I think under McNamara. That's how that happened.

Well, then, you can imagine, here you have hundreds and hundreds of weapons being delivered, to be delivered in case the thing was implemented, that's if they pushed the button. You see this big wall map up there and you see all these red dots and everything where a nuclear weapon is going to go down, and not any little A-bomb like Hiroshima, these are these tremendous H-bombs. It boggles the imagination to think what would be the result of all of this or why it was actually necessary -

Q: And before that the potential!

Adm. J.: Yes. Or why it was actually necessary to go to

that extreme of destruction, but the thing just kept building up, building up. The SAC people never seemed to be satisfied that to kill once was enough. They want to kill, overkill, overkill, because all of this built up the prestige of SAC, it created the need for more forces, for a larger budget, and so forth, and that's the way their thinking went.

Creating the plan itself wasn't particularly difficult, even though it was a very voluminous thing and complex, but the job was a very difficult one, probably the worst one I ever had because of the difficult people you were working with, many of whom were really dishonest and always had some ulterior motive.

Q: And very reluctant to have you on the scene?

Adm. J.: On, sure. If they couldn't get their way in a policy committee meeting, they would do an end run on you under the table. You had to be constantly alert to this, at the same time saying, "this is in the national interest. For goodness sake, can't we get together on this and do something objective?' But you didn't find very many people like that. I was on the verge of going over the cliff many times because of the arguments and so forth - how far you should give, how far you should keep your stand and not give. George Anderson said:

"You go out there and work with these people. Don't sell the navy short, but get along with them."

Q: But you'd demonstrated in your past career that you could get along?

Adm. J.: Well, I did, and Tommy Power the day I left paid a compliment to me that he'd never given to anybody else who'd ever been out there. I don't think we sold the navy down the river. As a matter of fact, we were in a stronger position then than when we started out.

You see, Butch Parker went out there first but then suddenly he was yanked out to work with Dr. Foster on the disarmament committee, so that's when George Anderson said he was sending me out there and told me to get along with these people. Some of them were good people, but an awful lot of them I'll never forgive, I never will, for being as dishonest as they were, accusing me of going behind General Power's back and talking to people in Washington, which I never did, and I proved it. The two people in question at a party, in front of everybody, he had these people come up to me and apologize to me in front of all the others.

Q: Oh, really?

Adm. J.: Yes. That's the extreme that some of these people would go to. Tommy Power at that point, even though at times I had some doubts about trusting him, he wasn't as bad as I thought he would be.

During all the time that I was there, there was one period when it approached a crisis, in the Cuban missile situation, and SAC really went on almost max alert, maximum alert, particularly in the case of their airborne alert. They had a segment of B-52s set aside as the airborne alert. Depending on the situation and so forth, they may have none of those airborne, they may have one-fourth, they may have half of them, but in this instance they had the max number airborne. They were airborne from these different bases and that is, of course, to decrease the reaction time going to the target, plus getting them off the ground and reducing their vulnerability. They'd go up in a circle and then they'd head towards the target, on that course, reach a certain point and then come back; back and forth. They'd stay airborne twenty-four hours out of the day, and during this Cuban thing that's what they were doing, because our people weren't too sure that something wouldn't come out of this.

Then of course, you had the others on the ground. They were on max alert, and you had missiles in standby status.

That went on for several days, but it finally calmed down. I think SAC exaggerated the severity of the crisis, even though, I guess, based on what you've read since then, it was a pretty scarey thing at that time. Kennedy stood up to Khruschev and made him back down, but at that time the Soviet Union did not have very much in the way of a nuclear-delivery capability, nothing approaching the situation they have now. Furthermore, they had little in the way of a combatant navy, a very important lesson for them and they are now exploiting what they learned.

Q: That was the watershed period!

Adm. J.: It was. I think you're right.

I was there not quite two years, I think, and then about that time Admiral Sharp, Oley Sharp, was ordered out to CinCPac Fleet and called me and said he wanted me to come out and be his deputy. So that's when I left Offutt and went out to Pearl.

Q: In addition to the fact that you got along with these people who were somewhat hostile toward the navy, what would you say was your ultimate contribution in that period when you were there?

Adm. J.: First of all was the mere fact that you were able to get along with them, that's number one.

Q: That was a tremendous contribution!

Adm. J.: Then, number two, to finally get these people to some degree, not as much as you wanted to but at least to some degree, to really sit down and be objective and think in terms of what is best for the security of the country instead of the parochial viewpoint, and lay the plan down along those lines rather than always fighting for this - the air force should have these targets, they're ours, no Polaris on these targets. The survivability of Titan II is 5 per cent higher than that of Polaris, even though it's liquid-fueled, in a silo. In my office there was a great big picture in color of nothing but the ocean, ocean waves, and do you know what it says under that? "Polaris on station," and this used to get the SAC people!

No system is invulnerable. It's a question of relativity. But, relatively speaking, I think the Polaris system is more invulnerable than any other system, first of all by virtue of its being mobile. You've got to find it.

Q: Mobile and hidden!

Adm. J.: Yes. You've got the Minuteman in the silos, and, of course, the air force is always trying to find some way to get back in the picture, the B-1 bomber, but they're a manned bomber, they can't survive in an electronic environment. Now they want the MX. They're going to dig up this territory, all this real estate in two states and put these things in tunnels and so forth. You're not going to be able to hide anything like that. And the other principle that we've always pointed out in the case of any weapon system at sea for that matter, let alone Polaris, is the possibility of trying to remove these things from populations and industry, whereby they become automatically, as a side effect, targets of any nuclear weapons dropped. There aren't any people out there.

Q: Be hard on the whale population, but other than that!

Adm. J.: Anyway, the plan developed finally and, I would say, everything that was in it was about the best you could get.

Q: In retrospect, do you see a continuation of these efforts in the development towards what is for the good of the nation, rather than what is for the good of the air force?

Adm. J.: Very slow, creeping improvement, because anybody in their right mind simply would not buy the idea of the MX concept. Once again, and it happened before, once political reasoning begins to take over and pretty well obscure logical, objective thinking. Then you end up with something like that, and Reagan, of course, he's promised that they'll get the B-1 bomber and the MX system, and they probably will.

Q: You mean this is the new administration that's promised?

Adm. J.: Yes, particularly with Senator Tower, who is going to be head of the Armed Services Committee, replacing John Stennis, and this simply isn't in the best interest of national security. Think of the billions and billions of dollars it's going to cost, and what are you getting for the money you spend?

Q: Of course, it will be closely scrutinized and there may be a possibility of common sense prevailing?

Adm. J.: Well, it's getting pretty late for that because they're already setting up arrangements for the physical layout. There'll be cities, with that many people involved in all this, surveying the land out there. There's all kinds of money already being spent with the idea that they're going to get the approval to go ahead.

Q: Won't there be some opposition develop in the states involved?

Adm. J.: Oh, gee, there's a tremendous lobby on that already, Laxalt and the different people. They'll just ruin that part of the country, particularly in the case where all this cattle ranching is. That's no good.

So, unless there's a complete, absolute, urgent necessity for it and there is no alternative, you should look for some other out, some other option. Granted, the Titan II should have been done away with, they just had this one explosion, you know and Minuteman in the silos, I think it is wrong in spite of the tons and tons of concrete that you have over it, but with the latest warheads that the Russians have with tremendous megatonnage, even those silos won't withstand that kind of over pressure.

Q: And their increasing ability to target?

Adm. J.: Yes.

Q: Spot the objective?

Adm. J.: Yes. Well, because of satellite reconnaissance you can, you can pretty well, in time. And you have the multiple warheads that come down and that assures you that you have your things spread out this way -

Q: So the trenches won't -

Adm. J.: You're pretty well assured, or have greater assurance that at least one of them is going to get that missile, find it. So what will come out of all this, I don't know. It will be interesting to see how the administration handles it. Dr. Brown, of course, SecDef, says he's all for it but that's because he was secretary of the air force, very, very partial to the air force. As somebody said, he thinks even in his sleep of how much he dislikes the navy. Publicly, he will say differently, naturally, but actually a very, very poor supporter of the navy. Except for Congress, we would never have gotten another nuclear carrier. Not with Brown, no way.

Q: Well, he will be out in another month!

Adm. J.: Yes. It will be interesting to see what happens. I don't know sho is going to be SecDef. That will be interesting, too.

Q: Those were momentous years for you, out there?

Adm. J.: Yes. It was a heck of a place out there. Omaha, of course, is a marvelous city, wonderful people there. The weather's absolutely awful in the wintertime, below zero, blizzards. Omaha is, I would say, real Americana.

Q: Yes, almost the heart of it.

Adm. J.: Pioneer spirit out there. It's a big insurance center, more than Hartford, Connecticut, the cattle, the stockyards. Omaha is the only place in the United States that has stockyards now. Chicago closed out.

Q: Yes.

Adm. J.: And Union Pacific headquarters.

Q: It's the focal point for those central plains, certainly.

Adm. J.: Yes, the midwest, grain, cattle.
Well, I left there and went to Honolulu.

Q: You were happy to leave there?

Adm. J.: I must admit that I was.

Q: You went out in July of 1963 to be deputy to the commander in chief of the Pacific Fleet.

Adm. J.: Yes.

Q: Who was PacFlt?

Adm. J.: At that time, it was Admiral Sides, Savvy Sides, really a wonderful man, tremendous person, and he was well named "Savvy Sides." He had a lot of qualities of leadership and he had a way with people, and, besides had this wonderful technical background. He was the first person in the navy to head up the missile division in OpNav, before Raborn. He more or less pioneered in that end of the navy. He knew he wasn't going to stay there very long.

Q: That was when Dan Gallery was -

Adm. J.: I think at one time he had visions that he might be CinCPac but that didn't seem to be in the cards.

Sharp came out and relieved him, and Savvy Sides was offered a job by Secretary of the Navy Korth to come back and be his special assistant, but about that time - and I remember when Savvy called me in and said, "I've got to make a decision because I have this offer, on the other hand Lockheed wants me to come to work for them, lifetime membership in the Riviera Country Club, a salary of $150,000, a paid-up life insurance policy of $100,000. So, weighing one against the other I think I'll take this," which he did. He was with them for several years.

Oley Sharp relieved him, and, at that time, I'm pretty sure Oley had in mind, even at the time he left Washington, that he would eventually move up and relieve Don Felt, because he'd been in that job quite a while and he was near the point where he would be relieved.

Q: What was your job when you came on the scene?

Adm. J.: His deputy.

Q: Yes, but what did that involve?

Adm. J.: Deputies on a staff like that can function and have functioned in one of two or three different ways, depending - once again, as we touched on yesterday - how much authority and responsibility the boss man delegates. But, in any event, one of your first jobs is to pull the staff, all these people, logistics, operational, intelligence, and all, together as a cohesive team efort and get the job done, cut through the red tape as much as you can, all the paper work, you always have a lot of that but I would separate the important from the minutia and get the job done. Things were beginning to build up then. Then, take as much of the burden as you could off the boss man, who had to worry about so many things, relieve him of as many of those as possible, which means trying to be as much as you can his alter ego in the situations that were appropriate.

Q: How did CinCPac fit into the picture of CinCPacFlt?

Adm. J.: CinCPac was a unified commander under the Joint Chiefs, the same as CinCLant. SACLant, of course, is NATO, but CinCLant is a unified commander, and CinCPac, as a unified commander, is required to have a joint staff, all services represented. And he has his component commands, PacAF, Pacific Air Forces; USARPac, U.S. army, Pacific; CinCPacFlt, that's the navy component. Those are the component commanders under the unified commander, and all responsible to the unified commander for the discharge of peacetime missions, and, of course, even more complicated and more important in time of war. You really get into a fuzzy area when you get into Vietnam.

Q: Yes, because no declared war.

Adm. J.: It was hard, even once we became involved - well, we were in hostilities, we were at war then. But here it was very difficult to draw any sort of chart because you had ComUSMacV, who was really in CinCPac's area of command and was really subordinate to him, but Mr. McNamara never saw it that way. He dealt with MacV on many matters directly. A lot of what happened and the fact that CinCPac was involved was due to the stubborness and the persistence of Oley Sharp. He insisted that he be cut in and be given certain responsibility, even though McNamara kept accusing him of always nagging. Well, he was trying to do his job and, at times, he had to watch ComUSMacV because he would tend to go around or right to Washington and get Buzz Wheeler, who was chairman or get Max Taylor in the act. These were the army guys and there they were. It was a difficult situation at times.

Q: McNamara came out to Hawaii periodically, didn't he, for conferences?

Adm. J.: Oh, constantly. So did LBJ. He was there one time, and another time they had a big conference on Guam. But I don't remember that McNamara ever stopped in Pearl on his way out. He always went to MacV, went to Saigon, and then he came back, with that lefthanded pencil of his, saying, "Here's what we discussed, here's what we decided." And not always, unless he injected himself into it, was Admiral Sharp invited to attend meetings in Saigon. That's the way he was operating. He violated all principles, accepted principles, of unified command.

Q: Don Felt was there when you first went out?

Adm. J.: Oh, yes, but you see the thing really hadn't built

up. He didn't have too many of these problems. All he had was the MAAG in Saigon. Harkins and Felt had little responsibility insofar as, as we mentioned yesterday, the recce missions over Laos, particularly when they started using a few navy aircraft. But the thing in Vietnam was just beginning to build up and he was in his last days as CinCPac. Felt was out there and the day before he had had a meeting with Diem -

Q: And left, and then he was assassinated?

Adm. J.: Yes. Felt hadn't even left Saigon.

Q: He told me that.

Adm. J.: So, here, all this was happening, and of course, he knew it because Cabot Lodge was keeping him informed through the right channels. One coup, of course, aborted because they didn't think they were ready. Then they pulled the other one off, though, and they pretty well knew that it was going to take place. A lot has been written to the effect that CIA actually - I'm just repeating some of the things I've read, I can't prove it to you, but I suspect it - encouraged the generals to pull off the coup. In other words, it's pretty much of a conclusion on the part of many people that, since Diem would not accede to some of the requests the U.S. government had made in terms of reforms and expanding his cabinet to include more Buddhists, he had to go. He had to go because his government was detrimental to the interests of the country and in confronting the threat of the VC.

Johnson #3 -264-

Q: That was the time when Buddhists were burning themselves?

Adm. J.: That was later on. That was part of it because they didn't feel that they had proper representation in the government in Saigon.

Q: Just as a footnote, in your opinion, how was the situation augmented and agitated by the actions of Madame Nu, as she traveled around the world -

Adm. J.: I think this was the woman behind the scenes. She exerted tremendous influence, there's no question about that, and not very good influence.

Q: Was she, as I recall -?

Adm. J.; She would have nothing to do with the Buddhists.

Q: She was very vocal, as she traveled around the United States and various other countries.

Adm. J.: A very forceful woman, a very attractive woman, very smart, but her thinking was a little bit off base, not for the good of her country.

No, the immolation and those things occurred from time to time. Of course, up at Hue, at one time, these people practically brought the U.S. and Vietnamese effort to a standstill. I remember flying up there and, on Route 1 that goes from Hue to Danang, for miles and miles were all these Buddhists lined up with all the fancy signs, colored signs and everything. They were not in favor of continuing the fight then. That was the big pacifist movement, which wasn't very good. You had to take care of that. You couldn't go up and shoot all these people. That would have made the situation worse. They finally resolved that, but it was just another one of the ancillary problems that didn't help the situation.

Q: Well, now, CinCPacFlt was a very large administrative unit and there were other duties in addition to Vietnam. How important were they at this time, 1962-63, what attention did you give them, to Japan, to Taiwan, and places like that?

Adm. J.: Well, you certainly had to give attention to them, but they began to pale and be of lesser significance compared to Vietnam. We had to keep in mind the commitments we had in Taiwan, the U.S. Defense Command in Taiwan, and working very closely with the Japanese, very close with the Japanese Navy, and with the senior U.S. naval officer in Tokyo, exchange of ideas, joint exercises. They didn't have much of a navy then, still don't even today, but it was important that they be assured of support from the U.S., including the U.S. Navy. But that wasn't any great problem because they were perfectly willing to work with us.

Korea, that was mostly army. I made a couple of visits up there. As long as the status quo remained, the navy would not be involved in it, even though we did have to engage in some contingency planning. All these different contingency plans because something could happen in Korea or Taiwan involving Quemoy and Matsu, which was still a touchy thing. Another contingency plan, suppose more than one of them happened at the same time, that sort of a thing. Then, of course, the contingency plans, what are you going to do about Vietnam. the first one that came up, of course, was when the first marines went into the I Corps. That was really an administrative over-the-beach operation because they didn't know what kind of resistance, if any, they would encounter when they hit the beach. As it turned out, they were met by people with flowers and things.

All these other areas, and you had some that were a combination of the political-military, which were very sticky. We still had SEATO, which really wasn't very active.

Q: It had been more so before?

Adm. J.: Yes, but anyway the British, of course, down in Singapore - they hadn't pulled out of Singapore yet - and then the Australians, more than the New Zealanders, they were content to sit on the side, they were still interested in SEATO, and, typical of the British, no matter how small the forces are in the area to be involved, they want to engage in a lot of combined planning. Joint planning was usually U.S. army, navy and air force. Combined, like the combined staffs, involves officials of another country. They had all these senior people down there, and every time I made a visit down there, which I never looked forward to, the British would want to have a briefing, a meeting, and so forth, and what is our next step to produce an overall combined plan, communications and things like that. I was told to lay off, don't commit yourself to anything, we don't want to get involved in that down there with the British and we never did.

We agreed on certain principles to avoid mutual interference-coordination-- that's as far as we ever went.

Q: What would have been the advantage of engaging in these conversations and the development of plans?

Adm. J.: There was none. We didn't want to get tied up with them at that point. All the political reasons, I'm not sure that I ever fully understood, but, anyway, that's one of the first things that I got from Tom Moorer, "When you go down there, you have to beware of that."

But, of course, in time the thing began to solve itself because Admiral Begg came out, a new boss, and the other people Admiral Desmond Dryer, who was a wonderful friend of mine —

Q: Desmond Dryer?

Adm. J.: Dryer, yes, British.

Singapore closed up. The Brits were gone, which was kind of sad, really. That was really their last outpost, real major outpost, in the Far East. Hong Kong is a crown colony. They have a military staff to the governor.

Q: A constabulary or something of that sort?

Adm. J.: Yes, that's all that amounts to.

Q: What about the interminable meetings up at Panmunjom? Was the Navy involved?

Adm. J.: No, except we had navy people in it; Arleigh Burke, Turner Joy, alternates. They were involved in that, but that was a U.N. thing.

Q: Had Victor Smith at one point, too?

Adm. J.: Yes, Victor Smith was up there. They alternated. But we were never involved in anything connected with these continuing talks. I don't know if they ever had any more of these things or not.

Q: Oh, yes, they went on.

Adm. J.: The same harangue that they go through. Once the armistice was signed, the navy pretty well pulled out of there, but just to keep contact with them and discuss things with them, be on good terms with them, I used to make trips in there. Actually, the marine guy would have a big parade for me, then I'd go see the Korean Navy guy, then I'd go see President Park. Of course, later on he was very cooperative. He sent one division of Korean troops to Vietnam and was willing to send more, if we'd taken them.

Q: How effective were they?

Adm. J.: Don't fool with them! The stats that I've read show that they took, or had, fewer prisoners than any other division in Vietnam. They didn't take prisoners. They used to tell the story - I was never around but "Brute" Krulak told me the story. He said if you were downwind you could pretty well cite the location of the Korean division many miles away, with their kim chee. Have you ever eaten kim chee, the cabbage they keep underground?

Q: It smells?

Adm. J.: Oh, boy. Highly seasoned stuff.

No, they were great fighters and that in itself created quite - not a problem, but serious discussion with the Gimo, the Generalissimo. Of course, you know, the Australians had a combat regiment in there, too, and nobody's better than the Aussies.

Anyway, every time I went in to Taipei, the Gimo would want to have an audience with me - or he requested I have an audience with him, that's what it was. One time I went up to Grass Mountain - that's his summer home - and Jerry Wright was the ambassador then, so we went up there and the Madame, she was up there also, Peg was along. She'd go along with me on most of these trips. I was told, "Well, you're limited to fifteen minutes, and then I will terminate the audience."

Q: Was he in poor health?

Adm. J.: No, heck no, not at that time.

Q: Well, why the fifteen minutes?

Adm. J.: Oh, well, they were just putting up a lot of formality. They didn't know what the Gimo had in mind, anyway, neither did I.

He used an interpreter, S. K. Hoo, a wonderful guy, very smart, Chinese, and we started talking about Quemoy and Matsu and the Chinese mainland, the usual. He loved to talk about that, you know, that some day they'd have a revolution over there. Then he gets around to Vietnam and, of course, he wants to send two or three division into Vietnam. Well, we'd run this through the State Department long ago many times and they said absolutely no because the Chinese are traditional bitter enemies of the Vietnamese and to put Chinese into Vietnam would create more problems than it would help. But, of course, I couldn't come out and say that, so I said this was up to the ambassador and the State Department.

Q: Who was that? McConaughy?

Adm. J.: No, that was before McConaughey relieved Jerry Wright. It was Admiral Wright, he was the ambassador, and he said the policy of the State Department is no, "Your force is better used here on Taiwan, in the defense of Taiwan." So we got away from that.

He never understood why, and I kind of agreed with him and I had trouble answering this question and statement, why we didn't go in and almost completely obliterate Haiphong and Hanoi. They would quit, and President Park of Korea said the same thing. I was up there with him and Park said:

"You go in, you drop nuclear bomb."

The ambassador said:

"Well, the admiral doesn't have anything to do with that. That comes from higher authority."

He said:

"Admiral, you should go in, drop nuclear bomb, then resign."

Q: And get your head cut off!

Adm. J.: Yes! Those people could easily see that we just weren't fighting the war the way a war is supposed to be fought if you had any idea of winning.

Q: Was Madame a part of the conversation?

Adm. J.: Not very much. She spent her time with the ladies, serving them tea. I remember one time, though, we were sitting around with the ladies, not very many of them - one time just Peg and Madame - and she joined in the political discussion. She was well informed. She lives up in New Jersey now, you know, a completely isolated recluse.

Q: Does she really?

Adm. J.: Yes, a great big estate and a guard force of dogs. You can't even get close. Very mysterious.

Q: Why did she go over here?

Adm. J.: I don't know.

Q: That is not her son, is it, the present head of Taiwan?

Adm. J.: Chung-kuo, no, I don't think so.

Q: He's the generalissimo's son, but not hers?

Adm. J.: Yes, I think so. Of course, she was one of the Soongs, you know, very wealthy Chinese family.

Q: What was your impression of President Park?

Adm. J.: I thought Park was a very, very strong man, and with the problems that you had in South Korea, together with North Korea, I thought the man did a good job. There was a lot left to be desired on the economic side, particularly, as I said yesterday, trying to take care of some of the populace that lived pretty much, well, in abject poverty. He could have done more in that regard. He was a dictator but, once again, he was a very strong man, even if he was a dictator and so forth and he is violently opposed to communism and will fight it. They'll stick by him. We made that mistake and that's how we got Castro, so for that reason I would go along with Park.

Q: There you have the problem of the American attitude toward human relations –

Adm. J.: Human rights, which is overdone.

Q: Yes, in contrast to realism.

Adm. J.: Yes. You've got to be realistic about it and the manner in which you apply it to different countries. You cannot apply it the same way. It's like saying, "Well, part of this is that you have to reform and be a democracy." Some countries will never be a democracy, they're not cut out to be that. They're ill suited to it and if you try to force them into it, the first thing you know, the leftists are going to move into control, and that's what you have in Central America.

Q: Hasn't that always been an American attitude, however, since the nineteenth century?

Adm. J.: We've been wrong.

Q: We always thought in terms of the idea that they should have exactly the kind of government we have.

Adm. J.: Completely wrong, completely wrong approach.

Q: During that period, when we were getting more heavily involved in Vietnam, and the Chinese apparently were being concerned about that situation down there, was there any discernible lessening of mainland Chinese pressure against Taiwan?

Adm. J.: I didn't see any difference at all, except from time to time, when they could digress from their internal problems, they would express the age-old thing, there's only one China, it belonged to them. They never gave up expressing that any more than they do now. But there was no thought, which people were fearful of at one time, that they were actually going to invade it and try to take the island back. Taiwan itself would be a very, very difficult nut to crack in terms of an amphibious invasion.

Q: With any kind of defending force?

Adm. J.: Well, the Chinese in Taiwan, the Chinos, have a good military outfit and with the limited amphibious capability that the Red Chinese had, there wasn't very much they could have done. I think, once again, we were overly concerned about what they might do, what the Russians might do, about our actions in North Vietnam. Completely exaggerated. The Russians weren't going to get involved in that. They were going to supply them, yes. The Chinese - everybody was saying, well, don't forget Korea. That was a completely different situation.

Q: That was always an attitude that was expressed in high circles in the U.S., they didn't want to endanger the situation and get the Red Chinese involved. But was that an actuality, do you think, or was it an excuse?

Adm. J.: Well, Jack, at some levels in the State Department I think it was really a sincere worry, typical of a lot of the people we have in the State Department. On the other hand, later on, when Mr. McNamara first said, "Let's don't carry the bombing too far, let's be careful how far we carry it," he was using that as an excuse, I think.

Then, of course, later on, for the Tet pauses and other things, he was talking right away of restrictions. Then he was saying, "It's not effective anyway." He was using that excuse then. But there were people in the State Department who seemed to be sincerely concerned that we might antagonize or intimidate the Red Chinese to the extent that they would come in, more so than the Russians. The Russians preferred to let the surrogate outfits do all the fighting. They were going to help them militarily with supplies and so forth as they could and with political rhetoric, and they were convinced that eventually they would win out.

Q: That's the usual pattern of their behavior.

Adm. J.: Sure. They'll bide their time, two steps forward, one step back. They weren't going to worry about it.

Now, as we've seen in the last year or so, once again the Chinese hate of the Vietnamese, and that's why they invaded Vietnam, went in there. And, of course, no surprise, North Vietnam has gone into Cambodia and Laos, which is a tragic situation, but it shouldn't be any surprise. That was their announced goal, reunite Indochina.

Q: Now, in this time when you were deputy to CinCPacFlt, what relations did you have with the Philippines?

Adm. J.: Oh, we were involved with the Philippines all the time, particularly when it came to renegotiating base rights.

Q: Were they uppermost at that point, 1962-63?

Adm. J.: Well, yes, because they were making noises, in effect almost blackmailing us for many, many millions more of money for rental of Clark and at Subic. Those were the important ones. We finally gave up Sangley Point because it was mostly a seaplane base and, of course, seaplanes were phasing out. So we got out of Sangley and Cavite, after we'd built all the beautiful quarters and barracks over there for enlisted people. We finally got out.

The matter of base rights is a very touchy thing. It seems to have quieted down right now, but as long as you have Marcos in there he's going to bring it up. And you have the idea that you have two commanding officers at Clark, a Filipino and an American. The same thing at Subic. In all these places, you have two flags flying. They want more and more concessions and more and more money. You're always involved in a lot of these discussions with the Filipinos and still trying to remain on friendly terms with them, because a lot of times, through the medium of the military, you can advance understanding and friendship a lot better, more effectively and easily, than you can at the political level. I've seen that happen many times. So, yes -

Q: Well, there's an international fraternity of military?

Adm. J.: Yes, you have more of a common denominator for conversation, to start with.

Q: You made trips to Manila and - ?

Adm. J.: Oh, many times, oh yes. Not as deputy I didn't travel very much.

Q: Oh, you didn't?

Adm. J.: I stayed behind and the boss did the traveling.

Q: I see.

Adm. J.: A deputy doesn't travel. The travels I'm talking about are when I was commander of the Seventh Fleet, then CinCPacFlt, and, of course, you must remember that we did have a mutual defense treaty with the Philippines, the same as we had with the Chints. Whether or not this treaty with Taiwan had been abrogated, I don't know. I think in effect it has, but we still have it with the Philippines, of course, a mutual defense treaty, and we were always reviewing that, updating it, not so much the strategy of it, but the commitment of forces to it and the command structure.

Q: In this time frame, was Indonesia a problem?

Adm. J.: No. Indonesia had killed anybody who ever said the word communism and thrown them in the river. They'd settled down.

Q: It was Sukarno who had -

Adm. J.: I almost got in trouble one time in Saigon because you'd go to a press conference there and there'd be a couple of hundred people representing all the countries of the world, in view of what was going on there. A couple of times I requested permission to visit Indonesia and was told no by the State Department. They wouldn't let me go.

Q: What was their reason?

Adm. J.: They just didn't want to get involved in anything down there because, at that time, they were reluctant to even talk about any commitment in the way of a mutual defense thing in Indonesia. So, this one guy - he was from India, I think, said:

"What does the United States have in the way of provisions for mutual support of Indonesia in the event that it becomes involved in any difficulty?"

I said we had none. No, it was in Taipei, that's where it was, Teipei. So the Taipei newspaper, which was always distorting what I said, anyway, "Commander Seventh Fleet states United States committed to defense of Indonesia."

Q: Committed to it?

Adm. J.: Yes. Well, you can imagine, in a matter of hours I was on the phone, talking to Washington. These people have no integrity. You just can't trust most newspaper people.

Q: Why would they do a complete flop?

Adm. J.: Because he wants a scoop, something to make headlines - a big scoop. They have no ethics, a lot of them. Very few of them do.

Another time, in Saigon MACV's PAO said, "We're going to have a big breakfast here. You're the man they want to talk to, and it's nonattribution." In other words, they'd ask me questions -

Q: Off the record.

Adm. J.: Pretty much off the record.

Well, I soon found out, don't fall for that. Either you have it on the record or you don't talk. So, this one fellow, he was American - I forget what newspaper he represented, said:

"Do you have any nuclear submarines, U.S. nuclar submarines stationed off the harbor at Haiphong?"

I said: "It is the policy and always has been never to imply or in any way to disclose the location and the operational nature of any submarines, particularly nuclear submarines."

Well, gosh, here come the Saigon people, saying that I made a statement that we did have nuclear subs off Haiphong. I had to get on the phone and talk to McNamara's office on that. He'd have clobbered me on that one, but that's the way it is. Of course, actually, we didn't have any nuclear submarines off Haiphong. We had submarines that would go up into the channel between the mainland and Hainan Island. They would go up there and observe Hainan Island because there seemed to be reliable reports that they were putting missile sites there. Well, we kept a submarine up there and we had one guy who went up there - and, you know, when they go on that kind of a mission, he's supposed to report "sub safe" within twenty-four hours. Well, this guy went in there and we didn't hear from him. We didn't know what had happened to him.

I remember I got on the phone with Dave McDonald and the secretary of the navy and I said:

"I'm sending patrol planes and destroyers into this area and see if I can find out what's happened, what happened to the guy, did he go aground, or what."

They started out and about that time I got a report from that guy. Do you know what he had done? He was rigging a Soviet merchantship, which means he was going in there to take photographs through the periscope." Well, he came up to periscope depth under the freighter and really clobbered himself. The conning tower was sheered and the freighter sank.

Q: A novel way of sinking a ship!

Adm. J.: I don't know whether this has ever been revealed to many people or not. About four days later the word came out, "Russian freighter sinks after hitting uncharted reef"!

Q: This was in what year?

Adm. J.: This was when I had the Seventh Fleet, 1964 or 1965, in there. The guy came out and he had to make a jury rig antennae and report to me what had happened to him.

Q: How could he do that, anyway?

Adm. J.: Just doping off, he was doping off, a little bit too enthusiastic about what he was trying to do.

Q: Referring to what you said about reporters, did you ever inaugurate a system such as Tom Moorer told me he did? He had a habit, and I think still does, and that is he never had a press conference without taping the whole thing, so that he had-

Adm. J.: Sure, it's the only thing that saved me.

Q: In Taipei?

Adm. J.: Yes.

Q: So you had the record?

Adm. J.: I had Paul Trahan, my PIO, in and, boy he wouldn't let me get up and say anything unless he had that thing going. No, I learned that early in the game.

Q: And the language difficulty?

Adm. J.: Yes, language difficulties. With the Chinese in Taipei, that was a big problem. they would honestly make a mistake, but a lot of it was deliberate. They loved to distort it and come out with big, flashy headlines.

Q: Also, was there not a decided bias on the part of many of these reporters in Saigon? I mean they were anti-involvement, weren't they?

Adm. J.: Not when I was there, no. They wanted to try to get a true picture of actually what was going on and what progress, if any, we were making towards securing South Vietnam winning the war, are we actually in a stalemate, are we actually losing the war? Some of the good ones were pretty smart and they could see through a lot of the stuff that was being fed to them and it simply didn't wash. Of course, the principal source for this kind of information was in the five o'clock follies in MAC2 Headquarters.

Q: Five o'clock follies?

Adm. J.: Yes, that's what Westmoreland called his five o'clock briefing to his staff, and in a lot of cases he would bring in the press, the media. He had it then because by then he would have gotten, would have had the benefit of, reports from the field, of this patrol or this incursion, they'd killed this many, etc. This was the famous body count and bomb tonnage. He seemed to be trying to use that as a measure of what success they were making in the countryside against the VC, in pacifying the hamlets in the varius provinces. He showed all these elaborate charts. I've been there several times and seen this, and how the body count was going up.

Well, you can't use that as a measure of the kind of success you're having in any one particular area. Sure, he killed a lot of them because they had the bodies, I've even seen a lot of them, but a week later they're back in there again, it's the same force, so what's the net effect of that? It was really a misleading thing.

Q: He was not realistic, was he, about that whole situation? He could see it, too.

Adm. J.: I don't know but I had serious doubts. He and Lew Walt didn't see eye to eye as to how to go about trying to clear the countryside and pacify the areas at all. I think Lew Walt, together with some of Bruce Krulak's thinking, had a better idea, to go in and secure the area, and this is pretty much the hamlet program, which originated up in I Corps, and make them feel secure. Then build up their own security forces secure the market place, and let them go to bed at night and sleep securely, and keep it that way. Don't do it as a fleeting thing and then pull these people out, because the VC will be right back in there. Some of the families in there had boys who were out with the VC.

Westy had this idea, tremendous numbers of helicopters, the First Cav Division making a great big move through the jungle, cleaning it out. Well, they, the VC, went under cover, these people had gone underground. It's amazing the network of caves and everything they had - hospitals, even, places where they manufactured ammunition. They'd clean out a lot of that and destroy a lot of these things, but then you pulled back and, in a short period of time, they were in there again. About that time, he would ask for 150,000 more troops. Then he had about 400,000. At the end, you know, he had 450,000 troops in there plus the Korean division, and he asked for 250,000 more. He already had two marine divisions in there. That many hundreds of thousands of troops in a place like that? He just had to change his strategy. Namely, you cannot fight this kind of a war, guerrilla war, on the ground that way. You've got to find some way to get at the source of all this and sever that jugular vein to win.

That's what it is and that's what Sharp kept harping on. McCone saw it. Rostow saw it. You've got to get into North Vietnam because you know they're providing all this support. You've got to go up there and wipe them out. Otherwise, it's going to go on and, pretty soon, it's going to get to a point of no return and you're in a bad position with the American people. That's how the thing escalated to a very, very bad situation.

He was just naive about it. He didn't know how to fight a guerrilla war. I hope that at least somebody has learned the lesson about that sort of thing. A fight for the minds of the people, in effect. That's what it is, a big part of it; the hamlet program. You have to do something about the threat before you can really begin to appeal to the minds of these people. They want to be freed. A lot of them came down there.

Q: When you look at it objectively, that's precisely the tactic that the North Vietnamese used against our people in this country?

Adm. J.: Sure. They sure did.

Q: They got the minds of the people behind them.

Adm. J.; We'd go down in the delta, and we muffed it down there. We had an effort down there that was not very effective pitiful. They went in there and they got the key people - in the case of the province chief, if he didn't come around, the next day they'd find him without any arms, legs, or head. There's one city down there, Cantho, and it's really the rice capital of the delta, that's where all this rice, thousands and thousands of tons of it, were brought in there to market. Well, we didn't have enough sense to go in there and try to get control of this. Instead, we let the VC do it whereby it was all brought in there and, except for about 15 or 20 per cent of the money they got, the rest of it went to the VC. They were in there, collecting it.

Q: That was a source of income for them?

Adm. J.: Sure, certainly.

Q: For supplies:

Adm. J.: Plus getting all the rice they needed. We never came close to starving any of the VC. He could exist on practically nothing for days.

So, as I've said before, we missed the boat. It wouldn't have been decisive, but it sure would have helped. The marines wanted nothing to do with it. They wanted to engage in ground force combat, just like the army did.

Q: Well, now this leads you to the riverine warfare. Will you talk about that?

Adm. J.: Sure. We pushed this all along, riverine warfare. That's why we went out and we got the PBR boats. We got LSTs in there with the helicopter platforms. We sent ou these patrols and, in a limited way, this was very effective, yes, but it wasn't big enough, it wasn't expansive enough, to really fully get control of the area. You need more than that because comparatively speaking, it was a relatively small number of people involved in it. They did a tremendous job, those people. and here, in the amphibious commands, we've pretty well dismantled, done away with, all elements having to do with riverine warfare. And it's something that should be kept alive, it's a different means of warfare that you might be involved with, who knows?

It was a very interesting thing, the development of what happened down there, the tactics and everything. The U.S. Navy was in command in this one small area down there, under Ward, of course. He was the component commander. He stayed up with Westmoreland, but he made visits down there. Paul Grey was the guy pretty much in charge, and he had the smallest carrier in the world, he had an LST with a landing deck on it, where he operated all these helicopters and from there he sent out these patrols.

Symington came out and wanted me to go with him on a trip down there. Well, I'd met him before, knew him quite well.

Q: He was then secretary for air?

Adm. J.: No, he was a senator then. Yes, I'm pretty sure it was after.

Q: Yes, it must have been.

Adm. J.: So, we went to Danang and then went to Saigon. He got a briefing from Westmoreland, and he wanted to go down and look at the delta. We flew all over in a helicopter and were shot at a couple of times. Then we landed on board this

LST. and here Paul Grey and he had ten of the worst-looking things you've ever seen. Their faces were all charcoal-black, camouflage suits, and there was a patrol that had just returned two hours early and they had these four VC prisoners tied up on deck.

Q: Still kicking and alive?

Adm. J.: Oh, yes, they were alive and looking at you in a very mean way. Of course, you couldn't get any more absolute proof than that of what they could do. This impressed Symington very much - we ought to do more of this, why don't we expand on this?

Well, MACV was convinced there was a potential there for doing some good, but once again he injects the army into it, and here they set up this tremendous base, with all the logistic tail, you know. The army can't handle anything unless the logistic tail is about five times as big as the operational outfit. All this stuff built up and everything, and all the different kinds of water craft were brought in there and so forth - helicopters, and, to my knoweldge they never accomplished but very little of anything.

And we had all these different PBR bases in the delta along the river and in different places there. The COs did quite a job, really. They were the unsung heroes. I used to tell a story of a fellow named Dale Meyerkord. There was a Meyerkord Hotel in Saigon at one time. They sent Meyerkord down there - he was a young lieutenant called up from the reserves, he volunteered to go down there in charge of a Vietnamese unit, going in the LCMs, in these boats, going along the river, trying to ferret out the VC.

Well, he came into this one place. He was in charge of the boat. He was the only American in there. He had these Vietnamese all armed and everything. They went up against the shoreline, and they were ambushed, VC opened fire on them, and Meyerkord got up there and even manned a carbine himself. He was able to extricate that LCM out of there, backed it out, and started down the river. Well, he died shortly after that, but I think that was one of the greater acts of heroism that anybody heard of down there, and that's why they named a hotel after him. These people loved the man, they respected him because he would talk to them, and they would say, "Listen to Meyerkord. We know why he's here, what he stands for. Therefore, we will fight with him - freedom. He knows what he's talking about."

Q: How effective were the Vietnamese in operations like that?

Adm. J.; Unless they had leadership, they were relatively ineffective. They simply had to have leadership.

Q: And it couldn't be Vietnamese leadership?

Adm. J.: No, not as a rule. They had some few, very, very few it simply didn't work. The reasons for it, I don't know. The ones who were good in the military who were the leaders and trained by the French, these people were killed off or were assassinated. I knew, and I have a couple of plaques from the fellow, he was head of the Vietnamese Navy, a wonderful young fellow, a commodore - I've forgotten his name now. I used to go to his headquarters, I used to take visits out with the junk fleet. They had a wonderful junk fleet. The guys got paid about fifty cents a month. They'd go out with these junks and try to counter the activities of the VC. But, here, this fellow was well educated, he knew what he was talking about, and we gave him all the assistance we could, more up-to-date landing craft and so forth, and, with one of these coups, they came in there and they killed him.

Q: He had the rank of a captain, I believe?

Adm. J.: Well, he was a captain, but they made him a commodore since he was head of the navy. He was a wonderful person. I used to go to his headquarters and, boy, he'd have the honor guard out there, and they were a sharp bunch! They'd give you the honors, you know, with a bugle and everything!

Q: Somebody told me that the U.S. Navy had real difficulty in getting any public notice of what they were doing and what they accomplished.

Adm. J.: In country?

Q: In Vietnam, South Vietnam.

Adm. J.: Certainly, mainly because this was all controlled from Saigon, MACV's outfit, and they weren't going to play up that, no way. It was hard for the marines to get any recognition. Pretty soon Lew Walt had his own press conference.

Q: I guess it was Bill Mack who told me that, he was involved with publicity in the U.S. or something at that time.

Adm. J.: He was the head PAO guy in CNO.

Q: He told me he arranged with the Seventh Fleet people to get some kind of public -

Adm. J.: Well, you could get coverage from the Seventh Fleet because you had people, reporters, off and on the flagship all the time, but they had no knowledge of anything going on in country, what the navy was doing or in the coastal surveillance with the Swift boats coming down the South Vietnamese coastline. Most of the coverage they got was the activity that originated from the carriers, like the flights over North Vietnam. Then, later on, of course, Westmoreland insisted we put a carrier down south. They called it the Dixie Station. There was one carrier down there sending these flights in there. At times, they couldn't find any targets, and here were all these aircraft, more than he could really use effectively the way he was trying to use it. He didn't need a carrier down there. But, what MACV wants, McNamara gives him!

We put these Swift boats in there. They finally got the coast guard to put patrol vessels in. We had patrol planes going up and down daily, night and day. They might get a fishing boat, maybe, with a few rounds of ammunition or some food, taking it in maybe to the VC. We weren't even sure of that. And here you'd go and talk to Westmoreland or to

McNamara, and even in his book Westmoreland was saying that at least 75 per cent of all supplies were coming in over the coastline, when everybody knew they were coming in over the Ho Chi Minh trail or across the DMZ.

I'll never forget - and, heck, we had four DERs on station, DERs, together with the Swift boats. Once again McNamara came from Saigon, he didn't come through Pearl, and we had a big luncheon and conference out at Kehroo Lagoon. We were sitting out there at tables, after a couple of drinks, and, as it was, I was sitting next to McNamara. I asked him:

"Mr. Secretary, what do you think of the surveillance effort down there?" He said:

"It stinks."

I said: "Well, could you explain to me? If it does, we'd better do something about it."

"I said it stinks. You talk to Westy." That's all he said. Well, at that moment, a great damned big cocoanut fell and almost hit him on the head. People at the other end got up and, when they did, the bench went up like that and he fell with all his food on him. I laughed, I couldn't help it!

That's all he's say, "It stinks." What do you do when somebody acts that way? He didn't give any further explanation

Q: Pretty frustrating!

Adm. J.: Oh, gee.

Q: There was a change when Abrams came in, wasn't there?

Adm. J.: Well, yes. Abe came in in the midst of the Vietnamization program. The decision was made in Washington to turn it over to the Vietnamese and pull the U.S. troops, marines out. It's their fight, let them take over. Everybody was convinced, not necessarily Abrams or Oley Sharp, by any means, that they could handle it, but that was the way to pursue the war. We were losing too many people because casualties were really beginning to mount up, and the American people wanted something different. That was Nixon by then, and he figured he had to do something, and that's about all he could do, I guess, even though I think in the minds of a lot of people it was destined to failure. No one in Washington would go for bombing Hanoi or mining Haiphong. He sent the incursion into Cambodia, the Parrot's Beak, and he got into trouble with Congress on that. They rescinded the Tonkin Gulf resolution. Then, about the time of the peace treaty, and he thought they'd agreed to release the POWs, which was becoming a touchy thing in this country, too, more so than with the hostages.

Q: But played down for a very long time, wasn't it?

Adm. J.: Well, yes because people were thinking more then of stopping all the killing, the loss of soldiers in South Vietnam - get out of the war. That was the big movement back here, the communists, Jane Fonda and those people.

Well, of course, you had the problem in making those people really do what they said they would do. That's when he sent the B-52s in there and really clobbered them. Then, they were released after that. We should have done this long before.

Q: Here's a citation to the effect that, when you were CinCPac Fleet, you supervised the landing of 78,000 marines. Do you want to talk about that phase of the war?

Adm. J.: We just cranked up the plans. That's what I talked to you about a while ago, when these marines went into the I Corps.

Q: Yes.

Adm. J.: And it was more of an administrative landing. It wasn't a combat landing. The marines did conduct some limited amphibious operations in certain areas where they thought there was intense VC activity. They would land in daylight and go in there and try to sweep them out, surround the area, and mop it up.

Q: Was this in the delta?

Adm. J.: No, they wouldn't go into that. This was in I Corps, that's the area. I Corps belongs to the marines. In many cases, this wasn't too effective. You had to notify the province chief, you see, that you were coming in there, and a lot of times he told the VC or they found out some other way, so they'd flown the coop, they were gone!

Q: That was just an added handicap, wasn't it?

Adm. J.: Oh, gee, we finally got permission - well, first of all, naval gunfire north of the DMZ. If you don't think that took a lot of doing, and that's when we pulled the New Jersey back out of mothballs and sent her out there, even though I think the 8-inch guns would have done as much or even more damage.

Q: Who made that decision?

Adm. J.: It originated, of course, with somebody back in CNO. I didn't originate it and neither did Sharp. I was all for gunfire, but the cost of putting the New Jersey back in commission and putting people in here and so forth just didn't make sense when we had so many 8-inch cruisers and they could send a shell just as far as the 16-inch guns on the New Jersey, unless they started another production line. That's when they decided this wasn't too good an idea after all.

Q: The reserve supply of shells had been exhausted?

Adm. J.: Yes. Oh, they were throwing these things in there hour after hour all night long. I guess they probably killed a lot of people, but what good it ever did, I don't know.

But, anyway, down south we had destroyers going in there and putting gunfire in areas where we knew there were VC. You had to clear this with the province chief and a lot of times, with the communications, that was quite a few days. Well, by that time they were gone.

Q: That doesn't really make sense. We were fighting the battle for them and yet -

Adm. J.: Don't kill any of our friendly people! This was the country team, you see. The State Department guy insisted on that. But here, once again, this is typical of some of the completely nonsensical rules of engagement you had to abide by.

Q: How did the province chiefs react to this?

Adm. J.: Oh, sure, he says, I will let you know as soon as I look around and notify my people. Well, once he started notifying the people -

Q: The secret was out!

Adm. J.: Sure. He says, "I'll make sure none of my civilians are in that area'! He didn't know who was who, really, in his province. You can't tell them from anybody else. They'd come into the hamlets at night and the men would sleep with the girls, get food and everything, then leave before daylight - they're gone. Some of the things they would do- in this one hamlet, in the market place in the daytime, absolutely peaceful. And here, the marines had an outpost and they had all these warning things. They had wires strung up, you'd touch that and a bell would go off, and you had the tin cans and all these things that you struck and they'd make a noise. Here in this place, they had two Vietnamese women doing their laundry. They were pretty good, they had all this help and everything, cook, laundry, and everything. Here was a little girl, her arms were off like this -

Q: Both arms off?

Adm. J.: She'd been tortured because she wouldn't tell them where so and so was. You saw many examples of that. So, it was an ugly war and they certainly didn't seem to have any idea of how to fight it. They just could not come up with an overall strategy that made any sense, particulaly since we were under the imposition of so many restrictions and rules of engagement imposed by civilians who knew practically nothing about fighting any kind of a war. They simply would not, and Westmoreland was almost at fault as much. He could not see t necessity for really pulling together, integrating the business of the bombing of the north with his operations down south.

Q: Somebody told me that when units of the Seventh Fleet were operating in Tonkin Gulf, engaged in perhaps bombardment of the coastal areas, they had also to be concerned with another potential enemy off the stern in terms of Russian possible action. Was this a reality?

Adm. J.: I don't know what kind of action they had reference to, certainly not any combat action.

Q: No, but it was a potential. Were there Russian submarines or anything of that sort out there?

Adm. J.: Russian submarines off the Chinese coast a couple of times, and there were Russian ships in transit, going around, and a good part of the time there was always one of these Russian trawlers, an intelligence-gathering one. You could always depend on that guy being around. He was always there, sure, but he was unarmed, he was just collecting intelligence, just like the guy who sits off Guam. He's anchored there. He watches the Polaris submarines come in and out.

Q: Traffic monitor!

Adm. J.: Yes, the pattern of operations and what pictures he could get. The admiral in charge there used to have a great big spyglass trained on the Russians. We could see the women in bathing suits, bathing on the stern! They had women on board. They stayed on station about six months and then somebody else relieved them. He stays there all the time - at least, he did when I was there. But we're about to abandon Guam as a Polaris base, of course, with the increased range of the missiles, the same as over in Spain and Scotland.

So, as CinCPacFlt - well, I was with the Seventh Fleet ten months or so, then came back and relieved Tom Moorer once again.

Q: You certainly were admirably qualified to go up to CinCPac Fleet, weren't you?

Adm. J.: I think I knew the situation out there firsthand.

Q: This was in March of 1965, March 30?

Adm. J.: Yes and, of course, I was there just a short time prior to the August 4 Maddox Incident in the gulf.

Q: Yes, you told me about the Maddox.

Adm. J.: Yes, right.

Q: Well, now, Tom Moorer hadn't been there very long, had he?

Adm. J.: In Seventh Fleet?

Q: Yes.

Adm. J.: I was trying to think who he relieved. Bill Schoech I think. I think he'd been there - he had the job longer than I did. He had it about a year and a half.

Q: Then he was CinCPacFlt?

Adm. J.: Yes. He came back and relieved Sharp and Sharp relieved Felt.

Q: He was there for a very short time, wasn't he?

Adm. J.: He was there the same length of time that I was commander of the Seventh Fleet.

Q: Oh, yes.

Adm. J.: This was about ten months, and then they sent me back there and he went to CinCLant.

As CinCPacFlt, of course, I would make many trips out to the Far East, always to Vietnam, but in conjunction with that to Taiwan and the Philippines. Of course, once again going back to Japan and talking with those people back there.

Q: What kind of a plane did you have to travel in?

Adm. J.: It was a four-engine prop airplane. Among other things, as CinCPacFlt, I was the military governor of the Bonin Islands. We had those under trusteeship.

Q: Oh yes.

Adm. J.: Iwo Jima and Chichi Jima. Policywise and so forth, it was part of the trusteeship we assumed after the war. We didn't have any active U.S. administrator in those islands, so that's why they put it under a military governor.

What reminded me of being such was that I used to talk to Ambassador Reischauer in Japan and, of course, in his sentiments, sympathy, and everything he was very, very pro-Japanese. There's no question about that.

Q: Yes.

Adm. J.: Every time I went out to talk with him, he would have a joint military-diplomatic conference. He would have ComUSJapan, who was an air force general, he would have me, commander of the Seventh Fleet, and the senior U.S. naval officer ashore, ComNav Jap, who was Walter Price at that time. So we discussed all the things in cooperation with the Japanese, how we could help them and so forth, and then he'd get into the broad political aspects of the thing.

First of all, you simply cannot expect to continue base rights in Japan---. We had Atsugi, we had Yoko, which was a very important base for the carriers and all the other ships there. There was -

Q: Sasebo?

Adm. J.: Sasebo, yes. By that time, not too much at Sasebo. But two or three air bases, U.S. air bases. The bigger one was outside of Tokyo - I've forgotten the name of it now. Anyway, he said:

"You cannot expect to continue these base rights and so forth unless you have a quid pro quo. Namely, you've got to return the Ryukyus to the Japanese."

Well, first question, OK, maybe we'll concede that. From a military point of view, of course, we needed the base rights in Japan.

Furthermore, if you return the Ryukyus to Japan, from the military point of view, what happens to the bases we have there, which are very important. Kadina, we had a patrol squadron there and this was a staging area for the marines. All marines staged into Vietnam, in and out, staged through the Ryukyus. He says:

"Well, you just have to accept the facts of life. I'm telling you that you are going to have to give it up."

He pursued that and, of course, we finally did give it up.

Q: Was there any obvious agitation on the part of the Japanese at that point?

Adm. J.: I think, at times. There was one prime minister who was making noises about it, yes. He knew that he had a receptive audience in the ambassador, so he'd bring it up and talk about it. Oh, sure, they had it in mind. They wanted to recover all their pre-World War II possessions, so they'd bring it up at a propitious moment. Then, of course, he'd bring up the Bonins. Well, the people of the Bonins got wind of it, and the poor people were terrified, really. So I decided I'd better make a trip down there. They'd been after me to make a trip, because the last military governor, the last CinCPacFlt, who had been down there was Admiral Radford. Hopwood and these other people had never visited the place. So I said, OK, I'll go.

I started out, landed at Guam and picked up Admiral Jones to take with me, who was ComNavMarinas, in my plane, and we landed at Iwo Jima. That was as far as we could go in a land plane. We got a search and rescue seaplane to go in to Chichi. So there were two planes to go in there. The pilot came in, and he aborted the first landing, went around, and came in on a different approach, whereby he was committed to landing. He couldn't go around because of the mountains - it's very mountainous, Chichi Jima - got too high, pushed over, got too much speed, hit the water, ripped the bottom wide open, and that thing sank in about twenty seconds up to right here.

The wings held up fortunately, and there was the wife of the senior naval officer, with her skirt floating up over her head, just as calm as she could be.

I went over and finally got the door open and got out. We were swimming around quite a while before they sent a boat out to get us.

They were prepared for all this because at Radford High School over there, named for Admiral Radford, here were all these little kids lined up there by the American flag, and here was their special committee, along with all the citizens. The total population was only 403. They had begun to forbid any further intermarriage because of genetic diseases. Many of these younger people said they couldn't do anything there, so they'd go to Guam or the States and get an education. Some would come back, but not many.

So, here I was, all wringing wet. I didn't even have a toothbrush with me, so I went up to Commander Johnson's quarters and he found some khakis and dried my shoes. He was really a wonderful person. So I went down and got up on the porch of the school, made a speech to them, and the other little kids were reciting the pledge, you know, and everything. It was really an impressive thing. Then I went in to talk to the special committee. These people, the Kings, the Washingtons, and names like that, all missionary names, and that's how many of them arrived there. During the war, of course, the Japanese ocupied it. There was over a division of troops. I remember going in there on an air raid. Finally, the place was blockaded and they were practically starved to death. There were American citizens still there.

So, I met with the committee and said:

"I know your feelings, I sympathize with them, and so forth, but this is in the hands of negotiations between the State Department, the ambassador in Tokyo, and the Japanese. I'll do what I can, I'll appeal it as much as I can," which I did, and how much could I do? I didn't know. We'd helped these people quite a bit because we collected a lot of money by patrol vessels from the Japanese who were encroaching on their territorial limits and catching their fish. Every time one was caught, we'd bring him in, confiscate the fish, and fine him. And, with that, we built a great big refrigeration plant, which, as an economic thing, was a big help to them. We built a better school, we built roads, and a lot of things like that, to help the people. So, they said:

"Well, we are very apprehensive of the whole thing because, as you know, the Japanese were in here and there was actual proof that they resorted to cannibalism. Three American pilots were shot down and they were cannibalized."

These people testified against a Japanese general, and he was hanged. So they said, with the Japanese taking over and coming back in there, you can well imagine the situation we're going to be in. And, of course, pretty soon the State Department had the final word on this type of thing. They turned it over to Japan, they came in there, and quite a few of these people got out and went to Guam, and they said it was a horrible situation, besides being a sad one, when we had to leave.

I stayed there about four days because one plane was cracked up and the pilot wouldn't take off in the other plane then. He was scared. Of course, they had a big dinner, a big reception, then a dance, and they'd catch two of these great big turtles. That's where I got that great big shell. They'd have a big feast and everything. Finally, I told this guy:

"Look, if you've got your wind up and you aren't going to take off, I'm going to find some other way to get out of here. I can't stay here any longer."

So I told the aide:

"Look, you contact the people in Yoko and any carrier coming out of there, I don't care where she's headed for, you divert here and bring her by here."

So, the Intrepid came by and launched three helicopters and they came in. That was a big event there. They'd never seen a helicopter.

Q: I guess it was!

Adm. J.: They landed and I got aboard one of them and left with the poor people there, waving good bye.

During that time, I went fishing and I toured the island. It was very interesting to see what the Japanese had done by hand. They had underground railroads all over that island, all the underground storage for ammunition, for food supplies, and even a tea house, where they had the geisha girls.

Q: Was this hollowed out of rock, or what?

Adm. J.: Pure rock, and a lot of it lined with copper, lined with copper!

Q: Where did they get that?

Adm. J.: I don't know.

Q: Extravagant ideas! What would the copper do?

Adm. J.: Well, it would insulate it, keep the moisture out, and keep stuff from falling down. They had a little narrow-guage railroad through there. One favorite pastime was to go up to this place where they had the geisha house, which was no longer there. I guess the custom was, you know, toasts and all this from a cup and then throw it over the side. And, of course, there were thousands and thousands of different design and shapes of saki cups. You could find a lot of these things around there. I was just trying to think who it was who had a tremendous collection of saki cups. The marine general who was the hero of Tarawa, Dave Shoup. He had several hundred of them, each one completely different. He made a collection of them.

Q: Quite something!

Adm. J.: I'm sure it's pretty valuable.
    That was that episode, being the military governor.

Q: Suppose you talk about the role of the Seabees? You mentioned them off-tape this morning.

Adm. J.: Well, the Seabees, once again, for anything that they did they never received the credit and recognition that they deserved. They went into many of these places before you got the big construction companies in there. They constructed Chu Lai, the marine air base. Chu Lai means Krulak in Chinese.

Q: Oh, it does?

Adm. J.: Yes. He picked it out and named it after him.

So, they went in there and built the place. It was marston matting before they could put the more solid stuff down and provided their own security now. Think of that. In many of these places where they went, they provided their own security.

During this time, of course, there were all kinds of congressional medals of honor being given to people, all in the army. Here, at one point, there were navy people doing things that were really not enough to merit the congressional Medal of Honor but certainly as much as some of the army people had done. Every time we sent a recommendation in, he would downgrade it. Finally, we got one approved for one of the bravest actions that anybody ever heard of. A fellow named Shields, a Seabee. He was way out in the boondocks, there were not too many of them there, constructing this outpost in the jungle and he was surrounded by the VC. There were only about twenty of them. They stayed there and they were fighting these people off day and night, and, of course, they would send in word for help because they were really in a bad situation. It came daylight and Shields was still there, very badly wounded and all his buddies killed, and he was still shooting them. Right at the very end, when they went in there, he was still alive, but he died in the helicopter that was taking him back. He was a Seabee, and Westmoreland approved and got the Medal of Honor for him. He was the first navy man to receive the congressional Medal of Honor in Vietnam since the war began. There's a ship named after him. I remember writing to his family.

They were a great outfit of people. Up in Danang, the port facilities, and then the port director and the stevedore battalions, which were part of the Seabees. They could do this sort of a thing, they were professionals. They could build anything, build a field hospital. They built one at Danang and one for the south, and that brings up another thing, the matter of hospital care, because actually, the ratio of people who died to the ones wounded was the lowest of any war we'd ever fought. Why is that? Because, either in the field and later on, I was able to get two hospital ships activated, the Sanctuary and the Consolation, the wounded received almost instant care.

Q: Activated? They had not been in commission, you mean?

Adm. J.: Oh, sure, in World War II, but they were in mothballs.

Q: Yes, they were in mothballs.

Adm. J.: They were activated, and we kept one on station all the time, and, depending on the intensity of action and so forth, we sent it to I Corps or down south. MACV said,

"You favor keeping it up for the marines."

I said, "Well, they're doing more fighting and more people are getting wounded than there are among your troops."

Anyway, my point is that a man would be wounded right on the battlefield and a chopper would lift him and bring him right to the fantail of the hospital ship. They had a blood bank and they had surgeons there to take him below, and they stopped the bleeding. He didn't bleed to death. The day I was on board the ship, they brought in one double amputee and they saved his life.

Q: The helicopter was a tremendous advantage, wasn't it?

Adm. J.: Made all the difference.

Q: The helicopters were under - the marines had theirs?

Adm. J.: Oh, yes, they insisted, also the marine air. That was another big fight, because the Seventh Air Force, which was under MACV, wanted control of all air in Vietnam. At one time, he was talking about controlling all air strikes from the carriers. It's interesting how people think.

Q: Well, that's the unification fight all over again, isn't it?

Adm. J.: Well, worse than that, but the marines wouldn't give at all. In the case of Danang, you see, the Air Force wanted control of the F-4s in there, even though they said, OK, you're responsible for providing the air defense of the

Danang air base. Well, of course, that didn't make any sense, so they accepted responsibility for perimeter defense and air defense. But they would have operational control of all the combatant elements involved in there.

The carriers - that was a big fight. Gee, that went on and on. The Seventh Air Force, he wanted to do the selection of the targets, the designation of the targets to be hit. You see, after we got the targeting broadened a little bit, we could go in there almost on a continuous basis and use a big target list. It was a matter of selecting them out. 7th Air Force wanted to do that from Tan San Nhut, Saigon. There was a task for the air force with their 104s, which was coming all the way from Thailand, and there were the carriers up there, half the distance they had to go. They would say, "We're going into this area there, and by virtue of that, you go into this area." Well, that was no good.

So, there was a big conference, and Admiral Sharp prompted this, whereby we came up with package areas, Package Area 1, 2, 3, 4, 5, and the air force was assigned to some of them and the navy to the others, and these were our areas of responsibility for hitting targets. Furthermore, we finally forced them to agree to our sending a contingent from the Seventh Fleet in to Saigon to sit by the Seventh Air Force to coordinate all this. They didn't like that.

Q: No, to see that -

Adm. J.: We were spying on them. Well, in effect, we were, and we had good reason to be. These guys would cut you out of the pattern if you didn't watch them. So we sent some pretty sharp people down there. One of them was Buddy Yates. I'll never forget. The air force guys said, "Thank God, that guy has gone." Were they glad to see him go! He kept right after them, you see. They were so narrow-minded.

Q: At one point, the riverine people wanted helicopters and they couldn't get them and, to this day, blame Tom Moorer for not being able to get them. He told me that he tried awfully hard but he couldn't.

Adm. J.: They finally did get helicopters, but for a long time they couldn't get them, couldn't get them allocated.

Q: The air force had all of them?

Adm. J.: The air force had hundreds and hundreds in South Vietnam. The type they wanted, of course, was the attack helicopter. But, anyway, they finally did get some and they were the ones that were landing on this little LST, to support them. On call - if they got into trouble, call the helicopters. Well, it was a natural thing to have.

Q: Off-tape this morning, you were talking about Camranh Bay, and I wish you'd tell me on-tape about it, the development of the base.

Adm. J.: In the early days of when I was ComSeventhFleet, we were attracted to the possibilities of Camranh Bay and its future use. We were studying the map and looking around for potential anchorages and seaplane operating areas, because we still had some seaplanes out there then. I went into Camranh Bay with the mining outfit, the Seventh Fleet Mining Force. They went in there and pretty well surveyed the place. It's a beautiful harbor, well protected, mountains on almost every side, except the north, where it was flat. It had been a pretty big French anchorage, and then the Japanese took it over. So we surveyed it, depths of water, and even put in places for anchorages, where you would anchor if we sent a lot of ships in there. We also checked it out for seaplane operations, anchorages for seaplanes, etc. We got approval to do all this, of course, from the State Department and from the Vietnamese.

Q: What was their job, the seaplanes operating there?

Adm. J.: Patrol, coastal patrol. We had four or five squadrons out there.

Then, of course, as the war in Vietnam began to escalate, the marines were up in Danang, which became a tremendous base. It pretty soon was congested because they got a lot of air force people in there. At that time, going back to this argument I pointed out a while ago, they said, "We have air-defense responsibility to put our planes in there." They did until the marines took it over. So, as someone said, it was probably the busiest airport in the world, take-offs every second.

That was Danang.

Then, of course, the army took over Chu Lai, which the marines had built. Then they had a big base at Qui Nonh, four or five places down the coast, where they had their enclaves Camranh Bay was one, and this was one of the biggest complexes of all. The navy had a coastal surveillance unit in there, that's all we had. They put in these long piers, the DeLang pier so big freighters could come in there. They had plenty of water. And they built these runways, several thousand feet long. They built this great big tank farm, ammunition storage, barracks for two divisions of troops. That's what LBJ went through and made his famous speech to all the army troops. Do you remember that?

Q: Yes. It was reported in the paper.

Adm. J.: They even had a hospital there, and all of this was done under contract with the famous RMK outfit, Raymond, Martin, Knudsen combine a tremendous construction outfit.

Q: Where were they based, in Hawaii?

Adm. J.: Somewhere in the United States. They're international, they built stuff all over the world. They'll build anything. They went in there pretty much with a blank check, get it done immediately, all horizontal infrastructures, and they'd go in there and do this. It was a crash program. They did a wonderful job and, of course, with all this equipment, all kinds of cranes, earth-moving equipment, bulldozers, trucks and everything. When they finished it, everything was left right there, never moved a thing. They moved on to another place and brought in new equipment. It didn't make any difference. That was the easy way to do it.

Q: Was that their equipment or was it government equipment?

Adm. J.: It was their equipment but we were paying for it, millions and millions of dollars.

Q: And they replaced it when they went on to another project?

Adm. J.: Sure. It was amazing to see it. The last time I saw the place, it was still there, all over the place. Of course, there was jungle growing up around it.

That was another casualty of the Vietnam War. Goodness knows how much equipment like that, aircraft, trucks, tanks, helicopters, fell into the hands of the Vietnamese when we so hurriedly pulled out of there. We left a lot of stuff in there for the Vietnamese. Our troops were coming out.

Q: Hearing you tell this, I don't feel so badly about - I've heard the story about the Korean contingent down there, and when they went home, they just went back with the greatest amount of booty. But, if it was going to be left, why, I guess it was just as useful to them as it was to anybody else.

Adm. J.: That seems to be the thing to do in a war. When we went in to take Samar - of course, that was a MacArthur operation even though they were supported by PacFlt. So, when they went ashore there were literally thousands of trucks and jeeps, and you see the jeeps around Manila today. They were taken from this tremendous stockpile that was left and was never taken out.

Q: Is this strictly an American policy or do other nations do the same? Did the British do the same?

Adm. J.: I doubt it. I don't know. I think they're a little big more frugal than that. It's just a matter of wasting it. You would think they would certainly try to salvage some of this stuff. Some of it hadn't even been uncrated. It was brand-new.

Q: I know the argument raised by some man who said that - Admiral Cook - the argument was raised that American industry did not want these things to come back to the mainland.

Adm. J.: Of course not. They wanted to keep on manufacturing things, to keep the production lines going, so they could make more money. They knew that the production line was going to be severely cut back, anyway, when the war was over.

Now you go to all those islands and you'll find the jungle growing up around airplanes and trucks that we operated in southeast Asia, in Guadalcanal. A group went down there not too long ago who had actually been in combat in Guadalcanal, and told about the things they found down there.

Q: They recognized them?

Adm. J.: Yes, reminiscent of the days when they were there.

Q: When you were CinCPacFlt, you received a citation for an award that was simply spectacular, I've never seen one like it! There are various points mentioned in it that I'd like to bring up with you. In a general sense, they say your ability to master the complexities of integrating and applying new techniques was outstanding, and then they go on to enumerate various things and, under new tactics, the nuclear-powered ships that were in the fleet at that time. Do you want to say something about them and the problems that they raised?

Adm. J.: About the only nuclear-powered ships we had then, Jack, were the submarines.

Q: Didn't we have the Enterprise, the carrier?

Adm. J.: That's right, the Enterprise did come out later on. She came all the way around and we put her on the Dixie Station.

Q: Hank Miller brought her out there?

Adm. J.: That's when he had his famous conference on board with the press and, before the eyes of the press, two F-4s ran out of fuel and went in the drink.

In spite of this flowery language here, there was no problem involved in integrating nuclear ships into anything in the way of naval operations, task-force operations, or anything. If anything, the traditional problems are eased because you don't have to worry about refueling air planes.

The only worry is the avgas.

In the way of new tactics and so forth, we were always trying to improve on the way we operated the carrier forces up in the Gulf of Tonkin. I had some concern that we were getting into bad habits because, here, in a relatively confined space for fast carriers your breathing room in terms of radar detection and so forth gets pretty cramped, so I wanted to make sure we didn't try to get too close, even though that would simplify your operations. So you had to be constantly thinking about the optimum in air-defense formations and making optimum use of the kind of ships you had, which was always changing. We were getting a different mix all the time of missile ships versus the conventional, trying to make optimum use of them in formations and tactical equipment, plus you had the problem of identification and avoiding mutual interference using surface-to-air missiles at the same time you had combat air patrols, fighters from a carrier. You couldn't just go ahead and start firing these things with fighters up there, flying around. You had to have some means of separating this out and coordinating it.

Q: They had enough flak aimed at them from the SAMs, didn't they?

Adm. J.: Oh, sure against aircraft but this is about the task force. How far out to extend the fighter defense, that's what we were to do, extend them beyond the inner missile defense, except then you had something like Talos that could go way out to 100 miles, so you didn't want to send the fighters out much beyond that. It was a matter, really, of having some sort of doctrine whereby, up to a point, you depended on the pilots and if, at that point, the bombers or whatever it was were still coming through, you pulled them off and turned them over to the missiles. That doesn't sound too efficient but it was almost the only thing you could do, unless you wanted to try to separate them by altitude, which wasn't feasible. So that became the problem and we were always working on that. Even when I left, I didn't think it was completely satisfactory. There will always be a problem as long as you have airplanes and missiles mixed up in the same operations around a carrier task force. Once again, in addition trying to get something in the way of reasonable ASW defense. When we were up there, there were no submarines but, at times, we'd get a scare that maybe the Chinese had given the North Vietnamese some submarines, so, in desperation, they'd come out and there you are.

A couple of times we were given a scare on this and actually criticized all the way back - this was when I was Seventh Fleet - in Honolulu and Washington about how vulnerable we were to submarine attacks. There were some holes in the defense we had, so they didn't want to see anybody get into a compromise because your disposition of support units is completely different for air defense and ASW. In air defense, you tend to move them out, in ASW, you pull them in. Normally, you're not going to have enough to put them in both places, so you have to find some compromise and hopefully have something in the way of ASW air. Well, initially, we had ASW air, an ASW carrier. As long as we had him, I would send him up ahead and pretty well try to sanitize an area of sea of submarines. Well, pretty soon, we just had him about half the time, so you had to depend on patrol planes then.

Q: You never actually found any submarines, did you?

Adm. J.: No. Oh, we had a few false detections, I think they were whales or something else, but these people seemed to think, based on some intelligence that I never had access to, that there were actually submarines down there that maybe had been given to the North Vietnamese by the Red Chinese. At one time, there was a pretty good scare on that, but nothing ever came of it.

Those were some of the tactics. Also, in some ways, it was more important to keep trying to evolve new tactics, different tactics, and at the same time introducing the new equipment we were getting, to minimize your losses, the vulnerability of the aircraft. Once they introduced the SAMs that was a bad deal. We could pretty well tell where the thing was coming from, and there they were down there, but had no authority to attack on the spot.

Q: But you couldn't attack the base?

Adm. J.: We couldn't attack the battery. We began to get countermeasure equipment. In other words, you'd get a beep and a red light when a SAM was approaching, then, of course, he would be thrown off and aborted.

Q: That was part of the electronic equipment that came in?

Adm. J.: Oh, yes, you'd get the beep, you see, and that told the pilot he'd better do something because, otherwise, he was going to get it.

The air force tended toward a more action approach. In other words, they carried all this massive equipment, one plane equipped with this in every three or four, whereby in an area where suspected SAMs were being launched they would turn these things on and they would completely jam or throw out of kilter the whole homing mechanism in the thing. That's all right, but we went the other route - the passive concept.

We developed the Piraz, what we called the Piraz system, and this was the pilots' identification zone thing, to make sure that anything that came in, we identified it as friendly or enemy, because we never knew when one of these MIGs around Hanoi might come out, and at times they did.

Q: That was much more of a threat than submarines?

Adm. J.: Oh, sure, because it was there, you see it there, and, of course, it was a long, long time before McNamara let us send airplanes in there to attack the MIGs. They were sitting there and, when I left - well, anyway, to go back to Piraz, that was a matter of disposition and putting certain kinds of ships in certain locations to assist in sanitizing these aircraft coming in and determining whether they were enemy or friend. Then, at the same time, having two SAR units up forward, thereby they'd be in a position, if anybody came back with his plane shot up, wounded, or something, to pick them up.

Then we got the Long Beach. She was all-missile, with the Talos missile. By that time, with the advance elements of this formation, the Talos was in range of Hanoi. Well, we tried and we tried and we tried, and with the detection on the Long Beach they could actually get a lock on to fire these Talos at airplanes circling above Hanoi. No, you can't do that! After I left, they finally got approval and they knocked one down.

Q: Did they really?

Adm. J.: Yes. Why the reluctance there? They were just afraid they were going to scare up, intimidate somebody, and they'd come rushing in. Simply no way of understanding. No one ever understands. I bet if we prepared one mining plan, we prepared ten. I'm not exaggerating, mostly back at CinCPacFlt, different ways, but the more economic way to do it and the least costly, probably, was the airplanes. They'd go in there and drop a relatively few mines with all kinds of different devices on them whereby they can't be swept, whether they be pressure, magnetic, or acoustic.

So, it's an easy thing, it's a very effective thing, and it doesn't cost you very much to put in in there.

Q: Was it like the actual mining of Haiphong?

Adm. J.: That's what we're talking about.

Q: Which was a very simple operation.

Adm. J.: It didn't take many mines and it was closed.

Q: There were only five or six mines, I understand, weren't there?

Adm. J.: Oh, there were a couple of dozen, but airplanes did that in a couple of minutes.

Q: Those plans had been in existence for a long time?

Adm. J.: Oh, years. We planned that idea a long time.

Q: When Tom Moorer talked about it, he implied that Nixon was really shocked when he said, "How long will it take you to plan an operation," and he said, "Those plans have been in existence for eight years." It took them fifteen minutes or something like that!

Adm. J.: Tom Moorer said it, you have to give him credit. He sold Nixon on that idea.

Q: Yes.

Adm. J.: Before that, of course, they said, "Well, we'll let you mine. You can go into the estuaries and the waterways that empty into the Gulf of Tonkin and you can use the Destructor" which was a 500-pound bomb with a contact detonator, I guess. And we did, we dropped hundreds and hundreds of those things, but, heck, they were easily disarmed. I think we sank one ferry.

Q: Do you want to say something about the tactical data system?

Adm. J.: Well, there was a number of sophisticated tactical data systems in the Fleet. I'm sure there were. But what we had on most of the big carriers was a system which operated in conjunction with the RA5C. The RA5C is the old Vigilante, which was converted into a reconnaissance airplane. They were very sophisticated electronic reconnaissance, photo reconnaissance and had a means of getting back all the data acquired automatically to the ship. They could take these data and put them into a computer, and store them or analyze them, and bring out instant intelligence to be used against the enemy, against defense installations, and, in some cases, against SAM sites or other targets. This was an extension of the NTDS, but it was related to it, computerized and everything. It was a very effective way that the RA5Cs had.

Q: It would have been wonderful, if not impeded by Washington?

Adm. J.: Well, not necessarily Washington - more at regional level. In other words you couldn't always exploit it in a real time basis. And, of course, we had the EC-121, which was the Connie, the Constellation. They must have had twelve or fifteen console radars. People who knew Vietnamese, you see. They were always listening on station in the Gulf of Tonkin. This is the airplane that was shot down off Korea, you know, after the Pueblo incident.

They would pick up all this intelligence, and furthermore it's not stale. That is good new raw intelligence.

Then they would send it back. Well, here, these people insisted, because it was there and MACV wanted to get in the act, that all of this had to go through some land-based outfit to be scrubbed. Then they'd take out what they needed from it and would pass it on to the carrier task force commander, which was utter nonsense since it was no longer current. We finally got that changed but it took a long time to do so.

So, the tactical data system had come of age, really, it was beginning to at that time, even though you've got to be careful with computers. First of all, they don't always function the way they should. If you put garbage into a computer, you're going to get garbage out.

Q: Communication by satellites was coming in, too, wasn't it?

Adm. J.: Yes, but we weren't making any extensive use of it then that I know of, because most of that, you see, was probably what you'd call starategic communications. Ours was tactical.

Q: It could be used in terms of ocean surveillance, however?

Adm. J.: Oh, yes and then you could use it tactically. You could bounce it off and it would come back and it would probably be more reliable and maybe less subject to jamming, certainly less subject to any weather interference. But we were using mostly UHE. It had been tried and was proven, and the other was just coming in. By now, I'm sure they do it all the time.

Johnson #3 -324-

Q: Did you have SEALs down there in Vietnam waters?

Adm. J.: Oh, sure. They operated in the delta under Paul Grey.

Q: Yes, I see.

Adm. J.: Two or three of them were lost. Several of those boys were lost. They were really an elite group of people.

Q: They had a raid on a cadre of the VC, didn't they, caught them at a funeral or something?

Adm. J.: They made several raids on one VC outfit. They came in and I think a helicopter let them down. They could parachute onto airfields, put them in the water - they had on their UDT suits - and went ashore underwater and really cleaned out this outfit. It was a surprise and they could usually get away with it, but it was a hazardous thing. I don't think I could have gone for that. They're a wonderful outfit. I hope they still keep them in existence, even though they did away with riverine warfare as a force in being.

Q: You had to be pretty young to be a member of that outfit, didn't you?

Adm. J.: Yes and very dedicated.

Q: Yes!

Adm. J.: The UDP people have a training outfit at Fort Story They're still in existence. They're physical outfit, too.

But I repeat, it's just too bad that at one time they did not keep a nucleus of riverine warfare craft and people to keep the state of the art alive. They tested and made improvements, innovations, and so forth. This was a relatively new thing. It was done, but not on a very large scale in other operations.

Q: Well, in a comparable sense, mine warfare is something the navy doesn't seem to keep up with either in peacetime.

Adm. J.: No, both the minelaying and the minesweeping. They have certain techniques, but actually, in terms of their capability, it's very limited. They did sweep Haiphong and the Suez Canal, very true, and I guess as long as you have airplanes that can carry the mines, they're probably good enough for minelaying and that's the most economic way to do it. But minesweeping causes a lot of worry. Submarines can come in and lay a lot of mines and you'd never know it, then you've got to get rid of them. They've been experimenting with this towed device, towed by a helicopter that comes over and is supposed to sweep most of the mines, not all of them. They can sweep the pressure mines without any doubt, and, of course, they explode them right there.

Q: Yes, so as not to endanger the plane.

Adm. J.: Right. Now we seem to ignore that branch of warfare. They used to come under Commander, Mine Force, Atlantic, at Charleston. I don't know whether he's still in existence even. I doubt it.

Q: That goes back to what you said yesterday, it's not very glamorous!

Adm. J.: No, but, of course, there are some enthusiasts like the fellow who wrote the prize essay of the Naval Institute about mine warfare and the Navy neglect of it.

Q: Bob Salzer was very interested. I tried to get him to write a story, too.

Adm. J.: Well, you trace the history of mines and they've been used effectively in so many different instances. You take the North Sea minefield. That really gave the Germans a bad time.

Q: The thing that we should be concerned about, I believe, is the fact that the Russians obviously have always been interest in mine warfare.

Adm. J.: We know from intelligence that they're continually manufacturing large numbers of mines. Of course, they're also mixed up in germ warfare. We've pretty much forsaken that.

Q: Do you have anything to say about intelligence-collection in the Vietnam conflict? How useful was it to you as CinCPacFlt?

Adm. J.: Well, we depended on it quite a bit, and we had special "spooks", as we called them, whereby these people collected special intelligence by intercepts, you know and then they would analyze it. That's intelligence-gathering at the tactical level, not the national level. Many times, I think that at the CinCPac level we were too slow to do much good. What they had at the time was good.

The best element of intelligence-gathering, I think, during the Vietnam War was in the case of North Vietnam. They had real good information and photographs of all these possible targets. Of course, we weren't allowed to hit them, but that's another matter. But they had a very good collection of that. You were using drones to fly over and take pictures. Where the intelligence broke down very badly, and I don't know what you could do about it, was in the field in South Vietnam, on the movements, the concentrations, and so forth of the VC and of the North Vietnamese when they moved down. It was woefully inadequate.

Q: It was pretty hard to pinpoint that sort of thing.

Adm. J.: Yes. It was different. It was a different problem than they ever had before. You almost have to have something in the way of dedicated, brave, sort of coast-watcher-type persons to infiltrate and have little radios, and they could detect all this and send it back. They had some of that but not enough. Of course, that was a pretty hazardous thing.

Some of the other intelligence-gathering, as I said before, from the RA5C and the EC-121 was very good. It wasn't always made available as soon as it should have been because somebody else was injecting himself in the chain of communications and slowing it down.

Q: Will you say something about the service force and its operations in the Vietnam conflict?

Adm. J.: This was another outstanding effort on the part of the navy. We finally created Commander, Service Force, Seventh Fleet, and put him down in and around the Gulf of Tonkin. He was in command of all the Service Force ships down there. Before that, all these ships were out there at random with ammunition ships, oilers, AKs, beef boats, and what not, and it was left up pretty much to TF-77, the carrier guy, to coordinate what they were doing and to replenish all the ships in there, which, pretty soon, became quite a number. That's why we established this task force designation. He was in charge of all these ships and he kept them together and went up there, and all the carrier force people had to do was let him be aware of what their needs were and when, and he would work out the schedule and send these ships up there. That improved the efficiency of this a hundredfold. That was at sea.

The other big job the Service Force did, and I think I mentioned that yesterday, was the resupply in places like Danang, Camranh Bay, and Saigon. That was a very tricky operation. Even in Saigon. It was under the navy for a long time.

Q: They maintained supply dumps and what have you in the Philippines, didn't they, Guam?

Adm. J.: Yes, there was quite a stockpile in there. Of course, some items were in short supply a lot of times, like aviation spare parts, you had to bring them direct. You couldn't wait for them to be stockpiled.

Practically all your ammo came out of Cubi Point, Subic. A lot of your stores, canned goods and all that stuff, that was put on the ships, and a lot of that came out of the Philippines, too. Not, of course, the ideal thing, and we began to get one-stop replenishment. Had a helicopter platform - it was a big ship, a helicopter, and with the pilots you'd do the replenishment of a lot of things by the helicopter over to the carriers, to the cruisers, and so forth. You could take on black oil, you could take on aviation gasoline, food supplies, aviation spare parts, and you'd get everything in just one stop at a ship, so that was the ideal ship to have.

Q: Like a commissary, isn't it!

Adm. J.: Yes. Of course, they were using an enormous amount of ammunition, with all the tonnage of bombs they were dropping and rockets they were firing. And, of course, there were casualties at times, the airmen, and it really came to light in a very important way that the massive amount of ammunition and ordnance that we were using, in some cases without knowing that you were violating almost self-evident safety precautions. You were beginning to get overconfident and careless and that's what happened on the Forrestal when a rocket went off and pierced a fuel tank on a jet. Things really exploded in a hell of a hurry. Then it became obvious that we did not have the right kind of firefighting equipment. First of all, we had nothing to get rid of these things that were burning. That's why they put these big bulldozers in, so they could just throw all this stuff off the flight deck. We were using the wrong type of liquid to put on the fires. Foam is all right, foam's OK on a gasoline fire. So they came out with what they called Purple K. That's much more effective in really smothering a fire and getting it out. The answer to all of this, of course, is getting the initial stage under control before it spread into a conflagration, getting it under control. Those things are found on the carriers now, as a result of the experience we had on the Oriskany and on the Forrestal. That's when they lost all these pilots. They had all these flares stacked up, some guy went down and tripped one. Well a flare with a magnesium you know the kind of a blaze that makes, and all this smoke. It went into the officers' country and these pilots suffocated. There was no alarm and they had no way of getting out of their staterooms.

Q: It almost seems, however, Admiral, that you have to have an experience like this in order to learn?

Adm. J.: Yes.

Q: No one had the foresight to anticipate.

Adm. J.: I won't argue with it at all. I think that's - people keep saying, well, why didn't you think about this before. Well, they thought the equipment they had was adequate because they had had some instances where they had controlled the fire. Something like the Forrestal. That was different, though, because they lost 106 men. I'm president of the Forrestal Memorial Educational Foundation. All the crew on there contributed money, and they now have $89,000. Fifty-three little kids were orphaned, and the money is to be used for their education. Amazingly enough, some of them never applied for it. Six people were retired for physical disability, and two of them who were entitled to $1,500 out of this never claimed his money.

Out of the fifty-three kids, they're beginning to get to the age of high school and junior college. The number now is about sixteen, so we take the $89,000 and say we have fifty of them left, you divide fifty into that, and that's what they get to help them with their education. From time to time, we get contributions from other people. We have it invested, of course.

Q: Oh, yes, and probably drawing good interest.

Adm. J.: It's pretty good. Part of it's in bonds and some of it in stocks. We did have trouble with the IRS, of course. You know the court ruling that foundations cannot escape under the non-profit hiding, you see. They were trying to tell us we were a profit organization because we were making money in this investment.

Q: The end result was charity.

Adm. J.: True. They finally gave us a favorable ruling.

There were so many lessons that came out of Vietnam on survival. Survial of equipment and aircraft, they lea ed a lot of lessons in that regard.

It's a heck of a thing to see a pilot come down with a parachute being dragged by the parachute on the water and drown Of course, now they have this thing that's acted upon by salt water and automatically releases the parachute. I saw a pilot drown that way. We picked him up but he'd drowned. A parachute in a strong wind, you know, with waves, and it doesn't take long, if you're on the water, you're going to drown.

Q: Say something about the rescue operations that were effective.

adm. J.: Well, as I said the other day, this is one of the great stories of the war -

Q: You didn't say it on tape. That's why I asked.

Adm. J.: That has never been fully told. I suppose some of it, in the usual official language, is contained in some of the battle reports and so forth, but probably not all of them were told in a manner that really gives you the human side of it and the sacrifice in the things that were involved in rescuing these people, not only on the part of the people in the rescue helicopter or whatever it was, but also the guy who was being rescued.

One kid, the pilot of an KD5C bailed out, and they saw him walking on the beach, so they were going to pick him up. Well, for the North Vietnames, that's a prize thing, to get the pilot.

Our men had these little pencil lights. You could press this thing and it would fire its projectile. It was a pretty lethal thing. This Vietnamese came up. (The pilots weren't wearing pistols, we wore pistols in World War II). The pilot took this thing and shot him right through the head; he got rid of him. Then he was able to survive by runing along the beach. The chopper got him, pulled him out.

Q: He was just in time!

Adm. J.: Yes. Of course, there were many, many other stories- the ones you wonder about and some of the kids that I knew actually talked to you. They had this little radio. They could talk to somebody in the airplane, on the ground. The chopper was circling and they saw one pilot and talked to him, and they came in with a helicopter but they never saw him again. His body has never been recovered, never returned.

Q: You can speculate on how he disappeared and why.

Adm. J.: Well, the North Vietnamese got him and I'm sure in many cases they were killed. They wouldn't last very long, depending on what happened.

Q: They're the unrecorded ones we hear about from time to time.

Adm. J.: Yes, and, of course Dieter Dingler came out, the only one who really escaped overland by himself.

I told the story about how they picked him up. There are so many, many more, all these different stories of the people were saved.

Q: After their long incarceration, those who were made prisoners the story of the navy's handling of them when they came back is a tremendous story. The navy just did a beautiful job and still does, I think.

Qdm. J.: Yes, and it's amazing how quickly these people were able to rehabilitate, absolutely amazing. A lot of them didn't make it through.

Q: Don't you think some of them still bear the scars?

Adm. J.: To different degrees. The strongest, you'd never notice it, even though they keep signs because they still bear some of it mentally, if not physically.

Well, of course, talking to Dick Stratton, Jerry Denton, and some of these people, these were the strong ones, of course and there were some, they just didn't make it. They couldn't hack it, and they broke. Unless you were a strong person like Jerry Denton.

Q: Oh, he carries scars too. Some of the others do likewise.

Adm. J.: Oh, yes, but, of course, with the communist techniques and tactics and the brainwashing they did, unless you're a very strong person and believed in certain things and stick with it, they can break you. After all, Cardinal Mindzenty was broke. I have a classmate, who was the son of a Marine Corps general. He was in Korea, a marine aviator and had a wonderful reputation, a colonel. He and this other marine were up, flying around getting flight time, and they wandered over the lines and they shot him down, so they took him in. They kept him in solitary for months and months, gave him the water treatment, which must be pretty horrible. They finally broke him and he confessed that we were using germ warfare - I don't know whether you know this story or not.

Q: No, I don't.

Adm. J.: Oh, yes. Of course, when the armistice was signed, this marine officer was returned. He was brought back and the Marine Corps court-martialed him. They were completely unforgiving in his case, and the sentence was that forever, for the rest of his career he could never have command of any unit that had marines in it. He lives in Washington. I see him every now and then. He was in pretty bad shape at one time but he's come out of it pretty well.

Q: Well, most of them -

Adm. J.: Since that time, the code for POWs has been modified.

Q: Necessarily!

Adm. J.: Yes. In other words, you could give them you name. Before, all you could do was give them your serial number and so forth.

Q: Most of them, as far as I can observe, were broken and recovered again, they weren't permanently broken. They simply had to give in.

Adm. J.: Some, but not too many. Some of them died, they couldn't stand it.

Q: Speaking of your tour of duty as CinCPacFlt, other than Vietnam, were there other elements that were of historical concern? Was there any discussion in your time of Diego Garcia?

Adm J.: No, not then, not there, but, when I was in Op-93, in long-range objectives planning, I had the job and I told you about Stu Barber.

Q: Yes.

Adm. J.: He was always thinking, always thinking ahead, so he picked out a place, he brought the map in to me and showed it to me, and I said:

"Oh heck, it's too isolated way down there. What the heck do we need with the place." He said:

"It's near the Persian Gulf, oil emirates. One day, we're going to be interested in something like this."

So I said OK, we wrote up position papers, made a study of it, and even mapped as best we could the geographic layout of the atolls and so forth. We submitted that to the CNO, and it was just more or less thrown in the circular file, no attention paid to it. Well, this guy would never give up, so he finally had this paper - it even went to the Joint Chiefs.

Of course, the first thing to do was contact the State Department, contact the British, and get an agreement for us to go out there and survey it. Then, if it showed any promise, go in there and develop it, assuming we could get the money. That was way back at that time.

Well, you simply couldn't get to first base until the obvious necessity for something hit you right in the face, and it finally did that.

Q: The Joint Chiefs had the same kind of imagination?

Adm. J.: Yes. Jack McCain pushed it when he was CinCPac.

Q: I know he did -

Adm. J.: We pushed it as much as we could. We even had ships go by there, go in there and photograph it, because that was part of the CinCPacFlt's area of responsibility.

Q: When I rode in Jack McCain's plane, he was using another plane to get out there, because he was going out to Diego Garcia to see what was going on.

Adm. J.: That was his Fifth Fleet concept, you see. That's what we have now, even though they don't call it that. I don't know why they don't.

I'll never forget Stu Barber. He's the first person I know of, and I think this was absolutely correct, ever to come up with ideas about Diego Garcia.

Q: Did you not, in your command, have cognizance of the South Pacific, the Antarctic? Doesn't that come under the -?

Adm. J.: Resupply, resupply of the Antarctic. Otherwise, it was a special operation under the CNO. But we had the resupply for it. I never had any desire to go down there.

Q: You were not a Byrd-minded man!

Adm. J.: No.

Howard Caldwell tells the great stories. He was in that plane that crashed down there, and kept all these guys from going to sleep and freezing to death. He was a pretty stalwart guy. He was the guy who kept them alive so they could be rescued.

In PacFleet, one thing we did there that a lot of other people copied - Of Course, CinCPac had its own photointerpretatio and would make up all the different intelligence packets for targeting and so forth. Well, we had within CinCPacFlt a couple of kids who were really experts in this, targeting, analysis, and so forth, and taking the benefit of all this intelligence coming in, and they could portray this in a way that even the ordinary layman could understand. Even Buzz Wheeler could understand, and from this, and part of it ran through a computer - you see, you could finally sift out of this the target worth of all these different things, the vulnerability to aircraft attacking, all these different things. Then catalogue that, and we'd send it out to the people in the carriers and they would use it. That was the basis for a lot of tactics and, if they had any choice, of the targets they selected to hit.

Q: It helped determine priorities, too?

Adm. J.: Sure, that was the first thing you went after, and that was created by CinCPacFlt. Buzz Wheeler came over with Oley Sharp and said:

"Oh, I'm sure the army has something that's much better than this."

Well, they didn't. Later on, they pretty well copied what we had. It was no better than what CinCPac had, even though they had all these grandiose facilities and all these data-processing things going on, and fancy equipment. It was something unique -

Q: Your staff there in Hawaii was very large, wasn't it?

Adm. J.: Oh, sure.

Q: Very complex. Do you want to say something about that? The staff meetings with CinCPac and that sort of thing?

Adm. J.: Well, within the ocean area we were involved in and all the forces under him,(which in the end numbered over 400,000 at one time,) and the variety of operations, all the planning that had to go along with this, together with the day-to-day operational things that you're involved in, even in peacetime, meant that you had to have a lot of professional people - the intelligence part of it, the operations part of it, the plans part of it, and logistics, even though you had Commander, Service Force, Pacific, who was Ed Hooper, a separate command in a separate building. He did pretty much of the nuts and bolts, the physical part of it, and organizi the ships, the rotation of the ships, and so forth, whereby in logistics we were tying together the requirements of this for the operational side of it.

So, you had a deputy for operations, you had a deputy for plans, you had a deputy for intelligence, logistics, and, of course, it was up to the deputy to pull all this together through the staff meetings. You'd have a morning briefing to bring you up to date on what the situation was, particularly, of course, in Vietnam, but we would have done it before that. And, from that, certain directives would be issued, certain decisions made, and people would go off and do their business.

Meetings with CinCPac? Not very many special meetings, unless there was a special crisis, like McNamara was coming to town or Wheeler was coming to town, or Taylor, or somebody of some prominence. But, every other morning we had to go up to his headquarters for his very comprehensive briefing by his experts, with a great big wall map up there showing the whole area, and pinpointing the things that were happening and so forth. There, he could question the component commanders and in the back you had selected people who accompanied you, who knew about operations or other things. There was an exchange of ideas and cross communications.

Q: You had feed-in from the State Department, didn't you?

Adm. J.: Yes, he had Polad. He was from the State Department.

Q: I remember this was a controversy because Stump didn't want one!

Adm. J.; Felix didn't, but at times, depending on who it was - he'd never contribute too much, but a good one could contribute an awful lot, because he was the means of the navy getting a feel and understanding of something that, otherwise, you might have trouble with and take a long time to do.

Q: Yes.

Adm. J.: He had good Polads out there, as a rule. He talked with the ambassadors on occasion, including Bill Sullivan, who was just as bad as McNamara. He was over in Iran, you know. He was ambassador in Laos and then later on in Vietnam. Here in Laos he was the one responsible for these silly rules of engagement we had to conform to over there, like armed recces. You couldn't fire a gun unless somebody shot at you. You were looking for trucks carrying military equipment and, if they were on a road, moving, you could attack them; if they were not moving, no. If they were stopped on a bridge, you couldn't attack them. This sort of a thing.

Q: Who would know, other than the person on the ground?

Adm. J.: That's the stupidity of it, that anybody would come up with an idea like that. So, here he comes in, and somebody had mistakenly bombed a village and killed some natives. So he immediately assumed that it was a Navy pilot. He went to the Naval Academy, so he sent out his famous message, "Tecumseh weeps today," and he went on to really castigate the pilot for dropping his bombs on this village and killing the people. So I got Admiral Jack Monroe out of the Philippines and sent him up there to investigate. Luckily, he found parts of the bomb that had serial numbers on there and it said "U.S. Air Force."

Do you think Sullivan ever said anything about that after we told him? No. No apology or retraction. He blamed West Point.

He was pretty grim at times. He wasn't much better in Saigon, I don't think.

Q: How was Bunker? Was he there when you were there?

Adm. J.: It's like a supreme court justice. When people get to a certain age, I think the thing to do is get out of there, even though it varies with different ones. I think he ought to be retired because I just don't think his mind is as sharp as it was at one time or as it should have been, and I think Ellsworth Bunker was in this category. That's why I was so distressed when I learned he was going to negotiate the Panama Canal Treaty. I said:

"Well, if he's going down there, we've had it. With him and Linowitz, we've had it."

Out there in Vietnam - oh, gee, dealing with the North Vietnamese? Totally, woefully inadequate, really.

Q: Was Henry Cabot Lodge much better?

Adm. J.: Cabot Lodge was a good man, yes. I had a lot of respect for him. He had a lot of smarts on the diplomatic touch, he had a lot of good, common horsesense. He knew how to reason with people, he knew how to be tough with people, he knew how to negotiate with people, he knew how to work with the military. He liked the military, he respected the military. He was a good man. He was the best of any of them we had out there, including General Taylor.

You can send military people as a rule to a job and have them perform as ambassador. I guess Admiral Kirk probably did it as well as anybody. Then, who else? Admiral Standley, he was no good. He went over to Moscow.

Q: Kirk was no good in Taiwan?

Adm. J.: Kirk was in Moscow, not Taiwan.

Q: He didn't even speak to the generalissimo!

Adm. J.: You must be referring to Jerry Wright, a respected man. I have a very high regard for him.

In general, military men aren't cut out for that sort of thing. Fortunately, we don't have a real State Department academy or something. Where do we get these guys, career people? Where do they come from? Georgetown?

Q: Well, yes, Foreign Service schools, they're supposed to be trained at.

Adm. J.: Basically, we should have a national Foreign Service academy or something. One of the real good Foreign Service schools in the country was Georgetown. I don't know whether that's still good or not.

Q: It is. It's still paramount, I think. There are a couple of others, too.

Adm. J.: But then, where you become cross threaded on this whole thing is when you become involved with all the political appointees. Of course, some of them were probably better than some of the career people.

Q: Isn't that the fallacy of the system. It also involves some of these retired military people who have never been in politics.

Adm. J.: Yes, mature guys at the end of their careers. You see people like this going to big jobs. To me, if I was trying to be a career diplomat and so forth and read what I did yesterday that there's a strong rumor that Frank Sinatra is going to be ambassador to Italy, I would take a dim view of that!

Q: I didn't read that. I'm glad I didn't!

Adm. J.: I think, considering the source, it may be unfounded.

Q: Well, your tour of duty came to an end in 1967?

Adm. J.: Yes.

Q: Did it come regretfully?

Adm. J.: Yes. You know you can't stay on active duty forever. You've got to make room for the young guys coming up. But there's always a tinge of that, you know, sort of sorrow. You look back on things that you did, no regrets - I have none, certainly, but you kind of hate to leave when here is something that's still going on that isn't finished. Admiral Sharp felt very strngly about this when he had to retire, because he'd been fighting for so many things, you see, and still hadn't given up that maybe they could bail it out, salvage it. It had gone too far, and no way. Once again, he felt that way about it and I felt that way, too.

There are probably some things you might have done differently but I can't think of too many. You always think of people who worked for you and you think of people you worked for. That's kind of a varied mix of people and a variety of feelings. Some of them you learned an awful lot from and had respect for and all this. Others, you just wondered how they got where they did. I've always said that I think in terms of my getting as far as I did, it was because of the younger people, not only my understanding of them and the support that I got from them, better than anything I got from people up above. I got help from people up above, but more from the young people, the kids.

So, I saluted and left the quarterdeck in retirement. It's kind of hard to retire in some ways. Some people do it, of course, they retire and go to the farm. After all, you know, you've got to do something or else you die on the vine.

Q: And that's what you've been doing, you've been doing something

Adm. J.: Yes. I think I've contributed to the community. I don't go up here and just do nothing. I get involved in a lot of things.

Q: And you've been involved with the navy, in the Alumni Association.

Adm. J.: Oh, yes and I tried the consultant thing for a year. The money was good to have, but - this was with Martin Marietta Corp. But I've been on the receiving end of so many people coming to me in the Pentagon asking for favors and special treatment for this weapon system or this piece of equipment...so I was not going to go up and lobby in the Pentagon or on the Hill an I made it plain to the president of the company. And he said:

"OK. We'll use your background and so forth to help us and guide us to the men we should approach to get this weapon system, the Walleye or something."

Well, it wasn't too long before they were in trouble on Walleye too; "You know people up there, go up and help us." That's when I quit.

Q: That was the attitude of Admiral Nimitz.

Adm. J.: Really?

Q: He did not want to go, be a consultant or anything, because he felt that it was too much pressure to put on a man to use his influence.

Adm. J.: Right. And there are people doing this, they've been doing it for years. You see them around the Pentagon. A lot of them live in Washington. That's all they do.

Q: I suppose it's one way they try to guarantee a fairly good retirement income.

Adm. J.: Some of them made a lot in dipping jobs, like Chick Hayward. There are others - let's see, pretty big exectuve jobs, and, of course, Admiral Sides and Abe Vosseller before him, worked at Lockheed. They were in touch with people back in Washington, but they weren't beating their way on the footsteps to their offices or anything like that.

Q: Arleigh Burke went with Texaco.

Adm. J.: Yes, and he went to the board meeting and got $100 for every meeting he went to.

Q: Well, he contributed.

Adm. J.: Yes. I don't know how much, what kind of people on active duty ever did, talking to him. Admiral Carney never did.

Q: Admiral Fechteler was with General Electric.

Adm. J.: Oh, he was? There's an awful lot of them. Some of them went into Strategic Studies because Arleigh was with the Georgetown outfit. That's good --

Q: And Moorer is there now.

Adm. J.: Oh, he is, with the same outfit?

Q: Yes.

Adm. J.: I didn't know that.
    Well, Jack, that winds it up. It's been a pleasure.

Q: I'm delighted we finally got this on tape. It's quite a story and -

Adm. J.: Oh, well, I'm sure the other people had much more than that.

Q: As a matter of fact, it's rather unique.

Adm. J.: Much more dramatic and stirring than that. But I was involved in quite a few things.

Q: You were indeed.

There's a little addendum that you just told me and I'd like to put on tape.

Adm. J.: This is a matter which I expressed at the time of my change of command when I retired. It has been said many times that, particularly people in the military and the ones who have been in positions of great responsibility, high authority, and so forth, a big part of their success was due to somebody - sometimes maybe they didn't know who it was - behind the scenes, who was of tremendous assistance when things were in doubt and he didn't know quite how they were going to go, it was sort of a touch-and-go thing.

In my case, I can certainly point without any question to my good wife, tremendous stalwart that she was all during my whole career, which numbered every day that I was in the navy.

Q: I certainly feel privileged to have met her on this brief occasion. She's a lovely person.

Adm. J.: Of course, you see so much of the wives complaining of husbands being away, and that doesn't help the morale or the attitude of a naval officer, and that's why many of them are getting out. The loyal navy wife, she doesn't like to be separated, no, but at times - of course, in times of crisis or war and so forth - that's unavoidable and she's got to keep the home fires burning and back you up.

Q: The modern young person doesn't always feel that way!

Adm. J.: Now, it unfortunate they don't.

Q: Well, thank you again, Sir.

Index

to

Series of Taped Interviews

with

Admiral Roy L. Johnson, USN (Ret.)

ABRAMS, General Bernard B.: p. 292;

AIR GROUP 2: Johnson to Quonset Point (May, 1943) to form Air Group 2, p. 69; problems in organizing a group, p. 71 ff; training of night fighters, p. 78-9; shipped to Pearl Harbor, p. 80;

AIR WEAPONS SYSTEM ANALYSIS (Op. 05 W): Johnson becomes head of Op. 05 W in 1953 p. 149; a study on the future of the seaplane as a weapons system, p. 149-50;

ANDERSON, Adm. George W.: p. 54; p. 56; p. 65; p. 219; p. 224; p. 251;

USS BADOENG STRAIT (CVE): Johnson in command in the Yellow Sea, p. 118; p. 120; p. 124; p. 128 ff;

BARNABY, Captain Ralph: his experiments with gliders for training at Pensacola, p. 27;

BEAKLEY, VADM Wallace M.: his effectiveness in field of logistics p. 67;

BONIN ISLANDS: Johnson visits them as the military governor, p. 301 ff; his efforts to help prevent return of the islands to Japan, p. 301-2; has USS INTREPID call and take him from the islands, p. 304;

BROWNING, RADM Miles R.: skipper of the USS HORNET, p. 81-2; his differences with Jocko Clark, p. 83-6; removed from command because of incident involving man overboard, p. 86-7; p. 89;

BUREAU OF AERONAUTICS: Johnson in Washington - works on war supplies for the British, p. 53; speed up in plane production after Pearl Harbor, p. 54-6; a free wristwatch for aviators, p. 63-4; Johnson's mission to keep equipment flowing from manufacturers to plane production p. 64-6;

BURKE, Adm. Arleigh A.: as CNO - difficulties over the commissioning of the USS FORRESTAL, p. 164-5; p. 168; p. 188; his total opposition to the giving of operational control of POLARIS to the Air Force, p. 248-9;

CAMRANH BAY: the story of its development by the U. S. during the Vietnam war, p. 311 ff;

CAR DIV 4: Johnson relieves Don Griffin in Med - FORRESTAL is flagship, p. 288; problems with planes and losses, p. 209; problems with flexible positioning of carriers in the Med - because of NATO requirements, p. 212; back to Norfolk and the WSEG exercise - WEXVAL 9-10-11, p. 215 ff;

CHIANG kai-Chek: p. 270-1;

CINC PAC: Sharp's difficulties with Secretary McNamara who often tried to by-pass him and his command - and go directly to MacV in Saigon, p. 262;

CINC PAC FLT: Johnson becomes deputy to Sides and then Sharp, p. 259 ff; concerns of command other than Vietnam, p. 265; p. 277; Johnson relieves Moorer in command, p. 297 ff; Johnson's citation - a discussion of points raised in citation, p. 315 ff; discussion of tactics centering on operation of carriers in gulf of Tonkin, p. 316 ff; comments on intelligence and its use in fleet, p. 326-7; the Service Force - fleet organized and put under 7th fleet, p. 328-9; interfacing with CincPac, p. 339-41;

CLARK, Adm. John J. (Jocko): his differences with Miles Browning, p. 83-5; fires his air officer and names Johnson, p. 87-8; p. 91;

COMMAND: comments on naval command - the requisites, p. 180 ff;

DIEGO GARCIA: the first stirrings of U.S. interest in the island, p. 336-7;

DIEM, NGO-DINH: p. 227-8; p. 263;

DOYLE, Adm. Austin K.: (Artie) becomes skipper of the HORNET, p. 88-9; p. 91; p. 116; chief of naval air reserve training, p. 119; p. 125-6;

DUNCAN, Admiral Donald (WU): commander of 2nd fleet (Task Fleet) 1948, p. 101; p. 104-5; p. 112-3; his planning of the surprise attack on Tokyo, p. 114 ff; recommends Johnson for command of the USS FORRESTAL (1955), p. 160; p. 163; p. 171; p. 173-4;

DYER, VADM George: Task Group Commander in Korea, p. 120-3;

USS ENTERPRISE: Johnson joins Scouting Squadron 6 in the ENTERPRISE, p. 43 ff;

ENTHOVEN, Alain: p. 200-1;

FELT, Adm. H. D.: p. 203-4; p. 260; p. 263;

USS FORRESTAL: Johnson given command of the new ship, first of her class, 1955, p. 160; the trials and the commissioning, p. 162-3; the hassle over a speaker for the event, p. 164; the first fleet exercise, p. 169-70; bugs - and threatened delay in commissioning, p. 171-4; post commissioning repairs, p. 174-5; Johnson leaves command in 1956, p. 180; p. 208; p. 216; disastrous fire on board, p. 329-31;

FRANKEL, RADM Samuel B.: p. 61-2;

GATES, The Hon. Thomas: Secretary of the Navy, p. 202-4; his effort to get Air Force and Navy to resolve differences over POLARIS, p. 248;

GLENVIEW TRAINING COMMAND: Johnson takes command Jan. 1950, p. 1 calling up ready reserve pilots for the Korean war, p. 117 ff; p. 124-6;

GRIFFIN, Admiral Charles D.: p. 205; p. 207-8;

HAIPHONG: mining of the harbor, p. 320-1;

HALSEY, Fl. Adm. Wm.: as a flying student at Pensacola, p. 31; p. 91;

HAYWARD, VADM John T.: p. 157;

USS HORNET: Adm. Radford shifts Johnson and his air group to the HORNET with Miles Browning in command, p. 81; difficulties with change of plane types, p. 81; panic caused by a false alarm during a movie, p. 85-6; p. 94;

JCS: Johnson in immediate post war years on the staff of JCS, p. 95 ff;

JOHNSON, Admiral Roy L.: early history, p. 1; p. 6-7; marriage, p. 39-40; retirement in 1967, p. 345-6; a tribute to Mrs. Johnson, p. 349;

JSTPS - JOINT STRATEGIC TARGET PLANNING: Johnson serves as deputy director at Offutt Air Force Base (1962-3), p. 246 ff; history of the JCTPS, p. 247 ff; Air Force felt they should control POLARIS, p. 247; origin of JSTPS, p. 248; the creation of SIOP, p. 249; purpose of JSTPS, p. 249-5

KING, Fl. Adm. Ernest: his method of training senior officers to command carriers, p. 28 ff; p. 62-3; p. 100;

KOREA: calling up the ready reserves, p. 117-9; p. 128-31; the constant lookout for floating mines, p. 133; the use of former Japanese Imperial navymen as pilots to bring U.S. ships into Japanese ports, p. 134;

KRULAK, Lt. Gen. Victor H.: p. 230-1;

LAWRENCE, VADM Wm.: p. 12; p. 17;

LINCOLN, Lt. Comdr. Samuel A.: room-mate of Johnson at the Naval Academy - later administrative officer for Johnson in Air Group 2, p. 8;

LODGE, The Hon. Henry Cabot: p. 227-8; p. 263;

USS LONG BEACH: a missile cruiser used in Vietnam - equipped with TALOS missiles, p. 320;

LONG RANGE OBJECTIVES GROUP (Op. 93): Johnson takes over in 1956, p. 187-204; discussion of issues and problems, p. 188 ff; deal with ASW and use of carriers, escort vessels, p. 192 ff; use of intelligence in arriving at forecasts, p. 195-6;

MAC V - and the U. S. Navy in Vietnam, p. 289-91; MacV wanted control of all air in Vietnam, p. 308;

USS MADDOX: the Tonkin Gulf incident, p. 183-4; p. 234-5; the Tonkin Gulf incident, p. 237-240;

MARINES: problems with MacV over control of the air in areas occupied by Marines, p. 308-9;

McCAIN, Adm. John Sydney: p. 29; special student at Pensacola, p. 29-30;

McNAMARA, Robert Strange: his interference in the Gulf of Tonkin affair, p. 183; his tendency to by-pass CincPac and go directly to MacV in Saigon, p. 232; p. 262; p. 274; p. 279; p. 291;

MINES - MINE WARFARE: p. 325-6;

MINH, Maj. Gen. DUONG VAN (Big Minh): p. 227-8;

MITSCHER, Adm. Marc: p. 83-4;

MOORER, Admiral Thomas H.: p. 267; p. 310; p. 321;

NATIONAL WAR COLLEGE: Johnson attends in 1952, p. 137; p. 142-8;

U.S. NAVAL ACADEMY: Johnson takes examinations for West Point but ends up in Annapolis, p. 4 ff; years at the Naval Academy, p. 7 ff;

USS NEW JERSEY - BB: in Vietnam, p. 294;

NEWPORT NEWS SHIPBUILDING CO: see entries under USS FORRESTAL

NOLTING, The Hon. Frederick E. Jr.: p. 227;

NU, Madame Ngo Dinh: sister-in-law of President Diem, p. 264;

PARK CHUNG HEE - President of South Korea, p. 271-2;

PBY's: Johnson comments on effectiveness of the PBY, p. 47-51;

PENSACOLA: Johnson and flight training, p. 24 ff; comments on trial use of gliders in training, p. 27; discussion of the special senior students sent to Pensacola by Adm. King for qualification, p. 28 ff; Johnson has two years as an instructor, p. 28 ff;

PHILIPPINES: p. 275-6;

PIRAZ SYSTEM: for pilot identification over Vietnam, p. 319;

PLANS AND POLICY (Op 06 B): Johnson goes to Plans and Policy in 1960 - under Adm. Sharp, p. 225; the SHEEP DIP operation in Laos, p. 226; Diem and the situation in Vietnam, p. 226 ff;

POLARIS: p. 247 ff; p. 254; p. 255;

POWER, General Thomas S.: p. 252;

RADFORD, Adm. Arthur: in command of 2nd Fleet (Task Fleet) Atlantic, 1947, p. 99; in less than a year back in Washington as VCNO, p. 100-1; p. 121-2;

REISCHAUER, Dr. Edwin O.: Ambassador to Japan, p. 299-300; his insistence upon the return of the Ryukyus to Japan, p. 300;

RICKOVER, Adm. Hyman: p. 142-3;

RIVERINE WARFARE: p. 285-9; the problem of getting attack helicopters, p. 310;

SAC: Air Force looked upon POLARIS as in competition with SAC - so they wanted operational control, p. 247 ff; CincSAC is double-hatted, SAC and JSTPS, p. 248; p. 251-2; maximum alert during the Cuban Missile crisis, p. 252-3;

USS SALT LAKE CITY: Johnson sent to her, p. 34; as an aviator something of a step-child on board, p. 35 ff;

SEABEES: p. 305-6; the story of Shields, a Seabee- first navy man to be awarded Medal of Honor in Vietnam, p. 306-7;

SEALS - in Vietnam: p. 324;

SEATO: British efforts to accelerate joint planning in SEATO area in early 1960's, p. 266;

SECOND TASK FLEET: Johnson becomes operations officer for Radford in the Atlantic, p. 99 ff; Adm. Duncan (Wu) takes command - the cold weather exercise, p. 101-2; contour surveying trip to Persian Gulf, p. 104 ff; visit to Jiddah and Kuwait, p. 107-8; Turkey, p. 111-112;

SEVENTH FLEET: Johnson relieves Moorer in 7th fleet, p. 235; Westmoreland fails to give him a schedule of the NASTY boat operations in the Tonkin Gulf, p. 237; the incident involving the MADDOX, p. 237-240; p. 264-297; discourse on reporting events, p. 277-81; p. 289-90; p. 297; hospital ships and their value in saving lives, p. 307-8; MacV wanted control of carrier planes targets, p. 309-10; fleet air defense and ASW use of units, p. 317-8; also COM PAC FLEET entries.

SHARP, Admiral U. S. Grant: (Oley) head of Plans and Policies (1960), p. 225; calls Johnson as his deputy in CincPac Flt., p. 234; p. 254; p. 260; his difficulties with McNamara, p. 262;

SIDES, Adm. John H. (Saavy): p. 259-60;

SMEDBERG, VADM Wm. R. III: in command of 2nd fleet for WSEG exercise in Atlantic (WEXVAL 9,10,11) p. 216 ff; p. 218; his command ship the NORTHAMPTON, p. 218; p. 221;

SULLIVAN, Ambassador Wm.: his rigid rules of engagement in Laos, p. 341-2;

SYMINGTON, Senator Stuart: his tour of Vietnam, p. 286-7;

TACTICAL DATA SYSTEM - in the fleet, p. 322 ff;

TAIWAN: p. 269-273;

USS TENNESSEE: Johnson's first duty, p. 21; Johnson applies for flight training while serving in TENNESSEE, p. 21-23;

TOKYO: the B-25 attack, launched from the USS HORNET, p. 114 ff;

TONKIN GULF INCIDENT: see entries under:
SEVENTH FLEET
and
USS MADDOX

TOWERS, Admiral Jack: p. 54-5; p. 65;

VIETNAM: p. 242 ff; opinion of Chiang kai-chek on the war in Vietnam, p. 270;
see entries under:

<u>PLANS AND POLICY</u>
and
<u>SEVENTH FLEET</u>
and
<u>CINC PAC FLEET</u>

VIETNAMESE NAVY: p. 289;

VP - 12: Adm. Combs gets orders for Johnson to PBY squadron, p. 46; comments on the effectiveness of the planes, p. 47-51;

WESTMORELAND, General Wm. C.: his news conferences in Saigon, p. 282; his strategy for winning, p. 283 ff; p. 291;

USS WEST VIRGINIA: Johnson serves on her as a communications officer, p. 23;

WILSON, Comdr. Eugene: his foresight in early plane construction, p. 59;

WOMEN IN THE NAVY: p. 17; p. 18;

WSEG EXERCISE (WEXVAL 9,10,11): conducted by the 2nd fleet under command of Smedberg, p. 215 ff; p. 222;

ZERO - JAPANESE FIGHTER PLANE: p. 73-5;

ZUMWALT, Adm. Elmo: p. 140-1; p. 185;

www.ingramcontent.com/pod-product-compliance
Lightning Source LLC
Chambersburg PA
CBHW080620170426
43209CB00007B/1472